# 1 & 2 TIMOTHY TITUS, PHILEMON

# 1 & 2 TIMOTHY TITUS, PHILEMON

## A Commentary for Bible Students

**ROBERT BLACK & RONALD MCCLUNG**

Copyright © 2004 by The Wesleyan Church
Published by Wesleyan Publishing House
Indianapolis, Indiana 46250
Printed in the United States of America
ISBN 0-89827-275-0

Library of Congress Cataloging-in-Publication Data

Black, Robert, 1945-
    1 & 2 Timothy, Titus, and Philemon : a Bible commentary in the Wesleyan tradition /
Robert Black, Ronald McClung.
        p. cm.
    Includes bibliographical references.
    ISBN 0-89827-275-0 (hardcover)
    1. Bible. N.T. Pastoral Epistles--Commentaries. I. Title: First & Second Timothy,
Titus, and Philemon. II. Title: First and Second Timothy, Titus, and Philemon. III.
McClung, Ronald, 1943- IV. Title.
    BS2735.53.B57 2004
    227'.8307--dc22
                                                                    2004010010

# WESLEYAN BIBLE COMMENTARY SERIES

## GENERAL PUBLISHER
Donald D. Cady

## EXECUTIVE EDITOR
David W. Holdren, D.D., S.T.D.

## EDITORIAL ADVISORY COMMITTEE

Joseph D. Allison, M.Div.
Publishing Manager
Evangel Publishing House

Ray E. Barnwell
General Director of Sunday School
and Discipleship Ministries
The Wesleyan Church

Barry L. Callen, M.Div., M.Th., D.Rel.
University Professor of Christian Studies
Anderson University

Ray Easley, M.Div., Ed.D.
Vice President of Academic Affairs
Wesley Biblical Seminary

Dorothy Hitzka
National Consultant for Christian
Education
The Salvation Army

Arthur Kelly
Coordinator of Christian Education
and Congregational Life
Church of God Ministries

Stephen J. Lennox, Ph.D.
Professor of Bible and Chair, Division
of Religion and Philosophy
Indiana Wesleyan University

Bonnie J. Perry
Director
Beacon Hill Press of Kansas City

Dan Tipton, D.Min.
General Superintendent
Churches of Christ in Christian Union

John Van Valin
Free Methodist Pastor
Indianapolis, Indiana

## EDITORS
Lawrence W. Wilson, M.Div.
Managing Editor

Stephen J. Lennox, Ph.D.
Theological Editor

Darlene Teague, M.Div.
Senior Editor

# CONTENTS

# EXECUTIVE EDITOR'S PREFACE

L ife change. That, we believe, is the goal of God's written revelation. God has given His written Word so that we might know Him and become like Him—holy, as he is holy.

Life change is also the goal of this book, a volume in the Wesleyan Bible Commentary Series. This series has been created with the primary aim of promoting life change in believers by applying God's authoritative truth in relevant, practical ways. This commentary will impact Bible students with fresh insight into God's unchanging Word. Read it with your Bible in hand.

A second purpose of this series is to assist laypersons and pastors in their teaching ministries. Anyone called to assist others in Christian growth and service will appreciate the practical nature of these commentaries. Writers were selected based on their ability to soundly interpret God's Word and apply that unchanging truth in fresh, practical ways. Each biblical book is explained paragraph by paragraph, giving the reader both the big picture and sufficient detail to understand the meaning of significant words and phrases. There results of scholarly research are presented in enough detail to clarify, for example, the meaning of important Greek or Hebrew words, but not in such a way that readers are overwhelmed. This series will be an invaluable tool for preaching, lesson preparation, and personal or group Bible study.

The third aim of this series is to present a Wesleyan-Arminian interpretation of Scripture in a clear and compelling fashion. Toward that end, the series has been developed with the cooperative effort of scholars, pastors, and church leaders in the Wesleyan, Nazarene, Free Methodist, Salvation Army, Church of God (Anderson), Churches of Christ in Christian Union, Brethren in Christ, and United Methodist denominations. These volumes present reliable interpretation of biblical texts in the tradition of John Wesley, Adam Clarke, and other renowned interpreters.

Throughout the production of this series, authors and editors have approached each Bible passage with this question in mind: How will my life change when I fully understand and apply this scripture?

Let that question be foremost in your mind also, as God speaks again through His Word.

DAVID W. HOLDREN

# PREFACE
# TO 1 & 2 TIMOTHY

"Don't be a pastor," read the advertisement for a new book directed at members of the clergy. "Be a leader."

Somehow I never considered the two to be mutually exclusive. As I studied 1 and 2 Timothy, I became increasingly convinced that Paul didn't either. My admiration of Paul has grown as a result, and so has my appreciation for the modern Timothys (both men and women) to whom, through the Spirit, Paul wrote.

Pastoral and lay leadership in the local church are more important today than ever, and because they are, these epistles are too. They are first-century letters for the twenty-first century church.

God gave some to be pastors (Eph. 4:11), and to them, as well as to those who team with them in ministry, He gave 1 and 2 Timothy.
I, in turn, have been given the privilege of working with editors and a publisher of incredible patience, grace, and vision. Larry Wilson, Steve Lennox, and Don Cady have my heartfelt gratitude.

To the memory of my first and favorite pastor, I dedicate this study. My father, Dr. Watson C. Black, modeled ministry for me on a level I cannot attain but will always admire.

ROBERT BLACK

# 1 TIMOTHY

# INTRODUCTION TO 1 TIMOTHY

A cult at work within the congregation . . . the role of women in the church . . . money and materialism in Christian circles . . . integrity in the ministry. . . .

It reads like a checklist of challenges facing today's church, but it's actually an index of the issues dealt with two thousand years ago in 1 Timothy. The overarching theme of this letter resonates with our age too: *the need for spiritual leadership.*

Leadership is a prevalent topic in contemporary evangelicalism. It's a perennially popular subject at ministers' conferences, and books and tapes on Christian leadership sprinkle the best-seller list. But God is, as always, ahead of the curve on this matter. Long ago He gave us guidelines for spiritual leadership, guidelines on which the best of our modern books on the subject build. No early church publisher solicited this epistle with a generous author's advance, no advertising executive created a campaign to provide it with maximum exposure, and no booksellers' association charted its sales. Instead, the Holy Spirit inspired a beleaguered and besieged apostle to write this brief letter, championing the role of pastors and lay leaders in the local church. The result is a divine word on leadership for every generation.

The term *Pastoral Epistles* originated in the eighteenth century as a designation of the New Testament letters to Timothy and Titus, even though the word *pastor* does not appear in the biblical text. Written to a young minister in a strategic role, 1 Timothy deals with how to lead in the light of the truth on which all Christian ministry is based. There is, then, an emphasis on practical ministry here.

There is also a recognition that not all leadership in the church is pastoral leadership. Other categories of leaders are addressed, and the principles laid out are applicable on the various levels of leadership in the local church. Thomas Oden maintains that the term *pastoral letter* does not mean "to be ignored by laity."[1]

Every pastor and local church leader—in fact, every Christian leader in any field of service—can profit from a study of the Pastorals. The world has changed a great deal from the first century to the twenty-first, but people are still people, and leaders are still needed. In this letter, we have the opportunity to learn from one whose words on leadership transcend generations and geography.

But who wrote those words?

# AUTHORSHIP

In the opening verse of both 1 and 2 Timothy, the Apostle Paul is identified as the author, and, until comparatively recent times, that claim went unchallenged. Many scholars question it now, however. There is perhaps more controversy about the authorship of these epistles (and Titus) than about any of the other books bearing Paul's name.

## THE CHALLENGE TO PAULINE AUTHORSHIP

To some, 1 and 2 Timothy are pure literary fiction, start to finish. They believe that these letters were written by an author pretending to be Paul a century or so after his death. The supposed motive was to add weight to the writer's views. Those who hold this position see even the personal passages in these epistles as fabrications, finishing touches to the deception.

Others accept the personal passages as authentically Pauline but agree that the surrounding material is pseudepigraphal (falsely attributed to someone other than the actual author). According to this view, fragments of first-century letters from Paul survived into the second century when they were supposedly woven into an unknown writer's work, which was then purported to be Paul's. It is supposed that this unknown writer may have been a follower of Paul and may not have intended to deceive. Pseudepigraphal works were not uncommon in the second century, and this theory holds that the writer may simply have meant to apply Paul's thought to the problems of a new era. In either case, the books would be inauthentic.

Proponents of both positions appeal to the same evidence to support their challenge of Paul's authorship.

*Vocabulary and Style.* In places these letters sound different from Paul's writings in the rest of the New Testament. A considerable number of words not found in Paul's other epistles appear here; for example, he uses a different word for Christ's return (*epiphaneis*) than the usual *parousia*. Additionally, some phrases unknown in the other letters of Paul recur here. One is the formula "This is a trustworthy saying," which appears five times in the Pastoral Epistles and not at all outside of them. A total of 175 Greek words in the Pastoral Epistles occur nowhere else in the New Testament.[2] The converse is also true; some typically Pauline words or phrases are missing from the letters to Timothy and Titus.

These epistles seem both similar to each other and dissimilar in some ways to Paul's other letters. This linguistic issue has been considered a strong argument against Paul's authorship.

*Chronology of Paul's Life and Ministry.* According to 1 Tim. 1:3, Paul left Timothy in Ephesus while he traveled to Macedonia. That doesn't match Paul's travels as recorded in Acts or in his other epistles. Similarly, in 2 Timothy Paul alludes to stops at Troas, Corinth, and Miletus (2 Tim. 1:16–17; 4:13, 20), which apparently do not fit into the chronology of Acts.

If 1 and 2 Timothy are authentic, those skeptical of Pauline authorship ask, why aren't they consistent with the Bible's record of the movement of Paul and his associates?

*Ecclesiastical Development.* Some contend that the level of church organization displayed in these letters is too advanced for Paul's day. Because *overseer* (or *bishop*) usually appears in the singular here, some conclude that the letter was written after the use of a monarchical bishop, a single overseer for one church, had replaced the earlier system in which several bishops, overseers, or elders held joint leadership. The monarchical bishop dates to the early second century, approximately forty years after the death of Paul.

Critics go one step further. They claim that Paul, in his other letters, seems uninterested or uncommitted to the offices and officers of church government. That's evidence, they say, that he didn't write these epistles; they're too churchy.[3] Whoever did write them obviously considered church organization essential.

*Nature of the Ephesian Heresy.* According to 1 and 2 Timothy, false teachers in Ephesus were promoting a syncretistic blend of Jewish and Gnostic elements. Jewish myths (Titus 1:14; see also 1 Tim. 1:4; 2 Tim. 4:4) and what appear to be fictitious Jewish genealogies (1 Tim. 1:4), perhaps of Old Testament heroes, were taught by those who fancied themselves teachers of the Jewish law (1 Tim. 1:7). To this were combined principles sometimes associated with a heresy called *Gnosticism*: opposition to marriage (1 Tim. 4:3), abstinence from certain foods (1 Tim. 4:3), denial of the resurrection (2 Tim. 2:18), and boasting of a higher knowledge (*gnosis*) than the unenlightened possessed (1 Tim. 6:20).

Full-blown Gnosticism was the greatest competitor with biblical Christianity in the early church. It was a dualistic system that declared the existence of two gods, one good (the god of spirit) and the other evil (the god of matter), with a descending scale of emanations in between. Given that worldview, Gnostics disdained the material universe and anything not purely spiritual. Why, they wondered, would anyone think resurrection of a physical body was a good thing? In keeping with that worldview, some Gnostics considered the physical intimacy of marriage taboo, along with the enjoyment of certain foods which appealed to the physical appetite. (Interestingly, some other teachers who started with the same tenet—"matter is evil"—concluded that the physical body was irrelevant and could be indulged without harming the spirit. This philosophical spin led to a lifestyle of sensuality that was the polar opposite of their ascetic brothers.) Further, Gnostics believed that a mystical and intuitive knowledge (*gnosis*) was given to some but not to all. This secret knowledge was the path to salvation, they believed. Those bearing the *gnosis* constituted a spiritual elite.

But the Gnostic system took decades to develop, and critics suggest that the appearance of Gnosticism in the Ephesian church dates these letters to a time later than Paul's.

*External Evidence.* The earliest codex of Paul's letters that we have, the Chester Beatty Papyrus, ends with the Thessalonian letters and doesn't contain 1 and 2 Timothy, Titus, or Philemon. This early-third-century manuscript is cited by critics of Pauline authorship as evidence that the missing books were rejected by the church.

## THE CASE FOR PAUL

Is there, then, a case to be made for Paul as author of 1 and 2 Timothy? Absolutely. J. N. D. Kelly spoke for many commentators (among them Joachim Jeremias, E. K. Simpson, Donald Guthrie, Thomas Oden, Gordon Fee, and Philip Towner) when he concluded that "the strength of the anti-Paul case has been greatly exaggerated.[4] Not only is there the clear claim by the letters themselves that they are from Paul, but the unanimous witness of the early church fathers also supports his authorship. No serious challenges to Pauline authorship were mounted until the nineteenth century. The personal reflections certainly sound like Paul, and the supposition that they are authentic fragments in an otherwise pseudepigraphal composition is conjecture.

While it is true that pseudonymous works were common in the ancient world, it is also true that the church frowned on pseudonymity in sacred literature. One presbyter, or elder, who composed a pseudonymous Pauline letter lost his office for the offense.[5]

What responses may be given to the specific challenges to Paul's authorship?

*Vocabulary and Style.* Determining authorship by vocabulary and style is always highly subjective. The subject matter, the circumstances under which the author is writing, those to whom or for whom it is being written, and even the passage of time and advancing age of the author can affect vocabulary and style significantly.[6] All four of those factors come into play here, in fact. (1) Paul was writing on church organization and leadership, topics not prominent in his other letters. (2) He traveled extensively, perhaps as far west as Spain, which presumably broadened his vocabulary and may have affected his style. (3) He was writing to persons, not churches—and the persons were close personal friends and colleagues. (4) Paul is about seventy years of age as he writes these last letters; he wrote his first New Testament letter some sixteen or eighteen years earlier. It should be noted also that unmistakably Pauline phrasing—familiar salutations, athletic metaphors, word play—is found in the Pastorals. If it be argued that a pseudonymous author would be careful to insert some of these phrases, then it must be asked why that author, if he wanted to be taken for Paul, wouldn't have used *more* Pauline vocabulary and fewer words atypical of Paul. Thomas Oden makes a good point about Paul's personal testimony: "On what imaginable hypothesis would a forger have put in the mouth of Paul a claim to be 'chief of sinners' (1 Tim. 1:15 KJV)?"[7]

One solution to the linguistic difficulties in these letters may be Paul's possible use of an amanuensis, or secretary. We know that Paul had dictated letters before—J. N. D. Kelly thinks he used a secretary for all of his letters[8]—and in the adverse circumstances in which he found himself in Rome, he may well have depended on such assistance for the composition of these epistles. The use of a stenographer who simply took down Paul's dictation verbatim would not account for linguistic or stylistic differences, of course. But what if Paul allowed more freedom of expression to a trusted amanuensis who had his full confidence? Luke was with Paul when he wrote 2 Timothy (2 Tim. 4:11). Is it possible that Luke had a hand in the composition of all three Pastoral Epistles, though not to a degree that would substantially diminish Paul's authorship? If so, the variations in vocabulary and style may be partially attributed to Paul's penman. Add to that Earle Ellis's observation, cited in Stott, that Paul used pre-formed materials like hymns, creeds, and doxologies to a "surprising degree" in these letters[9], and many of the linguistic objections find their explanation well short of denying Paul's authorship.

*Chronology of Paul's Life and Ministry.* If we can rely on the writings of the fourth-century church historian Eusebius, the problem of chronology is removed without difficulty. Eusebius wrote that Paul was released from the house arrest described in Acts and resumed his missionary journeys, traveling as far west as Spain. (Paul had long wanted to minister there; see Rom. 15:28.) Later, Eusebius indicates that Paul was re-arrested, tried, convicted, and executed. Eusebius is not our only source for this information. In A.D. 95 Clement of Rome declared that Paul had journeyed "to the limit of the west." A little less than a century later, the Muratorian Canon agreed. To assume a second Roman imprisonment makes it unnecessary to reconcile the comparatively non-threatening circumstances of Acts 28, when Paul was optimistic about the prospects of release (Phil. 1:19, 25, 2:24), with his desperate circumstances in 2 Timothy. A second Roman imprisonment resolves the biographical, geographical, and chronological problems associated with the Pastorals.

*Ecclesiastical Development.* To deny Pauline authorship on the pretext that the writer had a second century view of church order and organization is untenable. Bishops and presbyters were not separate offices for Paul as they were for Ignatius and other church leaders after the first decade of the second century. For Paul, the terms *bishop* and *elder* (or presbyter) were used interchangeably (see especially Titus 1:5–7). The references to bishop in the singular are intended to be generic; they do not imply the use of a single bishop but are addressed to bishops in general. As for the contention that Paul had no interest in church organization, it should be noted that he and Barnabas ordained elders on their first missionary journey (Acts 14:23), that Paul decided it was important to summon and meet with the Ephesian elders (Acts 20:17), and that he opened his Philippian letter with greetings to the overseers (bishops) and deacons (Phil. 1:1)[10] "This sort of consciousness grew in Paul's writings with each succeeding letter," Oden observes, "the last of which were the Pastorals."[11] At the same time, it is certainly accurate to say that Paul was always more interested in church leadership than in church organization, and that is true of the letters to Timothy as well.

*Nature of the Ephesian Heresy.* Gnosticism was beginning to disturb the church in these letters, but it was not the fully developed Gnosticism of the second century and beyond. This was incipient Gnosticism, the early form of the heresy. "Evidence has indeed been forthcoming in increasing measure of the currency of incipient forms of Gnosticism in the first century, especially in areas where Judaism found herself deeply involved in dominant trends of Hellenistic and Oriental thought," writes F. F. Bruce.[12] The Gnosticism revealed in the letters to Timothy is actually very similar to the early Gnosticism described in Colossians and 1 Corinthians, two letters whose first-century setting is well established. Later Gnosticism would probably not have included the Jewish elements so apparent in the Ephesian heresy, since Gnosticism tended toward anti-Semitism.

*External Evidence.* On the whole, external evidence argues for Pauline authorship rather than against it. Traces of the Pastoral Epistles appear in the writings of the early church fathers, and the frequency of allusion to them from the era of Polycarp (first half of the second century) on compares favorably with most of Paul's other epistles. The letters to Timothy are included in every early canon list or collection except two, the Chester Beatty Papyrus being one. It's not at all certain that they were not originally contained in that papyrus; its final pages are missing, pages on which the Pastorals and Philemon would be found. It has been noted that not enough pages would have remained in that papyrus to copy all four books comfortably, but it is also true that the later books contained in that papyrus carry more lines per page than do the earlier ones, evidence that the copyist was aware he was running out of space. It is also true that some ancient books had pages added to them to allow for just such a miscalculation. It is possible that the Beatty may have contained such added pages; they would be among those missing. The other canon list from which 1 and 2 Timothy are omitted is the list of Marcion, the heretic, who omitted much of the New Testament when he found it in agreement with the Old. No doubt he would have found much to disagree with in these letters.

There is solid evidence for Pauline authorship, and support for it has been growing in recent years. It seems most probable that Paul did, in fact, author 1 and 2 Timothy.

## RECIPIENT

Timothy was Paul's co-worker and son in the faith (1 Tim. 1:2; 2 Tim. 1:2). A native of Lystra, Timothy was born to a Jewish mother and a Greek father. He was apparently converted on Paul's first missionary journey and joined Paul's team at a young age during the second missionary journey. (He is still considered young in the Pastoral Epistles, at which time he might have been in his mid-thirties.)

Timothy was ordained by Paul (2 Tim. 1:6) and "the body of elders" (1 Tim. 4:14) through the laying on of hands. He traveled with Paul and represented Paul on a number of special assignments. Out of Paul's ten letters besides the Pastoral Epistles, Timothy is listed as co-author (a largely honorary designation) in six, and he is mentioned in a seventh.

At the time of the writing of this first Pastoral, Timothy was in Ephesus as Paul's apostolic delegate or personal envoy, a position which carried considerable influence because of the authority of the appointing apostle. Timothy was pastoring the Ephesian congregation on temporary assignment. Ephesus, a city on the trade route that runs along the western coast of Asia Minor, could not have been an easy church to pastor. Paul had both extraordinary success and extraordinary opposition in Ephesus during his stay there (Acts 19). It was a center of the worship of Artemis (to the Romans, Diana), and her temple in Ephesus was one of the seven wonders of the ancient world. The Ephesian church was troubled, and Paul wanted Timothy there to bring stability and to ensure the triumph of orthodox theology and biblical beliefs.

Although 1 Timothy is a personal letter, Paul intended for the letter to be read to the entire congregation. (See the discussion of 1 Tim. 6:21 in the commentary text.)

## DATE OF WRITING

Paul was writing from Macedonia (1 Tim. 1:3) between his two Roman imprisonments (see discussion under Authorship), but the precise date is unclear. If Paul was released from the imprisonment recorded in Acts in A.D. 62 or 63, we may assume there was a period of freedom long enough for a fourth missionary journey before his re-arrest and execution in the mid- to late 60s. It is most likely that 1 Timothy was written during that period of freedom.

## PURPOSE

Several concerns lie behind Paul's words in this letter. First, he was well aware of the threat false teachers presented to the spiritual health of the congregation. (See the previous discussion of the Ephesian heresy.) Timothy needed to control these teachers and curb their influence. Second, Paul realized that Timothy's success in doing so would be linked in part to his wisdom in choosing congregational leaders who would stand with him in faith and integrity against the opponents of the truth. Third, underlying all of this was Paul's intent to strengthen Timothy personally. There are indications that Timothy was somewhat timid

(2 Tim. 1:6–7). Yet he needed to act boldly to guard the deposit of faith, both personally and on behalf of the church entrusted to him. He was not only teaching the faith but also modeling it (1 Tim. 4:16).

All of this leads to the purpose statement in 1 Timothy 3:14–15: "Although I hope to come to you soon, I am writing you these instructions so that, if I am delayed, you will know how people ought to conduct themselves in God's household, which is the church of the living God, the pillar and foundation of the truth."

## HOLINESS THEMES

Paul's experience of God's grace and his defense of God's truth are foundational to evangelical Christians of all varieties. Of particular interest to Wesleyans is the stirring affirmation that "God our Savior . . . wants all men to be saved and to come to a knowledge of the truth" (1 Tim. 2:3–4). There is in that verse an open invitation not to some whose salvation has been predetermined but to all. It supports the "whosoever will" theme of the gospel, a theme which found expression in the sermons of John Wesley and the hymns of Charles Wesley. That theme is still the heartbeat of the Wesleyan movement.

### ENDNOTES

1. Thomas Oden, *First and Second Timothy and Titus*, Interpretation Commentary Series (Louisville, Kentucky: John Knox Press, 1989), p. 1.

2. P. N. Harrison published an influential study in 1921 that employed statistical analysis of the vocabulary of the Pastoral Epistles to determine authenticity. A number of respected scholars have demonstrated that Harrison overstated his case and drew unwarranted conclusions. See John R. W. Stott, *The Message of 1 Timothy & Titus*, The Bible Speaks Today (Downers Grove, Ill.: InterVarsity Press, 1996), p. 25. Counterstudies have found that analyzing Paul's other, more widely accepted letters yields similar results in some categories. See Donald Guthrie, *The Pastoral Epistles*, Tyndale New Testament Commentaries (Grand Rapids, Mich.: William B. Eerdmans Publishing Company, 1957), pp. 212–228.

3. The term comes from John R. W. Stott, *The Message of 2 Timothy* (Downers Grove, Ill.: InterVarsity Press, 1973), p. 15. Stott doesn't subscribe to

that view, however. He supports Pauline authorship.

4. J. N. D. Kelly, *The Pastoral Epistles* (Peabody, Mass.: Hendrickson Publishers, 1960), p. 30.

5. Robert E. Picirilli, *Paul the Apostle* (Chicago: Moody Press), p. 233.

6. Guthrie, *The Pastoral Epistles*, p. 228.

7. Oden, *First and Second Timothy and Titus*, p. 15.

8. Kelly, *The Pastoral Epistles,* p. 25.

9. Stott, *The Message of 1 Timothy and Titus*, pp. 25–26.

10. Picirilli, *Paul the Apostle*, p. 232.

11. Oden, *First and Second Timothy and Titus*, p. 13.

12. F. F. Bruce, *Apostle of the Heart Set Free* (Grand Rapids, Mich.: William B. Eerdmans Publishing Co., 1977), pp. 408–409.

# OUTLINE OF 1 TIMOTHY

I. **Apostolic Greeting (1:1–2)**
II. **Leadership in the Worship and Witness of the Church (1:3–3:13)**
    A. The Doctrinal Authority of a Leader (1:3–11)
        1. The Ephesian Heresy (1:3–7)
        2. The Sound Doctrine of the Word (1:8–11)
    B. The Divine Call of a Leader (1:12–20)
        1. Paul's Personal Experience (1:12–17)
        2. Timothy's Commission (1:18–20)
    C. The Spiritual Responsibility of a Leader (2:1–15)
        1. The Universal Importance of Prayer (2:1–8)
        2. Rules for Ephesian Women in Worship (2:9–15)
    D. The Ethical Character of a Leader (3:1–13)
        1. The Office of Overseer (3:1–7)
        2. The Office of Deacon (3:8–13)
III. **The Church of the Living God (3:14–16)**
IV. **Practical Counsel for Church Leaders (4:1–6:21a)**
    A. The Godly Example of a Leader (4:1–16)
        1. Asceticism and Apostasy (4:1–5)
        2. A Good Minister of Christ Jesus (4:6–16)
    B. The Congregational Relationships of a Minister (5:1–6:2)
        1. Pastoral Care of Old and Young (5:1–2)
        2. Widows in the Congregation (5:3–16)
        3. Selection and Care of Elders (5:17–25)
        4. Slaves and Masters (6:1–2)
    C. The Personal Values of a Leader (6:3–10)
        1. False Doctrine and Financial Gain (6:3–5)
        2. Godliness and Spiritual Gain (6:6–10)
    D. Final Instructions (6:11–21a)
        1. A Charge to Timothy (6:11–16, 20–21a)
        2. A Word to the Rich (6:17–19)
V. **An Apostolic Benediction (6:21b)**

# 1 TIMOTHY

## Part One

Leadership in the Worship
and Witness of the Church 1:3–3:13

# APOSTOLIC GREETING

## 1 Timothy 1:1–2

P aul was a giant of the New Testament church. He was its primary theologian, its premier missionary, and its most prolific writer, but he almost always chose to introduce himself as **an apostle of Christ Jesus**. For him, that title described not so much an office as a mission.

Paul was not one of the original Twelve. He was "one untimely born" (1 Cor. 15:8 NRSV) to the ranks of the apostles. Unlike *disciple*, which is a general term for any follower of Jesus, apostle (one who is sent out) applies only to a select few in the New Testament. It refers to a small group of leaders who had been commissioned by the risen Christ for special service. Paul never met Christ in the flesh; his encounter with the Lord was on the road to Damascus years later (Acts 9), and Paul's mind would return to that life-changing experience whenever he reflected on his apostolic assignment.

After the Ascension, the apostles were the first line of leadership in the New Testament church, and Paul had occasion to exercise apostolic authority in church controversies (see 2 Cor. 10, 11). Timothy certainly did not need to be reminded that Paul was an apostle, but some did. There was a problem with false teachers at Ephesus. If this letter was intended to be read to the entire church, as seems likely, Paul's credentials would be important. After all, Paul served by divine appointment. It was **by the command of God our Savior and of Christ Jesus our hope** that he was an apostle. The wording is a bit unusual. For one thing, Paul typically says his apostleship is "by the will of God" (see the salutations in 1 and 2 Corinthians, Galatians, Ephesians, and 2 Timothy). The new phrase used in 1 Timothy elaborates on that thought and establishes a command theme, which runs through 1 Timothy. Paul was not self-appointed. No true minister is.

We know of two occasions when Paul related his Damascus road experience before a hostile audience (Acts 22:4–21; 26:1–23), and he alludes to it in the opening chapter of 1 Timothy (vv. 12–17). More than just a part of Paul's testimony, it was the foundational event in his life and ministry. He spoke, acted, and wrote in light of the Light which had interrupted his journey—his physical and spiritual journey—that day. No wonder, as Donald Guthrie writes, "He can never forget that he is a man under orders."[1]

Paul's reference to God as **Savior** should also be noticed. Ten times in his writings, Paul uses that term in reference to the Father, and six of those occasions are in the Pastoral Epistles. (See also 1 Tim. 2:3, 4:10, and three instances in Titus). It may sound strange to us, accustomed as we are to referring to Christ as Savior, but it is biblically and theologically sound to refer to God the Father in that same way. The cooperative effort of the Trinity in our salvation is in view here, and the First Person of the Trinity, who sent His Son to die is, in an ultimate sense, our Savior just as Christ is our **hope**.

Typically, letter writers in the Roman era employed a standard formula of salutation: *A* (the writer) *to B* (the recipient), *greetings*. Paul followed that pattern, but with Christian modifications. Timothy, to whom the letter is addressed, is his **true son in the faith**. If the rest of the letter provides a glimpse into the mind of Paul, here is a glimpse into his heart. Timothy was probably converted, discipled, and even ordained by Paul (2 Tim. 1:6), but those biographical facts barely hint at the richness of their remarkable relationship. Of all Paul's colleagues and co-laborers, Timothy was special. He was Paul's spiritual son, a tribute Timothy is given five times in the New Testament. (Compare 1 Cor. 4:17, Phil. 2:22, 2 Tim. 1:2, Titus 1:4). Some experts advise leaders to keep their distance from the people they lead, but those who take that advice miss out on the only kind of leadership worthy of the name. Paul the apostle was also Paul the spiritual father to this young pastor.

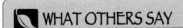

**WHAT OTHERS SAY**

Mercy expresses the heart of God, and grace expresses the hand of God.

—Alexander Maclaren

To the typical greeting of **grace** and **peace,** Paul adds **mercy**. (He himself had received mercy, as he recalls in v. 13.) Together these virtues form a triad of blessings. **Mercy** is related to God's compassion on us; because He is merciful, we don't get what we deserve. **Grace**, on the other hand, speaks of His loving favor toward us; because He is gracious, He gives us what we don't deserve!

**Peace**, then, would be the spiritual state of a person blessed with mercy and grace. It's Paul's prayer for all of his readers.

### ENDNOTE

1. Donald Guthrie, *The Pastoral Epistles: An Introduction and Commentary* (Grand Rapids, Mich.: William B. Eerdmans Publishing Company, 1957), p. 55.

# 2

# THE DOCTRINAL AUTHORITY OF A LEADER

## 1 Timothy 1:3–11

"Grace, mercy, and peace" was Paul's opening prayer for Timothy and his church, but because God's grace and mercy were being abused by a godless faction in the congregation, the church at Ephesus was hardly a church at peace. **Certain men** were promoting **false doctrines**; as a result, the church was torn by controversy. Paul never considered compromise or accommodation when revealed truth was at risk. Martin Luther was very much like him when he said in the midst of the turbulent Reformation, "Peace if possible; Truth at any price."

In this section Paul exposes the nature of the heresy (1:3–7) and contrasts it with the sound doctrine found in the Old Testament Law (1:8–11), which the false teachers claimed they were teaching but which, in fact, condemned their own beliefs and practices.

## 1. THE EPHESIAN HERESY 1:3–7

Paul was well acquainted with Ephesus and the Ephesians. He had stayed there for more than two years on his third missionary journey about eight years earlier, and if he was in fact released from his Roman imprisonment in A.D. 62 or 63, it's possible that he returned to Ephesus at that time to labor alongside Timothy before going **into Macedonia** (see Introduction). He knew the problem in this church so he repeats his earlier instructions to Timothy: **stay there in Ephesus** and stand your ground against it.

## THE NEED FOR PASTORAL AUTHORITY

Obviously, Timothy had considered leaving. Perhaps he, like many pastors, had paraphrased the Preacher in Ecclesiastes and concluded: There is a time to stay and a time to move. But Paul himself had remained in Ephesus against fierce opposition years earlier (1 Cor. 16:8–9), and he urged Timothy to do the same. Paul's words have an edge to them, as if by challenging Timothy he can strengthen his resolve. The language is direct, almost military. Serving by and under God's orders (v. 1), Paul the apostle, in turn, commands Timothy to issue a **command** to the false teachers; they are not **to teach false doctrines any longer**.[1]

This is pastoral authority in its purest, most biblical sense. There's no pastor-as-master model here; Timothy is not ordered to defend a personal power base or his own prestige against opposition from the congregation. With the authority of God's Word behind him and the welfare of God's church before him, he must defend God's truth, even if that involves a confrontation with error. Kingdom building in Ephesus relates to the kingdom of God, not the kingdom of Timothy. Like Jesus, who never worked a miracle for His own benefit, authentic New Testament leadership never seeks to profit personally from its own position. The modern church would have more credibility in our skeptical age if some of its most visible and vocal "leaders" could say the same.

Paul was so intent on making his point with Timothy that he never actually completed this sentence. It begins, literally, "As I urged you to stay on . . .," but no independent clause ever arrives to save the grammar. (English translations smooth out the syntax but lose the intensity.) Paul wasn't thinking of this letter as a polished work of literature. The church was under attack, and this was his battle plan.

For Timothy, the pulpit would become a key arena in this struggle, and most commentators see his assignment to combat false doctrine primarily as a preaching assignment. "Preaching up a storm" is an old expression, but it is often harder to preach in or through a storm. Yet that is when sound preaching is most valuable. In times of national, regional, or congregational crisis, people should be able to look to the pulpit for a word from the Lord. In this case, the crisis was doctrinal, and the corrective was doctrinal preaching.

We live in a day when theology is not considered PC—politically correct *or* pastorally correct—in the church. For many, doctrine is at best irrelevant and at worst divisive. But to downplay theology in favor of "practical" ministry is to forget how practical good theology is, and to create a dangerous dichotomy between the *foundational* and the *functional* aspects of ministry. Having one without the other leads to serious trouble.

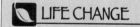

## LIFE CHANGE

### SPIRITUAL FOOD

*Doctrinal sermons* are one of the four basic homiletical "food groups" with which a pastor can feed a congregation. The others are *pastoral sermons, moral-ethical sermons,* and *evangelistic sermons.* All are important, and so is the balance among them.

**The goal of this command**, the aim of Timothy's preaching, **is love**, but love doesn't produce itself. It **comes from a pure heart and a good conscience and a sincere faith**—a second triad of graces (see chapter 1).[2] Timothy's goal, then, was to do something more than rebut error; it was to offer positive affirmation of spiritual health and well-being. In fact, Paul expresses the goal in the language of holiness, even though the term itself is not used. A lifestyle of love flowing by faith from a pure heart along the path of good conscience is holiness in action.

Timothy (1:19a, 5:22; 2 Tim. 1:5), Paul (1:12, 14; 2 Tim. 1:3, 3:10, 4:7), and, by implication in 1:6, the faithful members of Timothy's congregation all exhibited the spiritual wholeness characterized by these graces, which are listed in various combinations throughout the Pastoral Epistles. Those who hold leadership positions must exhibit them, of course (3:9); yet these graces are lacking in the false teachers, who **have wandered away** (some translations say "swerved") **from these,** having seared consciences (4:2) and corrupted values (Titus 1:5). Their wandering resulted in **controversies,** which are divisive, and **meaningless talk** (in the New English Bible, "a wilderness of words"), which is irrelevant. In other words, it is bad theology, not theology in general, which is irrelevant and divisive! Good, sound, biblical God-talk is the life-blood of a healthy church.

## ANATOMY OF A HERESY

What was the false teaching that so threatened the life of the Ephesian church? It was a syncretistic mix—a tossed salad of Jewish **myths,** elaborate fantasies based on Old Testament **genealogies,** and an unbiblical asceticism (4:3).

*Jewish Myths.* Four times in the Pastoral Epistles, Paul mentions the fascination with **myths** that marks the false teachers. (See 1 Tim. 1:4, 4:7; 2 Tim. 4:4; and Titus 1:14, where Paul specifically indicates that the myths in question are Jewish in their origin. The only other reference to myths in the New Testament is 2 Pet. 1:16.) Legendary accounts of Old Testament heroes and mythical stories built on Old Testament passages were common in ancient Judaism. Some remain today in the Talmud, a collection of Jewish traditions and rabbinic commentary on the law. These "secret teachings" of the Old Testament had a certain mysterious appeal, much like the apocryphal gospels that the church rejected from the beginning but which, unfortunately, are being marketed today as the "lost books" of the Bible. These counterfeit teachings were turning people away from the truth (2 Tim. 4:4) by encouraging the pursuit of legends and myths, which had no basis in God's revelation.

*Genealogical Speculation.* **Endless genealogies** are referred to again in Titus 3:9, also in the context of a Jewish problem (quarrels about the Law). Evidently, false teachers were concocting fictitious family trees for Old Testament characters, particularly the patriarchs. Like the myths, these genealogies appealed to the human fascination with anything labeled secret, hidden, or mysterious. Also like the myths, the genealogies were worse than a waste of time; they were dangerous detours from the truth.

*Extreme Self-Denial.* The third characteristic is not mentioned here but becomes clear in 1 Timothy 4: a spirit of asceticism, or severe self-denial. In this case, that took the form of forbidding marriage and requiring abstinence from certain foods (4:3). Asceticism is self-discipline taken to extremes, far beyond the bounds of either common sense or biblical requirement. Unlike the exercise of legitimate spiritual disciplines, asceticism is excessive and self-abusive—a lifestyle incompatible with **sound doctrine**.

*Denial of Resurrection.* One additional feature of false teaching in Ephesus deserves mention. Paul doesn't mention this in his first letter to Timothy, but from 2 Tim. 2:18 we understand that the doctrine of the resurrection was under attack. The sect taught that the resurrection of the saints had already taken place, probably based on Paul's reference to baptism as dying and rising in spiritual terms (Rom. 6:1–10). Apparently, some were telling the Ephesian Christians that rising from the waters of baptism was the only resurrection they would ever experience.

 **LIFE CHANGE**

SPIRITUAL FADS

In the church as well as in society, there is always a market for fads and novelties. Check out the hot topics on Christian radio talk shows and even the inventories of some Christian bookstores. Much of the content is frivolous; some of it is dangerous. Several contemporary cults and modern heresies got their start from just that sort of material. It's wise to steer clear of the spiritually faddish before it becomes, as it had for the Ephesian Christians, a spiritual fetish.

We could wish that Paul provided more details in his denunciation of this false teaching, but he does give enough clues to determine that it was a combination of Jewish and Gnostic teaching (see the Introduction). Both myths and the genealogies had Jewish roots. On the other hand, asceticism and denial of the physical resurrection are consistent with Gnosticism's rejection of the material universe. This link is confirmed by Paul's warning at the end of 1 Timothy about "the opposing ideas of what is falsely called knowledge," or *gnosis* (6:20)— the key word in Gnosticism.

First Timothy was written too early for this heresy to have been the fully-developed Gnosticism that threatened the church in the mid-second century, but it may have been an early form of that false teaching. In fact, the evidence indicates that Gnosticism developed from Jewish origins.

Timothy's Ephesus and Titus's Crete may have seen slightly different varieties of this heresy, but the descriptions are so similar that it's safe to assume the problem is essentially the same. It also parallels with the heresy Paul confronted in Colossians; it too, mixed Jewish and Gnostic elements (Col. 2:16–23; see also 2:8). We sometimes have romanticized notions about the first-century church, but it was not without its challenges to the truth.

## 2. THE SOUND DOCTRINE OF THE WORD 1:8–11

Paul wrote that the opponents of the truth in Ephesus **want to be teachers of the law but,** he notes with wonderful irony, **they do not know what they are talking about**—hardly a desirable trait in a teacher. The very law they claimed to teach condemned them; in fact, it condemns anyone and anything **contrary to sound doctrine.**

To drive home his point, Paul lumps the false teachers in with rather bad company: **those who kill their fathers or mothers, murderers, adulterers and perverts, slave traders** (KJV, "menstealers"), **liars and perjurers.** Clearly Paul had in mind commandments five through nine of the second table of the Decalogue, the portion of the Ten Commandments that deals with our relationships to each other. That puts his earlier condemnation of **the ungodly and sinful, the unholy and irreligious** into sharper focus. There he refers to the first table of the Law, commandments one through four, which concern our relationship to God. Enemies of God and enemies of humankind, the self-described **teachers of the law** were actually its targets (vv. 9–11). The whole picture stands in stark contrast to the virtues of v. 5—a pure heart, a good conscience, and a sincere faith.

In his dismissal of the false teachers, Paul makes a point that is often overlooked. He is sometimes assumed to be a critic of the law because of his emphasis on our freedom from it in Christ, but that's a simplistic and superficial interpretation of Paul's position. Here he proclaims that **the law is good** (compare Rom. 7:7–12, 14), but only **if one uses it properly** (literally, "lawfully"). Paul is an opponent not of law but of legalism. Legalism looks to the law for salvation and relies on the law for its sense of moral superiority. Paul identified the true purpose of the law in Gal. 3:24: "So the law was put in charge to lead us to Christ that we might be justified by faith." Followers of falsehood at Ephesus were not being led to Christ, and Paul would not allow them to camouflage themselves under the law.

## ENDNOTES

1. The command theme is more prevalent here than it appears to be in the New International Version. The word translated *instruction* in 1:18 is translated **command** in v. 5.

2. Thomas Oden, *First and Second Timothy and Titus* (Louisville, Ky.: John Knox Press, 1989), p. 57.

# 3

# THE DIVINE CALL OF A LEADER

## 1 Timothy 1:12-20

Unlike the false teachers in Ephesus, Paul seeks no camouflage or cover. In an intensely autobiographical portion of this letter, he revisits his past and recalls his violent persecution of the young church. As Paul's mind goes back to events he would surely rather forget, our minds go back to the accounts in the book of Acts that detail his campaign against those "who belonged to the Way" (Acts 9:2). No wonder Paul felt he was **the worst of sinners**. The wonder is that he was forgiven, or that any of us are—and not only forgiven but also **called to his service**. That's the wonder of God's grace, and it always prompts Paul to praise (v. 17).

Timothy is called to God's service too. Paul reminds the young man of his ordination service and challenges him to defend the faith by preaching the truth and maintaining church discipline.

A call to the ministry, someone has said, is a divine summons to the service of God. Paul and Timothy answered that summons. They are under the microscope of Scripture in this section, but it is God's grace and mercy, not their own flaws, that are magnified.

## 1. PAUL'S PERSONAL EXPERIENCE 1:12-17

Paul was a man with a past. He was unsparing of himself in his open admission that he had been **a blasphemer and a persecutor and a**

**violent man**. His role in the stoning of Stephen (Acts 7:58), his house-to-house manhunts for believers (Acts 8:1–3), his relentless pursuit of scattered Christians with intent to extradite them for trial in Jerusalem (Acts 9:1–2)—it was all part of the biblical record, and it was all on Paul's mind as he remembered how wrong he himself had once been.

## A TRUSTWORTHY SAYING

Paul's memory triggers a **trustworthy saying** and the first of five uses of that distinctive formula in the Pastorals (see also 3:1, 4:9; 2 Tim. 2:11; Titus 3:8; the phrase does not occur elsewhere in the New Testament). Here and in 4:9 Paul extends the phrase, noting that this saying **deserves full acceptance**. As a rhetorical device, the formula is exceptionally effective. It announces, "Reader, be alert! There is a vital statement ahead!"

This first **trustworthy saying** is vital, not only for this epistle but also for the entire New Testament: **Christ Jesus came into the world to save sinners**. How simple, yet how profound. From the moment the angels told the shepherds about the Baby who was a Savior (Luke 2:11), Christ's coming could not be separated from His saving work. Christmas has no meaning apart from Good Friday and Easter, or Advent apart from Lent.

## PAUL'S TESTIMONY

Paul personalizes salvation history in his testimony, as every Christian should. Christ didn't come to save sinners in the abstract, Paul says, but sinners like me; in fact, **I am the worst**. (Elsewhere he calls himself "the least of the apostles," 1 Cor. 15:9, and "less than the least of all God's people," Eph. 3:8.) And what a change that salvation wrought! The Greek word translated **a violent man** in 1 Tim. 1:13 is a

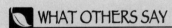

**WHAT OTHERS SAY**

He did not come to judge the world,
He did not come to blame;
He did not only come to seek—
It was to save He came,
And when we call Him Savior, then
We call Him by His name.

—Dora Greenwell

form of the word *hubris*, which means overbearing pride. It communicates insolence, arrogance, and the proud swagger of a bully. Contrast that with the deep humility of vv. 15–16: **the worst of sinners.** It's a before-and-after picture of Paul from Paul himself.

If we didn't know Paul better, we might think he was exhibiting false humility or even engaging in the perverse kind of witnessing that glorifies a sinful past. No, Paul had a valid point to make: if Christ can save me, he argues, no one is beyond His saving grace. Not only was God gracious in forgiving me, Paul marvels, but also in **appointing me to his service.** In the King James Version, that verse reads "putting me into the ministry." The New International Version is preferable. It captures the application to all who are **in his service,** lay people and clergy alike.

God's **mercy** and **grace,** which Paul claims for Timothy in the greeting of this letter (v. 2), were not textbook terms or abstractions for Paul; they came out of his own spiritual experience ( vv. 13–14). The Ephesians may claim them, also, but only if they **believe on** God, not the lies of the false teachers.

Paul's reference to his sinfulness serves another purpose. While he praises God for the patience God showed in Paul's ignorance, he doesn't seek to excuse his behavior. Sin is sin in 1 Timothy 1, whether it's the flagrant sin of the false teachers or the forgiven sin of the apostle.

Typical of Paul, his testimony ends in doxology. This beautiful prayer of praise is the setting for Walter Chalmers Smith's stirring hymn, *Immortal, Invisible, God Only Wise:*

> Immortal, invisible, God only wise,
> In light inaccessible hid from our eyes,
> Most blessed, most glorious, the Ancient of Days,
> Almighty, victorious, Thy great name we praise.

The God who displays those marvelous attributes is more than worthy of **honor and glory** (see Rev. 4:11, 5:12–13). To that the church in every age says with Paul, **Amen.**[1]

## 2. TIMOTHY'S COMMISSION 1:18–20

The chapter comes full circle with a repetition of Paul's reference to **Timothy, my son** (compare v. 2). As Timothy's spiritual father and mentor, Paul had invested much of himself in this young pastor and was committed to his success. As close friends often do, Paul alludes to a common memory of theirs which did not need elaboration in the letter because they both knew it well.

## AN ORDINATION REMEMBERED

**I give you this instruction in keeping with the prophecies once made about you,** Paul writes to Timothy. In 4:14, Paul adds that this prophetic message was given at what we might call Timothy's ordination, "when the body of elders laid their hands on you." As has been noted (see Introduction), Paul probably participated in and perhaps even presided over the ordination ceremony (2 Tim. 1:6).

Since the New Testament era, the program has been unchanged: God calls, the church ordains. In the simple solemnity of that ceremony reside centuries of trust and confidence in the people God has raised up for Christian vocation. Some churches teach apostolic succession, the theory that an unbroken line of ministry leads back to the apostles and transmits their spiritual authority to modern bishops. While not adopting that view, the church can recognize a related truth: those whom God has chosen and on whom the church has laid hands stand on the shoulders of others. Ordination is no trivial matter. If it were, Paul would not have made repeated references to it in his two letters to his son in the faith. "Remember your ordination" is always good counsel for a minister in crisis. "Remember the confidence of the church in your call. Remember your commission: 'Take thou authority to preach the Word and administer the sacraments. . . .'"

Timothy's ordination would not have included those time-honored words from the *Book of Common Prayer*, of course, but Paul does bring to his remembrance **the prophecies once made about** him. Biblical prophecy, in the New Testament as well as the Old, is not only prediction but also proclamation, or preaching. It is not merely foretelling but also forth-telling. We don't know what words were said to Timothy at his ordination, but Paul seems sure they will anchor him in this storm. The result will be a victory of character (**holding on to faith and a good conscience,** a glance back at the virtues of 1 Tim. 1:5) and conduct (**fight[ing] the good fight**, a foreshadowing of Paul's own famous testimony in 2 Tim. 4:7–8).

## SPIRITUAL SHIPWRECKS

As in 1 Tim. 1:5–6, Paul warns that **some have rejected** faith and a clear conscience **and so have shipwrecked their faith.** Nowhere else in the New Testament is shipwreck used as an analogy for backsliding; this single reference has been enough to make it a common metaphor in sermon and song. For Paul, it was something of a mixed metaphor: "fight the good fight" conjures a military image, and "don't shipwreck your faith" is a nautical one. Donald Guthrie quotes Lock: "The Christian teacher must be good soldier and good sailor, too."[2]

**Hymenaeus and Alexander** were neither good soldiers nor good sailors. Hymenaeus is mentioned again, in 2 Tim. 2:17–18, as one of the leaders

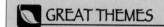

## GREAT THEMES

BACKSLIDING

John Wesley used this passage as evidence for the possibility of backsliding. He reasoned that Hymenaeus and Alexander couldn't have made shipwreck of their faith unless they had a faith to wreck.

of the Ephesian heresy. Alexander may be Alexander the metalworker named in 2 Tim. 4:14, who did Paul "a great deal of harm." Some have tried to identify him with the Alexander of Acts 19:33, but that Alexander was clearly not a Christian, whereas the one of whom Paul speaks in the Pastorals is a backslidden believer.

Paul's words **I have handed [them] over to Satan to be taught not to blaspheme** have prompted at least two interpretations.

(1) Some think Paul was simply referring to the expulsion of Hymenaeus and Alexander from the congregation, leaving them, in a sense, on the Devil's turf and outside the spiritual protection of the church (see Matt. 18:17 and Titus 3:10). Similar action was to be taken against the Corinthian man who was living in sin with his father's wife (1 Cor. 5:4–5.)

(2) Others think more is implied, both here and in the parallel case in 1 Corinthians. They read between the lines a prayer for the physical affliction of those who need the discipline of the church—affliction such

as Satan visited on Job—in order to bring spiritual restoration. The reference to "body" or "flesh" in 1 Corinthians 5 is offered in support of this view (in the New International Version, that reading is found in a footnote and not in the text).

Whatever Paul did (and F. F. Bruce says he must have done it "by remote control"),[3] he did redemptively and not just punitively. His aim was that they **be taught not to blaspheme**.

The word *taught* comes from the same root as the word *discipline*. Church discipline is hard to get right, judging from its inconsistent and uneven application throughout the centuries and even today. It is virtually non-existent in some circles and unreasonably, even illegally, harsh in others. The biblical model calls for the Church, as the Body of Christ and not as a cluster of Lone Ranger Christians, to administer discipline when necessary—but to do it remedially and redemptively. If everything is to be done in love out of a pure heart, a good conscience, and a sincere faith (1 Tim. 1:5), then church discipline is to be done that way too.

 **WHAT OTHERS SAY**

When the great pastor and evangelist Charles Spurgeon was asked, "How shall I defend the Bible?" he replied, "How would you defend a lion? Let it out of its cage and it will defend itself!"

As he wrote these lines, Paul had to be thinking of his own redemption. After all, he, too, had been a blasphemer (v. 13) and worse. Unlike Hymenaeus and Alexander, his sinful lifestyle preceded his conversion and was grounded in ignorance; Paul doesn't understand how these men can know the truth yet turn away from it. Still, this admonition is not a "There, but for the grace of God, go I" cliché for Paul. Rather, it's "There I went once, but by the grace of God, no more." The aim of his discipline is to make that true of his opponents as well.

In this opening chapter, Paul demonstrates the doctrinal authority of a leader summoned by God's call and serving under God's command. His charge is to teach and preach the truth, guarding, defending, and preserving it against error—a charge he passes on to Timothy. The good news for Timothy is that in the battle for truth, truth itself is the most effective weapon.

## ENDNOTES

1. *Amen*, along with *hallelujah*, is a Hebrew word recognized everywhere as a part of the language of worship. It is far more than a signal that the prayer has ended; it is a response, a word of affirmation meaning "so be it" or "truly." On the matter of ascribing glory and honor to God, Paul votes a resounding *aye*.

2. Donald Guthrie, *The Pastoral Epistles* (Grand Rapids, Mich.: William B. Eerdmans Publishing Company, 1957), p. 68.

3. F. F. Bruce, *Paul: Apostle of the Heart Set Free* (Grand Rapids, Mich.: William B. Eerdmans Publishing Company, 1977), p. 464.

# THE SPIRITUAL RESPONSIBILITY OF A LEADER

## 1 Timothy 2:1–15

The first chapter of 1 Timothy is largely introductory. In it, Paul reminds Timothy of a previous conversation about the threat from false teachers, gives his own testimony, and charges Timothy to be a spiritual leader. Now, in chapter 2, Paul introduces the heart of his letter with words about public worship. That is a subject on which the church has needed instruction in every age, ours especially. Today, leadership is defined mainly in management terms, and a leader's effectiveness is measured by head counts, bottom lines, and personal charisma. Paul was not unaware of the managerial aspects of leadership; he deals with them later in this letter. But "first of all" come prayer and worship (2:1–8). These are not add-ons or afterthoughts for a godly leader but are the very heartbeat of the church. As a pastor, Timothy had leadership responsibilities that went far beyond reporting statistics and chairing committee meetings.

Paul's instructions for women on the subject of worship, which complete this chapter (2:9–15), have proven both controversial and confusing. Yet all Scripture must be interpreted; we dare not ask "What does it say?" without also asking "What does it mean?" So what does Paul mean here? How should these directions be understood? How do they square with other biblical statements on the subject, including other statements by Paul himself? And are they timeless principles or specific rules for certain congregations in particular circumstances?

## 1. THE UNIVERSAL IMPORTANCE OF PRAYER 2:1–8

Worship was a priority for Paul, as he calls for prayer **first of all**. That phrase is not merely a literary transition; it indicates the primacy of the subject in the apostle's thinking. This counsel for a troubled church and its young pastor should be written into modern leadership manuals: first of all, pray and worship.

 WHAT OTHERS SAY

From the Christian philosopher and apologist Justin Martyr, we have this intriguing description of a worship service dating from approximately fifty years after the close of the New Testament era.

"On the day called Sunday there is a gathering together in the same place of all who live in a given city or rural district. The memoirs of the apostles or the writings of the prophets are read, as long as time permits. Then when the reader ceases, the president in a discourse admonishes and urges the imitation of these good things. Next we all rise together and send up prayers. When we cease from our prayer, bread is presented and wine and water. The president in the same manner sends up prayers and thanksgivings, according to his ability, and the people sing out their assent, saying the Amen. A distribution and participation of the elements for which thanks have been given is made to each person, and to those who are not present they are sent by the deacons."

—*First Apology*

## A PRIMER ON PRAYER

Each of the four words Paul uses for prayer has a different shade of meaning. **Requests** are primarily personal petitions, **prayers** are general conversations with God, **intercession** is made for others, and **thanksgiving** reminds us that prayer should never be divorced from praise and gratitude to God. It is possible that the Greek word *eucharistias*, thanksgivings, is meant to suggest the Eucharist, or Lord's Supper (see 1 Cor. 11:24). Paul's point, though, is not about specific types of prayer but about prayer itself. To Paul, prayer is of overriding importance in the life of the church.

That is why Paul urges prayer for **everyone** (v. 1) and then repeats by **men**

**everywhere** (v. 8). Note the circle of prayer that is formed as everyone is urged to pray for everyone else: pray, and be prayed for. The Christian community should be inundated with prayer, and so should society as a whole.

In fact, we are to pray especially for **kings and all those in authority**. Even in a pagan and godless culture, Christians were directed to pray for the officials of their government. The Roman emperor in power when Paul wrote these words to Timothy was Nero, the same Nero who later ordered the execution of Paul himself. Pray for Nero?

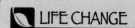

## LIFE CHANGE

### AUTHENTIC PRAYER

Modern worship services employ a variety of prayers, but often they are offered to God carelessly and with little advance thought. Andrew Blackwood Sr. once deplored the "sameness, lameness, and tameness" of our public prayers. Paul would applaud any effort to increase the quantity and improve the quality of our public prayers, judging from his emphasis here.

Certainly. Who needed it more! There is no room allowed here for picking and choosing those for whom we will pray. Paul urges prayer not just for leaders we like or with whom we agree, but for all leaders. Good or bad, they all need prayer.

Paul sees both practical and spiritual benefits in this Christian discipline. Even an evil government like Rome, if persuaded that Christians were committed to a spiritual and not political revolution, might allow them to **live peaceful and quiet lives**. If not, then those praying Christians, though persecuted, will at least be living **in all godliness and holiness** because they will have honored Christ's call to love one's enemies.

Lifting up **hands in prayer** was a common practice both in Jewish synagogues and in pagan temples, but to this practice Paul adds an ethical principle: the hands must be **holy**, meaning morally and not just ceremonially clean. Likewise, the heart must be pure, **without anger**. Evidently, quarreling and conflict were threatening the unity of the Ephesian congregation. Can you really worship together, Paul is asking, if there's something between you and a fellow believer that needs to be settled (Matt. 5:23–24)? Hands are never holy unless the heart is also. And if the heart is not pure, prayer is merely spiritual posturing.

## GOD OUR SAVIOR

God's heart is also on display in this passage. Paul reveals that God has a desire for **all men to be saved and to come to a knowledge of the truth**. That's why He provided atonement for all through the cross of Christ (2 Cor. 5:14, 15) and issued an invitation for all to come to salvation (John 3:16). Peter makes exactly the same point: "[God] is patient with you, not wanting anyone to perish, but everyone to come to repentance" (2 Pet. 3:9).

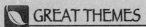

### GREAT THEMES

#### SALVATION FOR ALL

The "whosoever will" emphasis of Wesleyan theology finds a solid foundation in definitive passages like this one. There's no indication here that the offer of salvation is limited to a pre-selected few. On the other hand, it would be a mistake to read into passages like this an unbiblical universalism, which teaches that all will ultimately be saved, regardless of what choices they make. God loves all, makes provision for all, and invites all; but not all will choose to respond and be saved.

At this point Paul's focus shifts. *All* has been the key word as he has stressed inclusiveness: prayer by all, prayer for all, especially for all in authority, because God wants all to be saved. Gnosticism boasted of its exclusivity, teaching that some, but not all, have intuitive knowledge of how to be saved. Paul may have been taking aim at this notion that there is a class of the spiritually elite within the church. In 1 Tim. 2:5, however, the key word is *one*, and the tone is suddenly and unapologetically exclusive because the issue at hand has changed. No longer is the question "Who can be saved?" but rather, "Who is the Savior?"

## CHRIST OUR MEDIATOR

The classic tribute to Christ the Mediator contained in this passage appears to be a fragment of a hymn, creed, or catechism from the early church. As such, it's perfectly placed in a section devoted to worship. Other possible liturgical elements in 1 Timothy include the doxologies of 1:17 and 6:15–16 and the hymn to Christ in 3:16. Paul may well have been quoting words used by the church in worship in some or all of these cases. If not, his words certainly provided the church with new expressions for worship.

If the Ephesian heresy did contain Gnostic elements, this affirmation strikes them with a second blow, for Paul asserts that at the center of this inclusive circle drawn by the gospel stands the Christ, the one Way to God. Then, as now, cultic groups invariably mischaracterize who Jesus is. Paul leaves no room for wrongheaded ideas about either the Incarnation or the salvation it makes possible.

*A Challenge to Gnosticism.* Each phrase of 1 Tim. 2:5–6 answers ancient and modern critics of biblical theism, belief in the one personal, immanent, and transcendent God of the Bible.

- Against *atheism*, Paul insists that there is, in fact, a **God**.

- Against *polytheism*, Paul asserts that there is **one God**, not many. (Jewish readers would recognize this declaration as part of the *Shema*, the creed of Israel based on Deut. 6:4 that was repeated at every service in the synagogue.)

- Against *pantheism*, Paul points out that God and His creatures are not one and the same; they are separated by human sin and need a **mediator** to bring them together.

- Against *pluralism*, which sees every path as a path to God, Paul rejects all mediators but **one.**

- Against *deism*, the Enlightenment religion that views God as distant and uninvolved with His creation, this passage reveals a God-Man—**the man Christ Jesus**—who gave Himself **as a ransom for all men**. (Here Paul echoes Christ's portrait of himself in Mark 10:45.)

In this passage Paul also alludes to Christ's declaration that He is the one and only mediator between God and humankind. At the Last Supper, Christ described Himself as "the way and the truth and the life" and added, "No one comes to the Father except through me" (John 14:6). Such claims of unique authority are less than popular in our pluralistic age, but the fact is that truth is narrow while error is broad. How many right answers are there to a question like "What is the sum of 2 + 2?"

and how many wrong? Besieged as they were by Jewish-Gnostic error, first-century Christians needed to be centered on the finality of Christ. Besieged as we are by a host of modern errors that masquerade as truth, twenty-first-century Christians need the same centering.

All can be saved, yet only One can be the Savior. There is one Way, one Door (John 10:1–10), one Mediator, one Name under heaven given to us by which we can be saved (Acts 4:12).

*God's Perfect Timing.* The Incarnation was **the testimony given in its proper time**, a reference to the fact that God carefully chose the moment when He would send His Son. The Creator of time is its master, and His timing is always perfect.

The Greek language has two words for time. *Chronos* is the root of our word *chronology* and refers to calendar or clock time. *Kairos*, the word used here, refers to the quality of time. Paul's word choice shows that God was not watching a clock; He was watching a world. He chose to act at the **proper time**. First Timothy 2:6 parallels Gal. 4:4, in which Paul writes that God sent His Son when the *kairos* had fully come.

The God who acted at the right time also chose the right messenger. The call to ministry about which Paul rejoiced in 1 Timothy 1 was actually an appointment to be **a herald, an apostle**, and **a teacher of the true faith**. As a herald, Paul was to proclaim the truth. As an apostle, he was to champion the truth around the world. As a teacher, he was to instruct others in the truth, particularly **the Gentiles**. This, in a nutshell, is Paul's mission statement, and it was important to him that his readers understand and accept it.

**I am telling the truth, I am not lying** is a characteristically Pauline statement. Paul uses similar expressions in Rom. 9:1; 2 Cor. 11:31; and Gal. 1:20. A declaration of his truthfulness would not be necessary for Timothy, of course; but if Paul intended for the letter to be read to the entire church, including those being reprimanded, its use makes sense. Paul's credibility may have been under attack; this statement affirms his trustworthiness.

## 2. RULES FOR EPHESIAN WOMEN IN WORSHIP 2:9–15

In the second half of this chapter on worship, Paul shifts his focus to the women of the congregation. He sees two problems.

## DRESS AND APPEARANCE

The first problem involves the dress and appearance of the Christian women in Ephesus. In the original language, verse 9 shares a main verb with the preceding verse (our division of the chapter is topical, not grammatical) and may be read, "Likewise women to dress modestly, with decency and propriety. . . ." Paul's chosen verb back in v. 8 is really stronger than it appears to be in English; Paul expects his instructions to be followed.

Apparently, some of the women of the church were attending services dressed extravagantly and sporting elaborate hairstyles, **braided** with **gold** and jewels. Such ostentation might have been considered fashionable in Ephesian society or among the pagans worshiping at Artemis's temple, but it was not appropriate for Christian worship. John Wesley faced a similar situation in eighteenth-century England. He deplored the aristocratic custom of flaunting wealth and position by pretentious displays of fashion. An artist from Wesley's day has preserved for us the spectacle of a society lady whose hairstyle made generous use of wigs, which served as swirling waves for the tableau of a sea battle, complete with ships! Wesley condemned both the vanity and the poor stewardship represented by this custom along with the absence of modesty in the gowns many women wore.

Paul makes the same points here. His appeal is not for a legalistic plainness, although the passage has been read that way by some, but for an appearance that avoids excess and does not call attention to itself. True adornment, Paul argues, is a life of **good deeds**; that's what the "well-dressed" Christian woman should be wearing this and every year.

## PARTICIPATION IN THE KINGDOM

The second problem involves the participation of women in worship and ministry. This issue requires more attention, not only because of its complexity but also because of its consequences. Fully half of the church is directly affected by how this passage is interpreted, and the rest of the church is impacted by its repercussions—from pulpit ministry to public testimony, from the classroom to the church board, at home, and on the mission field. The issue: women speaking and teaching in the church.

Some regard Paul as a chauvinist. The charge is based largely on these verses and a similar passage in 1 Corinthians 14, in which he is thought by some to relegate women to second-class status in the church. Some others agree that Paul ranks men above women but accept this classification as the will of God, convinced that the subordination of women is one link in a divine chain of command.

There is a third way to understand Paul's words to Timothy, a way that not only takes seriously the problems in the Ephesian congregation but also gives proper weight to biblical passages that affirm women as partners in building the Kingdom and commend their ministry in the church.

When 1 Timothy 2 is studied, stress is usually placed on the idea that women should be submissive and silent. But the place to begin is where Paul begins: **A woman should learn** (or, in the New Revised Standard Version, "Let a woman learn"). That very concept—that women should be allowed to learn—was foreign to rabbinical thinking and Jewish custom in the first century. As a rule, rabbis would not even discuss religion with a woman. The early Christian church, on the other hand, recognized that Christ encouraged the full participation of women in the Kingdom.

Mary and Martha of Bethany were close friends of Jesus, and Mary even sat at his feet for instruction (Luke 10:38–42).

Other female disciples are known, including the woman at Jacob's well, whose witness led many people to faith (John 4:39). Luke 8:1–3 states that many women accompanied Christ during his ministry and supported Him financially, naming among them Mary Magdalene, Joanna the wife of Cuza, and Susanna.

Women were the last at the cross and the first at the tomb (Matt. 27:55–56, 28:1–8). For that reason, Jesus' first post-resurrection appearances were to women (Matt. 28:9–10).

Paul's own experience was consistent with Christ's.

Priscilla and her husband, Aquila, were colleagues of Paul and "fellow workers" (Rom. 16:3; *sunergos* is the term used, from which we get the word *synergy*). That puts Priscilla and Aquila in good company; among the others whom Paul calls fellow workers are Timothy, Titus, Mark, and Luke. Priscilla (or Prisca, her more formal Latin name) and Aquila tutored Apollos in the faith (Acts 18:24–26) before he became the pastor at Corinth.

Lydia, an independent businesswoman in Philippi, was Paul's first European convert and played host to him on his second missionary journey.

Phoebe probably carried Paul's Roman epistle to that church. He commended her to the Roman believers not only as a "sister" but also as a "servant of the Church at Cenchrea." The Greek word for servant is *diakonos*, which in other church-related texts is translated deacon or, more often in Paul's writings, minister. It's a word used by Paul to describe himself.

Junia (the New International Version renders it Junias, but it is a feminine name) is mentioned in Rom. 16:7 as one who is "outstanding among the apostles." Some take this reference to mean that she belongs in the same category as Barnabas and Paul (Acts 14:14)—designated as apostles although they were not among the original Twelve. John Chrysostom, the great preacher of the patristic period, thought so. This fourth-century church father wrote, "Oh! How great is the devotion of this woman, that she should be counted worthy of the appellation of apostle!"[1] At the very least, the statement that Junia was "outstanding among the apostles" means that the church held her in high regard.

In fact, of the twenty-eight people singled out by Paul for greetings in that final chapter of Romans, nine are women. Of those given commendation by Paul, more are women than men.

Galatians 3:28 flies like a banner over these notable examples: "There is neither . . . male nor female, for you are all one in Christ Jesus." How, then, should the restrictions of 1 Timothy 2 be understood?

*A Parallel with 1 Corinthians.* Paul's requirement of **quietness and full submission** parallels his comment on women's silence and submission in the first Corinthian letter (1 Cor. 14:33b–35). In the Corinthian passage, the instruction comes within a call for orderly worship in a congregation characterized by charismatic confusion; worship in Corinth was a cacophony of tongues and prophecy. In 1 Timothy the instruction for women comes within a call for orderly worship in a congregation plagued by false teachers. Both churches faced special challenges, and in both cases the challenges involved women in the congregation.

It appears that in Corinth, women who were not properly instructed were disrupting worship services by conversing among themselves or by asking questions of their husbands or teachers (1 Cor. 14:35). In Timothy's church at Ephesus, women whose learning was limited were attracted to false teaching (1 Tim. 5:15; 2 Tim. 3:6–7) and were heavily influenced by it. It's possible that some women were actually advocates of the heresy and were aggressively interrupting worship services with comments that were out of order. Having instructed Timothy to stop men from promoting false doctrine (1:3), Paul is determined to prevent certain uneducated women from propagating it too. The apostle writes to two churches in turmoil. To both he issues instructions intended to restore order.

One thing is certain: Paul does not impose an absolute rule of silence upon women in worship. Can anyone imagine that he would prohibit women, then or now, from singing? From testifying? From participating in litanies or responsive readings? From saying "Amen" at the close of a prayer?

That seems impossible, especially in light of 1 Cor. 11:5, in which Paul acknowledges the right of women to pray and prophesy in public worship. In that verse, Paul not only permits but expects public prayer and prophesy from women, stipulating only that their heads must be covered when they do so. Women prophets like Miriam, Deborah, and Huldah enjoyed divine approval in the Old Testament, and the New Testament declares that women will continue to prophesy. Peter declared on the Day of Pentecost that Joel's prophecy had been fulfilled: "I will pour out my Spirit on all people. Your sons and daughters will prophesy. . . . Even on my servants, both men and women, I will pour out my Spirit in those days, and they will prophesy" (Acts 2:17–18). Philip's four daughters demonstrate that reality, for they all prophesied (Acts 21:9).

For Paul, the gift of prophecy is second only to apostleship—he ranks prophecy higher than teaching in 1 Cor. 12:28—and women who have the gift of prophecy also have the right to exercise it, both in public worship and private conversation.

So the restriction in 1 Timothy 2 cannot be absolute; otherwise, Paul would be contradicting himself.

*Universal Principles versus Special Cases.* The clouds of confusion surrounding this issue lift if we view Paul's restrictions on women as special rules for extraordinary circumstances rather than as a universal requirement for every church in every age. That understanding can help us with the rest of this passage in 1 Timothy 2 as well.

The **submission** Paul expects is not to husbands in this case, as some writers suggest; husbands aren't even mentioned in the passage. (Eph. 5:22 does call for wives to submit to their husbands, but it's important to notice that the preceding verse, which is cited far less frequently, calls for *mutual* submission, including both men and women, to each other "out of reverence for Christ.") Nor does Paul specify submission to men in general in 1 Timothy 2. Given the context of this chapter, it seems clear that the women who were learning (v. 11a) were required to submit to their teachers and, beyond that, to the church and ultimately to God. That should be the attitude of any disciple, male or female.

In the same way, **I do not permit a woman to teach** need not be taken as a universal principle. If it is, Priscilla should have been reprimanded rather than commended for instructing Apollos. Like the requirement that women must wear a head covering in church (1 Cor. 11:2–16), the prohibition of women from teaching—which is mentioned only this one time in Scripture—seems to be a temporary injunction based on historical and cultural conditions.[2]

It would be wrong, of course, to make wholesale claims of "cultural conditioning" in order to dismiss biblical passages that make us uncomfortable. We have too high a view of the inspiration of Scripture to allow that. We recognize that in His Word God has given us timeless truths that never change. Yet we must recognize also that scattered among the Bible's timeless truths are time-specific customs and cultural practices, which apply much better to the time period in which they were written than they do today. How many Christians, for example, still greet each other with a holy kiss, as 1 Cor. 16:20 commands us? Paul, writing in a day when women were free in Christ but still poorly educated, was doing damage control on a church in crisis. These measures are best understood in that light.

Consider in that same light Paul's determination not to permit a **woman to have authority over a man.** For many sincere Christians, this is the line in the sand. They agree that women may be allowed to speak, sing, or serve in the church, but not in any capacity that would place them in leadership over men. Is that Paul's intent?

The verb translated "to have authority" appears only here in the New Testament. Instead of a more common word, Paul uses this harsher one which literally means "to usurp authority" (King James Version) or to domineer. Women who followed the false teachers at Ephesus would have been challenging the legitimate authority of Timothy and the leadership of the church. Paul would not allow a woman to "lord it over a man" by seizing authority not granted to her by the church, but it's doubtful that he would feel the same way about women today who are serving in leadership positions at the invitation of the church.

If women may not teach or lead, should women write books or articles on the faith, and should men read them? The hymns of Fanny Crosby, Frances Ridley Havergal, Charlotte Elliott, and Margaret Clarkson teach Christian doctrines; should men sing them? And what about foreign missions? Even some churches that strictly prohibit women from teaching men in their home congregations depend heavily on women's ministry on the mission field. The majority of Christian missionaries are women, and many of them

## GREAT THEMES

### WOMEN IN MINISTRY

Churches in the Wesleyan tradition have valued the contribution of women in ministry since the earliest days of the movement. "God owns women in the conversion of sinners," John Wesley said more than two hundred years ago, "and who am I that I should withstand God?" A generation later, Wesleyan commentator and churchman Adam Clarke agreed: "Under Christianity, [women] have equal rights, equal privileges, and equal blessings . . . and, let me add, they are equally useful." For more than a century, Wesleyan denominations have been ordaining women as ministers in the conviction that Paul's prohibitions are best understood not as a universal law for the church but as local measures limited to the particular situations to which they were addressed. This long-standing tradition is not a concession to radical feminism or feminist theology. It predates both by centuries. Rather, it is a logical and time-honored extension of what Wesley (and Wesleyans) saw as the biblical legacy of women in every age.

minister in one way or another to congregations populated by men as well as women. Is something that is forbidden at home somehow appropriate in another country?

*The Adam and Eve Argument.* Those who are convinced that Paul's words in 1 Timothy 2 should be understood as a universal principle argue that Paul makes his case using a universal illustration.

In vv. 13–14 Paul points back to Creation: **For Adam was formed first, then Eve**. By Paul's time Jewish rabbis had long declared that men should have authority over women in every sphere of life because men were created first. Paul knew this argument well, but in 1 Cor. 11:11–12 he acknowledges the interdependence of men and women (Eve came from Adam, but since creation all men have come from women!) and our mutual dependence upon God ("But everything comes from God"). If authority lies in the order of creation, wouldn't animals have authority over us all? Or wouldn't the Old Testament have authority over the New?

**And Adam was not the one deceived**, Paul's thought continues; **it was the woman who was deceived and became a sinner**. Some contend that by saying this, Paul asserts that all women are, by nature, more susceptible to deception and are therefore unqualified to teach. Yet would we then conclude that Adam was superior to Eve because he sinned deliberately and not by deception?

No, it is more likely that the conjunction **for** in v. 13 is explanatory rather than causative, so that it means "for example" not "because." Paul is using Adam and Eve as an example of his point but not using them as the theological rationale for it. Like Eve, many women in Timothy's church had been deceived by erroneous doctrine; Paul seems to be insisting here, very properly, that teaching is no role for the spiritually immature and ungrounded.

Incidentally, an appeal to the order of creation does not, in itself, constitute a theologically binding principle. Paul appeals to creation also in his argument for women wearing head coverings in worship (see 1 Cor. 11:8–9). Most Christians understand the requirement for women to worship with covered heads to be a cultural issue that had relevance in Paul's day but not ours.

63

Richard and Catherine Clark Kroeger believe this entire section of 1 Timothy is aimed combating at a Gnostic heresy that glorified Eve (along with the serpent), saw her as blessed instead of cursed after the Fall, and identified her with a number of pagan goddesses. This cult taught that Eve could enlighten (impart *gnosis* to) those in need of salvation and that, as the "mother of all living," she actually preceded Adam.[3] That this section was written with that heresy in mind is a distinct possibility.

It is true that the easiest conclusion to draw from 1 Timothy 2 is that women are disqualified from ministry and leadership not because of an absence of gifts or graces but because of gender. It is also true that that conclusion runs counter to much of Scripture. Apparently, the easiest conclusions aren't always the best.

Paul is the apostle of Christian freedom. Given his conviction that in Christ there is no male or female (Gal. 3:28), his recognition of women's right to prophesy (preach) in public worship (1 Cor. 11:5), and his commendation of the ministries of such women as Priscilla and Phoebe, 1 Timothy 2 is best viewed through the lens of Christian freedom.

## SALVATION AND CHILDBEARING

On one thing all agree: v. 15 contains the most perplexing statement in the chapter, if not in the entire New Testament. What could Paul possibly mean by writing that **women will be saved through childbearing**?

It should go without saying that Paul, the great proponent of salvation by grace through faith, would never suggest that childbirth could secure anyone's salvation. That would be another form of salvation by works. And if that were the case, what would be the fate of single women or married women without children? Clearly, a literal interpretation of this verse is without merit. Three other views have support.

*Safety in Childbearing.* Some translators suggest the rendering "be kept safe" in place of "be saved," maintaining that Christian women will be protected from harm in the bearing of children despite the curse of Gen. 3:16. (Moffatt translates this verse, "Women will get safely through childbirth,"[4] and J. B. Phillips's paraphrase is very similar.[5]) According to this theory, Christian women may not teach or serve in leadership roles, but God will give them His gracious guarantee of preservation in childbearing. The problem with that theory is that it simply hasn't proven true. Many Christian women have died in childbirth.

*Elevation of Motherhood.* Others note that the false teachers at Ephesus were challenging the validity of marriage and motherhood, portraying those roles as unworthy (1 Tim. 4:3). These commentators surmise that Paul's puzzling reference to salvation through childbearing is intended to restore the domestic and maternal roles of women to a place of honor and respect. By this interpretation, Paul is not talking about personal salvation but about personal fulfillment and a sense of self-worth. If that is Paul's intention, he uses the Greek verb *sodzo*, "to save," in a way not used elsewhere in the New Testament.

*Incarnation.* Many believe that 1 Tim. 2:15 refers to the Incarnation. In Gen. 3:16 God declared that women would experience pain in childbearing as a consequence of the Fall and Eve's role in it. But in the preceding verse, Gen. 3:15, God had promised a Savior. This *protevangelium* (first gospel) pledged that the seed of the woman would crush the head of the serpent. Because a definite article, *the,* is present in 1 Tim. 2:15, Paul could be saying that Eve and all women may be saved through *the* birth of *the* Child, the Messiah. Admittedly, this interpretation is a stretch; no major version translates the verse to reflect it. But it's an ancient interpretation first proposed early in the church's history, and it continues to have many proponents. It is theologically valid and provides a beautiful picture of the grace of God in turning the consequences of the Fall to our redemption: after centuries of painful and perilous childbirth, one Child is born who will lead us back to fellowship with God. Of course, if that is the point that Paul wishes to make, there are clearer ways in which he might have stated it.

Truth be told, no one is sure what this enigmatic verse means.

There's no debate, however, about the Christian virtues that close the chapter. Paul looks to Christian women for **faith, love, and holiness—**another triad of graces (see 1:2 and 1:5). Still concerned about decorum and proper behavior in worship, he adds **with propriety.**

## ENDNOTES

1. John Chrysostom, "Homily on Romans 16," in Philip Schaff, ed., *A Select Library of The Nicene and Post-Nicene Fathers of the Christian Church, II* (Grand Rapids, Mich.: Wm. B. Eerdmans Publishing Co., 1956), p. 555.

2. If Paul means for the prohibition of women from teaching to be a divine imperative, it is strange that he doesn't use an imperative form of the verb. Grammatically, "I do not permit" does not carry the same force as "Do not permit." Emphasizing his use of the present tense, some suggest that the thrust of Paul's words is "At present I am not permitting."

3. Richard and Catherine Clark Kroeger, *I Suffer Not a Woman: Rethinking 1 Timothy 2:11–15 in Light of Ancient Evidence* (Grand Rapids, Mich.: Baker Book House, 1992), p. 117 and following.

4. James Moffatt, *The Bible: A New Translation,* Revised and Final Edition (New York: Harper and Brothers Publishers, 1950), p. 3.

5. J.B. Phillips, *The New Testament in Modern English,* Student Edition (New York: Macmillan Publishing Company, 1972), p. 437.

# THE ETHICAL CHARACTER OF A LEADER

## 1 Timothy 3:1-13

After giving instructions for the church's worship, Paul turns his attention to the subject of the ministry—specifically, the offices of overseer (3:1–7) and deacon (3:8–13)—offering a checklist of the qualities and characteristics that the church should look for in its leaders. Little attention is given to their duties. It would be impossible to create a job description for either office based on 1 Timothy 3. That in itself makes a significant statement about Christian leadership: integrity and spiritual maturity are more important than ability, although both are essential. For the called, gifts and graces go hand-in-hand, but the Bible places much more emphasis on being grace-full than on being gifted.

In Paul's profile of these two ministerial offices, many of the required qualities overlap. Probably not much notice should be taken of any differences. The two have distinct duties, but excellence is the common standard for the spiritual, social, and moral qualifications of any Christian leader. In its leaders—clergy or lay, regardless of rank or position—the church dares not settle for less.

## REQUIREMENTS FOR OVERSEERS AND DEACONS

| Requirement | Overseer | Deacon |
|---|---|---|
| Above reproach/clear conscience | 3:2 | 3:9 |
| Husband of one wife | 3:2 | 3:12 |
| Temperate | 3:2 | 3:8 |
| Self-controlled | 3:2 | |
| Respectable | 3:2 | 3:8 |
| Hospitable | 3:2 | |
| Able to teach | 3:2 | |
| Not given to drunkenness | 3:3 | 3:8 |
| Not violent but gentle | 3:3 | |
| Not quarrelsome | 3:3 | |
| Not a lover of money | 3:3 | |
| Manages his own family well | 3:4 | 3:12 |
| Sees that his children obey him | 3:4–5 | 3:12 |
| Not a recent convert | 3:6 | |
| Has good reputation with outsiders | 3:7 | |
| Sincere | | 3:8 |
| Not pursuing dishonest gain | | 3:8 |
| Tested | | 3:10 |
| Keeps hold of deep truths | | 3:9 |

# 1. THE OFFICE OF OVERSEER 3:1–7

Another **trustworthy saying** appears to introduce Paul's discussion of leadership positions in chapter 3; however, some believe this saying belongs to the paragraph on women's roles, which closes chapter 2. Chapter and verse divisions in the Bible are not part of the original text and are not inspired. Paul's letter to Timothy was written as our letters are written, in one continuous flow from greeting to closing. The current chapter and verse divisions were not added until 1551, so it's entirely possible that what appears to be the opening thought of chapter 3 may actually be the final thought of chapter 2. The "trustworthy saying" formula can follow as well as precede the quotation it is intended to highlight (see Titus 3:8), and some commentators think this one does precisely that.

Grammatically, it is possible that the saying could be linked to 1 Timothy 2. Stylistically, it's unlikely. The statement that church ministry is noble work might not be the most quotable one in Scripture, but Paul's puzzling reference to women being saved through childbearing (2:15) is too cryptic to carry the weight of a trustworthy saying. Paul probably attached the familiar formula to 3:1 to indicate the high esteem in which the office of overseer should be held; perhaps it wasn't so highly regarded in those days. In a society hostile to the church, leaders in particular are exposed to persecution. And isn't the gift of administration ranked toward the bottom of the list in 1 Cor. 12:28, below other "more spiritual" gifts? If the Ephesians followed that logic, Paul might have been trying to elevate the offices of church leadership in the eyes of his readers and attract better candidates to those positions.

On the other hand, it's possible that Ephesus needed no persuasion. Paul may have been simply reinforcing an already popular opinion with an already popular proverb: **If anyone sets his heart on being an overseer, he desires a noble task**.

## LEADERSHIP STAGE ONE: A PASTORAL COMMITTEE

The Greek term for **overseer** is *episkopos*, which traditionally has been translated *bishop*. Our word *episcopal*, which denotes a system of church government that uses bishops, is derived from that root. It was not until after the New Testament era, though, that a single *episkopos* assumed personal and individual authority over a congregation, and, still later, over several congregations in the same geographical area (a diocese). When Paul wrote to Timothy, there apparently was not a single pastor or bishop per church but a governing board of overseers in each congregation, assisted in ministry by the deacons (1 Tim. 3:8–13). The arrangement was similar to the organization of the Jewish communities from which most Christians had come. Every Jewish synagogue was ruled by its council of elders, a tradition that was said to date back to the seventy elders appointed by Moses in Num. 11:16–17, 24–25. In the New Testament, the term **overseer** is synonymous with *elder*. The Greek word for *elder* is *presbuteros*, from which we derive the terms *presbyter* and *presbyterian*. When Paul addresses the leaders of this same Ephesian church in Acts 20, they are referred to interchangeably as elders (20:17) and overseers (20:28). Similarly, Paul writes of overseers in 1 Timothy 3 and of elders in 1 Timothy 5, both in the context of directing the church's affairs (3:5, 5:17). He also seems to equate elders and overseers in Titus 1:5, 7. Apparently, these are two titles for the same office—*elder* being a reference to the leader's age and experience and *overseer* a reference to the leader's responsibility or function. A first-century church would have been pastored by several such elders or overseers.[1]

## LEADERSHIP STAGE TWO: A SINGLE OVERSEER

By the beginning of the second century, however, a new system gained acceptance on the ecclesiastical scene. In place of a pastoral board, a single overseer was set over his fellow elders as first-among-equals and was charged with oversight of the entire congregation. Properly concerned about the problems of heresy and disunity in the church—the same kind of problems Timothy faced in Ephesus—leaders like Ignatius of Antioch elevated the role of this single overseer to paramount importance. On his way to martyrdom in Rome in A.D. 107, Ignatius wrote seven letters to sister congregations, offering a simple but potentially far-reaching prescription for the ills of the church: obey the (one) bishop.

But the rise of this powerful *monarchical bishop* came a generation after 1 Timothy was written. Since it's difficult for a modern reader not to think of that kind of bishop when reading the term, **overseer** is a less misleading translation of *episkopos*.

Timothy was not an overseer; however, he was an apostolic delegate, reporting directly to Paul. As such, he had authority beyond that of the overseers/elders and was considered the pastor of the Ephesian congregation, overseeing its overseers. He had the power to appoint and ordain overseers/elders (1 Tim. 5:22), as Paul and Barnabas had appointed elders in all the churches they had planted on their first missionary journey (Acts 14:23; see also Titus 1:5). Remember that 1 Tim. 3:1–13 is addressed to Timothy, not to the church. We are not told anything about the role of the church in the selection of its leaders.

Two observations may be made at this point.

First, the New Testament does not distinguish between the roles of the clergy and laity as clearly as we do; those separate classifications developed more fully later. But some distinction is implied in the very existence of the office of overseer/elder. That certainly doesn't imply the superiority of the one status over the other. It is merely a distinction of spiritual function. In the apostolic era, as in the subsequent history of the church, some were called to spiritual leadership and had the gifts, authority, and responsibilities required to perform it. All Christians are ministers in that all are servants, but some Christians, from Paul's day to the present, have been called to "the ministry," a specialized leadership role within the church.

Second, there has also always been a diversity of ministry roles. As an apostle, Paul had an itinerant ministry; prophets and evangelists traveled also. But the overseers and deacons Timothy was to appoint were stationary, serving a single congregation.

## CREDENTIALS OF OVERSEERS

From the *Didache*, a manual of church practice dating from around the turn of the first century, come these words: "[Choose] overseers and deacons who are worthy of the Lord." That's the theme of 1 Timothy 3 where Paul lists fourteen criteria for determining the suitability of overseers (vv. 2–7) and eight for deacons (vv. 8–10; 12–13), along with four for "the women" (v. 11). These qualities are the credentials for Christian leadership. The **noble task** of overseer requires not noble birth or rank but noble character; **likewise** for the men and women serving in support ministries (v. 8, v. 11). James Stalker writes, "The prime qualification for the ministry is goodness."[2] Timothy is to screen candidates carefully for behaviors that exemplify Christian character and integrity.

**The overseer must be above reproach**. Writers who wonder that the standards in this chapter aren't higher should revisit the very first one. It sets the tone for the rest of the list; all of the others should be read as areas in which the leader is to be blameless. Taken by themselves, many of the other expectations do seem elementary; surely all Christians should practice self-control and beware the lure of money, for example. But Paul is saying that leaders should be above reproach in their self-control and that they should have an attitude toward money that not even their critics can fault. Leaders aren't held to new spiritual principles, but they are held to greater accountability in the principles common to us all. Qualifications two through fourteen appear in no apparent order, but there is a reason this one heads the list. In every sphere of an overseer's life, this sets a standard of spiritual excellence.

The remaining qualifications may be examined topically.

*In the Home.* In the home an overseer must be a faithful spouse and a good parent. Much debate surrounds the requirement that he be **the husband of but one wife.** This should not be taken simply as the prohibition of polygamy; that would have been unnecessary because the church would have considered such a lifestyle scandalous for any Christian, not just for leaders. Nor can it be seen as a requirement that overseers be married, although some have taken it that way. Jesus wasn't married, and neither, apparently, was Paul (see 1 Cor. 7:8). If an unmarried man is disqualified on the basis of 1 Tim. 3:2, would a childless man be disqualified on the basis of v. 4? And if the question is merely marriage versus singleness, why the stress on **one** wife?

There is wide support for the theory that Paul was thinking of remarriage—either a second marriage after a divorce, where the innocent party would ordinarily be free to marry again, or even a remarriage after the death of a first wife. According to this view, remarriage was prohibited not for all Christians but for leaders (including deacons; see 3:12) as evidence of extraordinary spiritual discipline. It's true that remaining single after divorce or the death of a spouse was considered praiseworthy by some in first-century society, and it's true also that Paul himself had previously advocated singleness (1 Cor. 7:8–9). In 1 Timothy, however, Paul nearly insists that younger widows remarry (5:14), which is interesting because widows are held to the same marital standard as overseers. They are to be, according to the literal translation of 5:9, "the wife of one husband." Why would Paul encourage young widows to remarry if that were less spiritual than remaining single, especially if it also would disqualify them from inclusion on the list of honored widows?

The fourth and final option for interpreting Paul's instruction on marriage is preferred: it means that a leader must practice fidelity within marriage. The New English Bible translates it this way: "faithful to one wife." Curiously, the New International Version doesn't translate the instruction that way in the passage on overseers but does in the section on widows—"faithful to her husband" (1 Tim. 5:9)—even though the structure of the two passages is similar in the original language. Robert Anderson puts it more colloquially: an overseer must be "a one-woman kind of man."[3] This interpretation gives strong support to marriage and family without introducing the kind of ascetic regulation for which Paul criticizes the false teachers (see 4:1–3).

In his emphasis on sexual morality and marital faithfulness for ministers, Paul sounds a timely, and timeless, warning. Nothing less than being "above reproach" will do.

Interestingly enough, the debate over women in ministry in chapter 2 spills over into chapter 3. Many opponents of the ordination of women contend that the list of qualifications applies only to males since an elder must be "the husband of one wife." Churches that turn women away from the pastoral office, however, seldom forbid single men (who are not husbands, v. 2) or men without children (v. 4) from entering the ministry. Paul's assumptions are not necessarily Paul's requirements. (The translation of 3:1 shared by the King James and New King James Versions is particularly restrictive. It reads "If a man . . ." when the Greek pronoun means *anyone*.)

As a parent, the overseer **must manage his own family well** (v. 4). The same verb is used here of the family and in 5:17 of the church. The comparison is intentional, for **if anyone does not know how to manage his own family, how can he take care of God's church**, which in the same chapter is called God's household (3:15)? Scripture is filled with parallels between the home and the church, and in a Quaker phrase, the family is "the little church" (*ecclesiola*). It's not surprising, then, that Paul holds up the family—not synagogue experience or civic leadership—as the pattern for church leadership. That involves discipline, of course; the overseer must **see that his children obey him**. But the word that the New International Version translates **with proper respect** is best understood as applying to the attitude of the parent. In his loving faithfulness to spouse and his measured discipline of children, the overseer must be above reproach. Leadership in the family of God requires it.

73

*In the Inner Life.* The overseer must be above reproach in the way he manages himself. He must be **temperate**, developing a lifestyle of moderation in his habits and appetites. Synonyms include *clearheaded* and *soberminded*—able to avoid excess and find balance in every area of life. Temperance is usually associated with the consumption of alcohol, but since that vice is specified further down the list, the focus here is on moderation in other things, from eating to spending.

Closely associated with temperance is the requirement to be **self-controlled**. Many Christians would be surprised to hear that the Bible says more about self-control, self-discipline, and self-sacrifice than it does about self-esteem and self-fulfillment. A leader who lacks self-control is a leader incapable of leading himself.

**Not given to drunkenness** is an inelegant item in a list of qualifications for Christian leadership, but Paul evidently had reason to be embarrassingly blunt. We might suppose that some things would go without saying, but moral and spiritual decline set in when the church allows things that need to be stated openly to "go without saying."

**Not a lover of money** also might seem an unnecessary stipulation for someone in the ministry, where salaries seldom rival the pay for comparable work in the marketplace. But this issue is important enough to be mentioned six times in the Pastoral Epistles (see also 3:8, 6:9–10, 6:12–19, 2 Tim. 3:2, Titus 1:7). Paul knew that even those on a small income can love money. This is an especially appropriate warning for overseers, who would manage the church's funds.

Paul's point is clear: the minister must be above reproach in the private world of his inner life.

*In the Church.* In the church, too, the standard for a leader is moral, ethical, and spiritual excellence. To say that an overseer must be **respectable** (1 Tim. 3:2) seems to be a bland and unexceptional statement; over time that word has lost much of its strength and impact. Some translations suggest the word *dignified,* which at first glance doesn't look like much of an improvement. But there is a dignity to the ministry that is rooted in the nobility of the task (3:1). That dignity is always at risk of being lost because the best motives are sometimes coupled with the worst judgment. Gimmicks and glitter might draw a crowd, but they won't win a world. Consider the word *respectable* in this sense: in his words and in his work, the overseer must do nothing to lessen *respect* for the church and its leaders.

Paul told the Roman Christians to "practice hospitality" (Rom. 12:13). Hospitality is a Christian virtue (compare 1 Tim. 5:10; Heb. 13:2; 1 Pet. 4:9), so an overseer should be **hospitable**, modeling this grace for the congregation. In a day when inns were seldom safe and never reliable, an overseer would be called upon to play host to traveling Christians. In times of peace, the overseer's home might be used as a place of worship; in times of persecution, he might need to provide a refuge for the scattered flock. Today our circumstances are different, but a spirit of hospitality still strengthens churches and encourages believers.

Not all overseers were teachers (1 Tim. 5:17), but all should be **able to teach**. Quite apart from the formal settings of the pulpit or classroom, a leader will teach in dozens of informal ways—when counseling, for example, or meeting with small groups, or discipling new believers. Each setting represents a divine encounter with the Master Teacher and contributes to creating a biblically and theologically literate congregation.

An overseer must not be abusive (**given to violence**) but must be **gentle** (v. 3). An extended passage in the fourth-century Apostolic Canons sheds light on the problem: "A bishop, elder, or deacon who strikes believers when they sin or unbelievers when they do wrong, desiring by such means to terrify them, we command to be deposed; for nowhere has the Lord taught us to do such things. On the contrary, when he was reviled, he did not revile in return; when he suffered, he did not threaten."[4]

A combative nature is out of place for an overseer not only in action but also in attitude. An overseer is **not quarrelsome**, contentious, or argumentative, even with the most aggravating sheep in the flock.

One very practical requirement for an overseer is that he **must not be a new convert** (in v. 6). Apparently, our age is not the first in which churches have been tempted to put new believers at risk by rushing them into leadership positions. The reasons may be many: the church is short-handed, the new Christian is gifted, and, in the case of celebrity converts, can generate lots of attention to the cause. But whatever the reasons, the risk is greater. **He may become conceited and fall under the same judgment as the devil,** who also fell because of pride. Discipleship before leadership is the New Testament sequence for the development of new converts. We ignore it at our peril and theirs.

*In Society.* Finally, Paul looks past the church to the world. The overseer must be above reproach in society. **He must also have a good reputation with outsiders** (v. 7), which is no easy assignment. As a new religion on the world scene, Christianity had to be careful of its reputation. Paul's caution was well placed. Already, rumors and misinformation about the faith had spread among the population, and Roman society was eager to believe the worst about this new sect. Christians were thought to be cannibals because they ate their Lord's body and drank His blood; they were considered atheists because they did not believe in the gods of Rome; they were seen as cowards because they wouldn't fight in the Roman army (which required inductees to worship Caesar). Perhaps worse, these Christians spoke ominously of a world destroyed by fire. The emperor Nero made good use of this last misrepresentation of Christian teaching when he blamed Christians for the fire that swept through Rome in A.D. 64.

Despite opposition and persecution—or perhaps because of it—Paul thought the reputation of the church worth defending. As leaders, overseers would constitute the first line of that defense. Obviously, there is no guarantee that a Christian leader will not be lied about or libeled; godliness is no guarantee against malicious slander. But overseers could so live that when a lie was told, those outside the church would not believe it. The fact that the church survived three centuries of persecution is strong evidence that these early leaders did exactly that.

## 2. THE OFFICE OF DEACON 3:8–13

Like *bishop*, the term *deacon* is a familiar one, and it's easy to read the New Testament with a preconceived definition in mind. That can be misleading for two reasons.

First, the Greek word *diakonos* doesn't always indicate the office of deacon. A literal rendering of *diakonos* would be *servant* or *minister*, and in the New Testament, the word is used in a general, non-technical sense more often than not. Paul uses the word in that general sense referring to himself (Col. 1:25, for example ) and Timothy (1 Tim. 4:6), among others. In 1 Timothy 3, it's obvious that Paul is writing about a specific category of ministers called deacons; in some other passages, that is not so clear.

Second, it is important to realize that the office of deacon developed over time, as did every aspect of church government. Acts 6:1–7 is often identified as the origin of the office of deacon.[5] In Acts 6 the early church created a category of practical ministry to meet the physical, financial, and social needs of believers while freeing the apostles for the ministry of the Word and prayer. Judging from the activities of both Stephen and Philip, two of the seven chosen for that ministry, there was also room in their commission for the spiritual activities of preaching, evangelizing, and baptizing. The deacons mentioned in Paul's first letter to Timothy (1 Tim. 3:8–13) and to the church at Philippi (Phil. 1:1) are mentioned in connection with overseers/elders, and the responsibilities of those deacons had been modified from those assigned to the seven deacons in Acts.

The role of the deacon has continued to evolve in different ways in different denominations. In some denominations ordination as a deacon is one step toward ordination as a priest or minister; in others, deacons are not professional ministers but constitute a lay order of ministers with sub-pastoral and administrative duties. In both cases, deacons find their roots in the New Testament diaconate, but neither is an exact replica of that early office.

## CRITERIA FOR SERVICE

The qualifications for New Testament deacons closely parallel those for overseers. Several of the criteria are repeated or re-stated in slightly different words. Like overseers, deacons must be above reproach (people of **a clear conscience** with **nothing against them**, vv. 9–10). Like overseers, they are to be respectable (**worthy of respect**), not given to drunkenness (**not indulging in much wine**), faithful to their spouses (**the husband of but one wife**), and strong leaders at home (**manages his children and his household well**). Overseers must not be lovers of money; deacons **must not pursue dishonest gain**. Overseers must not be new converts; deacons must know and hold **the deep truths of the faith** and **must first be tested**.

Differences in the lists relate more to function than to character. The description of deacons does not mention teaching, and there is no indication that hospitality is an essential condition of their effective service. No specific reference is made to their reputation with outsiders, perhaps because the scrutiny of unbelievers would more likely be focused on the primary, rather than the secondary, level of Christian leadership. There is one additional quality expected: a deacon must be **sincere** (literally, "not double-tongued"), saying the same to one as he does to another. Positioned as they were between pastor and people, deacons would have special need to show one face and speak with one tongue to all.

## A WORD TO WOMEN

Women in support ministries are addressed in v. 11. This new category of service is addressed beginning with the same verbal connector used at the start of the deacons' list. It is translated **likewise** in v. 8 and **in the same way** in v. 11, but the Greek word is the same. Again, the lists overlap considerably. But there is a question as to whether Paul refers here to the **wives** of deacons (as the New International Version has it) or to women deacons (as it is rendered in the New Revised Standard Version).

The Greek word Paul used means *women*. The translators of the New International Version render it **wives** and add the possessive pronoun **their** because they judged that that was Paul's meaning. Yet if that is what he meant, there are several more obvious Greek constructions he could have used to convey it. Instead, Paul wrote simply "women."

J. N. D. Kelly raises an additional question: if these are the qualities necessary in a deacon's wife, why are there none mentioned for the wife of an overseer, who would be even more influential in the congregation?[6] It is most likely that Paul intended to address women who were serving as deacons, like Phoebe in Rom. 16:1.

Along with their male counterparts, these female servants of the church must meet the high standard of authentic leadership—moral respectability, **temperate** lifestyles, **trustworthy** character, and a Christian tongue.

The rewards for both men and women in support ministries are spiritual in nature. They will **gain an excellent standing** before God and the congregation and **great assurance in their faith in Christ Jesus**. What better remuneration for leaders committed to what has been called "administry"—administration as ministry?

These verses open a window on the shape of ministry in the first-century church. More than any other part of the New Testament, Paul's pastoral letters deal with the organization of the church, and all three major types of church government—episcopal, presbyterian, and congregational—have taken at least some of their inspiration from these pages. Still, details are tantalizingly few. There is no biblical blueprint here or elsewhere in Scripture for any single ecclesiastical system. Not one of our contemporary forms of church government springs wholly from the pages of the book of Acts or the epistles, nor is it necessary that it should. The shape of the church is variable; the soul of the church is

## TYPES OF CHURCH GOVERNMENT

| Type | Leadership | Authority | Clergy | Examples | Consensus/Autonomy |
|---|---|---|---|---|---|
| Episcopal | Hierarchy outside the local church, local authority vested in the ministers. | Based on hierarchy and church tradition, catechisms/creeds | Appointed by bishops | Roman Catholic Anglican/Episcopal Free Methodist United Methodist | High Consensus Low Autonomy |
| Presbyterian | Shared leadership between those inside (church board) and outside (bishop or superintendent) the church | Based on denominational Articles of Faith; autonomy within the broader parameters of official church doctrine. | Elected by congregation, subject to approval of authority outside the local church | Wesleyan, Nazarene, Christian and Missionary Alliance, Presbyterian | Moderate Consensus Moderate Autonomy |
| Congregational | Hierarchy inside the church, local authority vested in the laity | Based on doctrinal consensus established by the individual church | Elected by congregation | Independent, Baptist, United Churches of Christ, Disciples of Christ | Low Consensus High Autonomy |

essential. Appropriately, then, it is the moral integrity and ethical authenticity of church leaders that stand at the center of Paul's words to Timothy.

Those leaders may be called overseers, bishops, presbyters, elders, pastors, ministers, priests, deacons, superintendents, or directors. They may be clergy or lay. Yet whatever the title or status, the standard is spiritual excellence. If leaders in the church are not spiritual leaders above all other things, they have missed the point of 1 Timothy 3 and failed the test of true leadership.

## ENDNOTES

1. Thomas Oden suggests that all overseers were elders, but not all elders were overseers. He theorizes that some people from the board of elders were elevated in rank and given more duties. If so, Paul slights the other elders by addressing overseers and deacons in Philippians but not mentioning those ranked in between. That seems improbable. See *First and Second Timothy and Titus* (Louisville, Ky.: John Knox Press, 1989) p. 139.

2. James Stalker, *The Preacher and His Models* (Grand Rapids, Mich.: Baker Book House, 1967 reprint), p. 58.

3. Robert Anderson, *The Effective Pastor* (Chicago: Moody Press, 1985), pp. 5–6.

4. Alexander Roberts and James Donaldson, eds., *The Ante-Nicene Fathers VII* (Peabody, Mass.: Hendrickson Publishers, 1999), p. 501.

5. Although *diakonos* does not appear in Acts 6, the related terms *diakonein* (to serve) and *diakonia* (service or ministry) are used. The tradition that Stephen was the first deacon dates to Irenaeus, who wrote in the second century.

6. J. N. D. Kelly, *The Pastoral Epistles* (Peabody, Mass.: Hendrickson Publishers, 1960 reprint), p. 83.

# THE CHURCH OF THE LIVING GOD

## 1 Timothy 3:14–16

P aul's longer letters characteristically have a break near the middle, marking a change in the content and a shift in his emphasis. First Timothy is no exception. These verses form a bridge between the two sections of the epistle, and what a magnificent bridge it is!

In his transition, Paul quotes a fragment of an early Christian hymn, and a doctrinal hymn at that. To a church beset by false teaching, he offers the triumphant truth contained in its own hymnal. Although the practice might seem odd today, previous generations of Christians kept a hymnal by their Bible at home. Christians hymns are both theologically instructive and devotionally uplifting.

For Timothy, the message of this short section would have been unmistakable: the church of the living God exalts Jesus Christ.

So far as we know, Paul's desire **to come . . . soon** was never realized. There's no indication in 2 Timothy that he ever made it back to Ephesus; the appeal in that letter is instead for Timothy to come to Paul, who by then was in a Roman prison. This letter spoke for Paul, however, accomplishing his purpose: **that . . . you will know how people ought to conduct themselves in God's household, which is the church of the living God. . . .**

The Greek word Paul uses can mean either house or household, and Paul gives it both meanings. A house is suggested by his mention of **pillar and foundation**, the structural supports of a building. The church is the strong supporter of truth. In Matthew 16, Jesus indicates that His church will be built on Peter's confession of His Messiahship; here, that truth is in turn supported by the church. (Nowhere in the New Testament does the word *church* refer to a church building, but the analogy of the church as a building is common.)

The idea of the church as a family is continued from earlier in the chapter, where Paul writes of the families of overseers and deacons. Here, Paul is saying that the church is family to us all, and, like a good overseer, God knows how to manage His children and His household well (compare 3:5, 12).

It must have been encouraging for Timothy to be reminded that in spite of the problems they face, he and his people were in **the church of the living God** and participants in **the mystery of godliness**. "Great is Artemis of the Ephesians!" the mob in Ephesus had chanted (Acts 19:28). "Great is the mystery of godliness," Paul replies in his letter to the pastor of the church in that same city.

Almost twenty times in his epistles, Paul speaks of the **mystery** of the faith (see, for example, Rom. 16:25–27; Col. 1:25–27; and Eph. 3:2–9), although at times the New International Version translates the word as "secret things" (1 Cor. 4:1) or, as in this very chapter, "deep truths" (1 Tim. 3:9). In Paul's day, mystery religions promised secret spiritual insight to an elite few through secret ceremonies and rituals. These were the cults of the first century, outside even the pagan mainstream. But when Paul laid claim to the word *mystery*, he gave it a very different meaning. For the cults, secrecy was the secret of their appeal; for Paul, the Christian mystery was a secret revealed. God revealed Himself in Christ (John 1:18); and with the Incarnation, the mystery of the ages was made plain (Col. 2:2–3). God is not without mystery, for He is God; but He is not hidden. Clouds of mystery have faded into the clarity of the cross. God has told His secret to everyone.

Because Paul is lifting the fragment of poetry that he quotes here from the body of a longer hymn, it begins in mid-stanza with the relative pronoun *who,* for which no antecedent is given. (The New International Version has substituted **he** for *who.*) It is a hymn to Christ, of course, and it has the effect of a creed. Some see the rhythmic phrases falling into two verses of three lines each, but the poetry flows better in three couplets connected by the parallelism of their closing words: **body** and **Spirit**, **angels** and **nations**, **in the world** and **in glory**.

In the first line, Christ's appearance **in a body** is the wonder of the Incarnation, the beginning of what theologians call the Humiliation of Christ. He gave up heaven to come to earth as one of us. He was rejected, crucified, and buried (John 1:10–14, 19:30–42).

The second line speaks of His vindication **by the Spirit**, which probably refers to the Resurrection. Paul attributes Christ's resurrection to the power of the Spirit (Rom. 1:4; see also 1 Pet. 3:18). This begins the Exaltation of Christ: His restoration to glory, honor, dominion, and praise (Rev. 4:11, 5:12–14). For a classic passage dealing with the Humiliation and Exaltation of Christ, see Phil. 2:8–9.

The third line is ambiguous but may refer to the Ascension, which was attended **by angels** (Acts 1:6–11) and which is the next step in Christ's Exaltation. It's also possible that Paul had in mind Christ's entry into heaven, taking His place at the Father's right hand in the presence of angels (Acts 7:55, Rom. 8:34).

The fourth line recalls the day of Pentecost when the church was born, ten days after the Ascension on the Day of Pentecost (Acts 2:1 and following). Starting with Peter's magnificent sermon on that occasion, Christ **was preached among the nations** (Acts 2:5–11, 41–47; Matt. 28:19–20).

Line five recalls that as people who heard the message came to faith, Christ **was believed on in the world** (Acts 11:19–21, 13:12, 13:48, 16:34, to identify only a few examples).

The closing line refers to Christ's being **taken up in glory**. This reference to the Ascension seems to be out of sequence, if not repetitious. But the emphasis in this sixth and final line is on His permanent place in the realms of glory. Ultimately accepted on earth (line five), He is eternally enthroned in heaven.

Creeds may be sung as well as said. With this creedal hymn, Paul passes from the first to the second half of his letter on a bridge of worship and an affirmation of our common faith.

# 1 TIMOTHY

## Part Two

### Practical Counsel for Church Leaders 4:1–6:21A

# 7

# THE GODLY EXAMPLE OF A LEADER

## 1 Timothy 4:1-16

In 1 Timothy, chapters 1–3, Paul deals with principles. He discusses the call to ministry (1:12–20, 2:7), qualifications for leadership (3:1–13), the content of the Christian message (1:3–11, 3:16), and the primacy of proper worship (2:1–15). In chapters 4–6, he deals with practical matters: relationships within the church, spiritual models, materialism, the financial support of ministers, and even the importance of prayer before meals.

The close connection of principles to practice in this letter is neither awkward nor surprising; it fits the apostle's usual pattern. For him, nothing is more practical than Christian doctrine.

The passage before us tells more about the opposition in Ephesus. This group of individuals are austere in the extreme, requiring celibacy and a restricted diet (4:1–5), and their belief system is nothing but **godless myths and old wives' tales** (4:7). Paul's advice to Timothy is simple: **point out these things** (4:6), and **set an example for the believers** (4:12). By his word and by his walk, Timothy will save himself and his people (4:16).

Then as now, that's the way to be **a good minister of Christ Jesus** (4:6).

## 1. ASCETICISM AND APOSTASY 4:1-5

Immediately following his allusion to the household of God and his quotation of the hymn to Christ at the end of chapter 3, Paul refers to a revelation of the Spirit: **The Spirit clearly says that in later times some**

**will abandon the faith. . . .** The Trinity—Father (3:15), Son (3:16), and Spirit (4:1)—is engaged in the struggle of truth with error at Ephesus, and the outcome will have eternal consequences.

## ABANDONING THE FAITH

Paul's word from the Holy Spirit may have come through the Scriptures, which the Spirit inspired and in which Jesus predicts a falling-away (Matt. 24:10–14; see also Mark 13:22). Or the Spirit may have spoken to Paul directly, as was the case with the itinerary of his second missionary journey (Acts 16:6–7) and the imprisonment awaiting him in Jerusalem at the end of his third (Acts 20:23). Under the inspiration of the Spirit, Paul had warned of a falling-away in his address to the Ephesian elders (Acts 20:29–30) and had written a similar message to the Thessalonians (2 Thess. 2:3, 11–12). Whatever the route of the revelation, it demonstrates that the teaching and directing work of the Spirit promised by Christ was in effect (see John 16:13–15).

**In later times** is a variation on "in the last days" (2 Tim. 3:1), but the meaning is the same. Some argue that Paul is not referring to the end times in 1 Timothy 4 because the prophecies that he mentions were already being fulfilled. But that viewpoint assumes that Paul did not expect the Second Coming to happen soon. Every generation should live in anticipation that Christ will return but with the realization that we don't know when it will happen. The church must have a sense of urgency that motivates but doesn't immobilize, the kind of urgency that keeps all eyes fixed on Christ and not on the calendar. Paul has that sense of urgency. Whether he calls them "later times" or "last days," Paul makes it clear that Timothy is already living in them.

Returning to the discussion of false teachers begun in chapter 1, Paul warns that **some will abandon the faith** in these later times. Apostasy, or spiritual defection, is a tragic but real possibility. Some would say that anyone who leaves the faith was never genuinely saved; but that viewpoint contradicts the plain sense of Paul's words to Timothy (1 Tim. 1:5–6, 19–20; see also 2 Pet. 2:20–23).

There is no mystery about the source of the lie that leads people astray; Satan is behind it. He is a liar and the father of lies (John 8:44). Those who fall away **follow deceiving** ( or seducing) **spirits** in contrast to the Spirit of Truth whom Paul follows (1 Tim. 4:1; see also Acts 16:13). These people open themselves up to **things taught by demons**. These "devil-devised doctrines," in Roy S. Nicholson's words,[1] are diametrically opposed to the sound doctrine of the gospel (1 Tim. 1:10) and serve as evidence that spiritual warfare is real. The clear mind and sense of balance that Paul prizes in overseers are desperately needed here. Overreaction distorts our perspective; the outcome of this war is already decided.

Though the originator of the lie is Satan, his lying agents are flesh-and-blood people. These deceivers are not simply mistaken but are **hypocritical liars** who intentionally mislead; their **consciences have been seared as with a hot iron**. An alternative reading of the Greek is "branded with a hot iron." That translation suggestss the image of slaves or criminals in the ancient world who might have

## LIFE CHANGE

### RESISTING THE DEVIL

In his preface to *The Screwtape Letters*, C. S. Lewis says that there are two traps into which Christians can fall with regard to Satan. The first is to ignore the reality of the threat he poses. The second is to become obsessed with it. That spiritual warfare is real does not mean that the Devil is behind every flat tire or lost key ring, or that exorcism ought to be a regular ritual in our worship services. Popular novels about spiritual warfare may have confused more saints than they awakened. Yet it is true that there is an unseen world at war around us, and it is necessary that we choose sides. The defectors in 1 Tim. 4:1 made the wrong choice.

had an identifying mark burned into their forehead by their masters. By that reading of this text, these false teachers belong to Satan and bear his brand. In Eph. 4:19, however, Paul wrote of sinners who had lost all sensitivity, and that seems to be the best way to understand the phrase used here. Having made a career out of deception, these false teachers could deceive without suffering any pangs of conscience. Contrast that experience with the good conscience of God's servants described in 1 Tim. 1:5, 19.

Thomas Oden quotes Martin Luther: "It is the nature of all hypocrites and false prophets to create a conscience where there is none, and to cause conscience to disappear where it does exist!"[2]

## SPIRITUAL MASOCHISM

In 1 Tim. 4:3, Paul gives more details about the Ephesian heresy. Its leaders would **forbid people to marry and order them to abstain from certain foods**. The issue is asceticism, a stringent, occasionally extreme form of self-denial. By and large, ascetics over the centuries have had faultless motives but faulty judgement. They have rightly understood self-denial to be part of the cost of discipleship and a measure of their devotion to Christ. Since their love for Christ was great, they denied themselves in great, often extreme, ways.

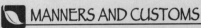

## MANNERS AND CUSTOMS

### ASCETICISM

Many in the early church practiced asceticism to some degree—for example, observing fasts and prayer vigils. Some took the practice further and became famous (or notorious) for their self-abusive behavior. One monk who lived not long after the New Testament era absent-mindedly slapped a mosquito and was so overcome with guilt that he stripped off his clothes and stood in a swamp, allowing mosquitoes to feast on his flesh. Another, Simeon Stylites, lived as a hermit in his search for holiness. Desiring to avoid all contact with people for fear of being distracted from his spiritual pursuits, he lived on a small platform atop a nine-foot pillar. As reports of his unusual lifestyle spread, crowds of the curious came to see this holy man, and the seeker after solitude became a tourist attraction. His response was to raise his platform even higher, and at the end of his life he was living atop a pillar sixty feet high.

In the church at Ephesus, a radical form of asceticism had arisen, based on bad theology. First, its promoters mandated celibacy among their followers. Although singleness has always been an option for Christians, it was never considered the norm, much less required. The Ephesians ascetics required it. While Paul has more to say about the heretics' view on food than on marriage, his positive attitude toward marriage is evident from 2:15 and 5:14. Titus 2:4 is another example.

Second, these false teachers insisted on abstinence from certain foods. The Jewish roots of this false teaching are particularly evident here; dietary laws were important in Judaism. As a result, food and dietary issues were a constant cause of controversy in the early church. Some examples of this are Paul's confrontation with Peter at Antioch (Gal. 2:11–21), the stronger/weaker brother debate in the Roman church (Rom. 14:1–4, 13–23), and the teaching on meat offered to idols (1 Cor. 8:1–13). The closest parallel to the ascetic teaching Timothy faced in Ephesus is the Colossian heresy. Paul wrote to the church at Colosse:

> Since you died with Christ to the basic principles of this world, why, as though you still belonged to it, do you submit to its rules: "Do not handle! Do not taste! Do not touch!"? These are all destined to perish with use, because they are based on human commands and teachings. Such regulations indeed have an appearance of wisdom, with their self-imposed worship, their false humility and their harsh treatment of the body, but they lack any value in restraining sensual indulgence (Col. 2:2–20).

The "harsh treatment of the body" Paul mentions was asceticism, and it was a common element in the false teaching at both Colosse and Ephesus because the seeds of Gnosticism had been sown in both congregations. Gnosticism did not reach its fullest expression until the second century, but early Gnostic influences were already undermining the faith of these two churches.

Gnostics had a dualistic worldview. They believed in two gods who were in eternal conflict—a good god who reigned over the spiritual world, and an evil god who created and ruled the physical universe. Gnostics considered things of the spiritual world to be holy, but they treated all matter as evil. Because of their hostility toward anything material, Gnostics variously chose one of two different approaches to the human body, particularly with regard to food and sex.

The first approach was asceticism. Some Gnostics became ascetics or even hyperascetics,[3] denying the "evil" body even the most basic appetites, needs, and comforts. They deprived the flesh to let the spirit soar.

The other approach was self-indulgence. Some Gnostics became libertines, living lives without moral restraint and engaging in all the sins of the flesh on the grounds that it didn't matter what the body did since only the spirit would survive. Their behavior was often scandalous, but they boasted of their spiritual virtues.

The false teachers in Timothy's church subscribed to the first view. Paul himself wrote often of the need for self-discipline—in fact, the later Gnostics loved to quote Paul selectively—but Paul had no patience with Gnostic practices because of the spurious theology behind them. (Gnostics never quoted 1 Timothy!) Paul affirmed self-denial but not spiritual masochism.

In response to the ascetics at Ephesus, Paul cites the very first chapter of the Bible. Although at first glance it appears that Paul is answering only the challenge to forbidden foods, his argument brilliantly covers the prohibition on marriage as well.

**God created** the foods in question; to reject them as evil or unworthy, Paul implies, is to reject the God who created them (Gen. 1:29–30, 9:3). The additional rejection of marriage indicates that the false teachers were not contending for Jewish dietary laws out of regard for their Old Testament heritage: they were making a negative statement about God's creation, despising the physical bodies He had created for them.

**For everything God created is good**, Paul adds; in fact, seven times in Genesis 1, God pronounced His creation to be good or very good. The only thing God said was not good was for the man to be alone (Gen. 2:18). In response, God created Eve and introduced the institution of marriage that these Ephesian Gnostics also despised.

**Thanksgiving**, mentioned twice in 1 Timothy 4, is the key to understanding Paul's argument. **Nothing**—food, marriage, or any of God's good gifts—**is to be rejected** (Moffatt says "tabooed"[4]) **if it is received with thanksgiving**. Paul expects **those who believe and know the truth** to realize that truth, since thanksgiving is one of the prayers he commends in 2:1. The false teachers were neither thankful nor receptive, so their claims to be teachers of God's truth ring hollow.

The commonplace table blessing gets a major endorsement from Paul in this passage. Whatever we eat, he reasons, is **consecrated** (literally, sanctified) **by the word of God and prayer**. It's not that our prayer somehow changes the nature of the food; rather, by praying we acknowledge that God has blessed the food, and all good things, for our use.

## 2. A GOOD MINISTER OF CHRIST JESUS 4:6–16

Paul's theme in this section sounds like the topic of a pastor's conference: how to be a good minister. Paul's advice, however, doesn't match the contents of some conference brochures. There's nothing here about marketing, for example, managing growth, or high profile leadership. Instead, Paul offers four biblical guidelines for effective ministry. Follow these, he urges Timothy, and **you will be a good minister of Christ Jesus**.

### KNOW AND TEACH THE TRUTH

Timothy had the advantage of a Christian upbringing; his mother, Eunice, and his grandmother, Lois, are saluted for their faith by Paul in 2 Tim. 1:5. So it is true that Timothy was brought **up in the truths of the faith**, but the participle in

>  **MANNERS AND CUSTOMS**
>
> SAYING GRACE
>
> Table blessings in the New Testament era were saturated with Scripture, which is why **the word of God and prayer** are linked together, and the saying of grace was treated seriously. Jesus blessed the bread and fish at the feeding of the five thousand (John 6:11), the bread and wine at the Last Supper (Luke 22:17–19), and the bread He shared with disciples in Emmaus after His Resurrection (Luke 24:30). Paul, while enduring a storm at sea, "took some bread and gave thanks to God. . . . then he broke it and began to eat" (Acts 27:35). A simple prayer of thanks at table makes a profound theological statement, and it puts us in rather good company—the company of Jesus, Paul, and **those who believe and know the truth.**

this verse is in the present tense and literally means "being nourished in." While his enemies were concerned with limiting the intake of their followers, Timothy was feeding on, living on, the truth. (Compare 1 Cor. 3:1, 2.)

Again, doctrinal truth proves to be crucial. Paul never views theology as optional or unimportant; he has seen what poor theology can do. Paul beautifully captures the two sides of the teaching task with his instructions for Timothy: **point out these things to the brothers** (1 Tim. 4: 6), and **command and teach these things** (v. 11).

In v. 6, Timothy is to be a persuader, convincing his hearers by quiet reason and gentle appeals in personal conversation. The word translated

**point out** is an up-close-and-personal one; it means to suggest or advise. As **brothers**, after all, Timothy's parishioners were members of the same family, the household of God (3:15). Timothy was not to be a pastor on a pedestal; this is a picture of true servanthood leadership, one brother serving the spiritual needs of another in the considerate and consensus-building way suggested by the verb *to point out*.

In 4:11, Timothy is to be a proclaimer, announcing God's truth with conviction, courage, and authority. From the pulpit he must insist with the confidence of a first-century Billy Graham that the church line up with the truth. The confident proclaimer and the quiet persuader are one and the same: two sides of the pastoral coin.

In stark contrast to the **truths of the faith and of the good teaching that you have followed** stand the **godless myths and old wives' tales** of Timothy's opponents, which are as profane and ungodly as they are silly and superstitious. The Ephesians have a choice, Paul is saying: faith or fables.

Verses 7b–8 borrow an allusion from the world of sport, which yielded so many rich illustrations for Paul (1 Cor. 9:24–27; Phil. 3:13–14; 2 Tim. 4:7–8; Gal. 5:7). Paul urges Timothy, **train yourself to be godly**. *Train* and *training* come from the same Greek root that gives us the word *gymnasium*. Like an exercise regimen, holy living requires daily discipline; the believer's devotional habits are like a regular workout in God's gym. **For physical training is of some value, but godliness** (*Cross*-training?) **has value for all things** because it makes us fit for life not only here but hereafter.

Ignatius of Loyola understood that. His classic devotional manual is entitled *Spiritual Exercises*. The heretics thought they understood it, too, but their abuse of the body (which may have inspired Paul's use of this athletic metaphor) was the very opposite of godliness.

It is worth noting that while we tend to contrast the physical interests of this world with the spiritual interests of the world to come, Paul makes it clear that godliness is a benefit in **the present life** too. God wants us to have the best of both worlds, and because He created both worlds, that best is found in Him.

The third **trustworthy saying** (see 1:5, 3:1) of 1 Timothy is found in 4:9. As in 1:15, it carries the augmenting phrase **that deserves full acceptance**.

As in 3:1, it can refer either forward (to 4:10) or backward (to 4:8). Both v. 8 and v. 10 have the look of a proverb or maxim, but v. 10 seems to be a weightier theological statement. Paul declares that **hope in the living God** is something for which we who are in the church of the living God (3:15) **labor and strive**. Nothing except salvation comes without effort, either in the gym or in the sanctuary; we work hard at our hope.

Once again God is called **Savior**—in fact, the Savior of all people. This is not universalism, the belief that all will ultimately be saved, but an echo of 2:3–4, which speaks of "God our Savior, who wants all men to be saved and to come to a knowledge of the truth." He is the Savior **of those who believe**; no one can be saved any other way or by any other one (2:5).

The remaining instructions in this section are not directly tied to Timothy's being "a good minister." But in a section that begins with the challenge to be a good minister (v. 6) and ends with the prospect of saving his congregation (v. 16), it is safe to assume that Paul would consider all of the material in between important for a pastor.

## SET AN EXAMPLE FOR THE CHURCH

Teaching is essential (v. 11), but more is caught than taught. Paul knows that leadership includes modeling the Christian life. Paul himself was a model (Phil. 3:17; 2 Thess. 3:9), and Timothy must be one too. As such, Timothy must **set an example for the believers** in public and private life.

As a public figure, Timothy must watch his **speech** and his **life** (conduct). People will listen to what he says and watch what he does. In his private, inner self, Timothy must be marked by **love**, **faith**, and **purity**. That is nearly a repetition of the Christian character described in 1:5. Those inner graces will have an outward expression. The bottom line is this: on the inside and on the outside, Timothy must be a worthy example.

Evidently, Timothy's age, or people's perception of him because of his youth, was a handicap. Although he had joined Paul some fifteen years earlier and was probably in his mid-thirties, some were evidently inclined to **look down on** him **because** he was **young**. Remember that age may be relative. Thirty-five may be old for a professional athlete but young for a bishop or general superintendent. In Timothy's culture, men of military age were considered young, and that included everyone up to age forty.

Many in Timothy's congregation would have been his elders, including some of his *elders*—the overseers whom he appointed and who were under his direction. It is possible also that Timothy lacked an assertive or forceful personality (see 1 Cor. 16:10–11), which may have compounded the problem. Paul's solution was simple: **set an example** that will silence your critics and win their support. Let your life speak for you.

## MINISTER THE WORD IN ALL ITS FORMS

A visit from the great Apostle Paul (3:14) would be a red-letter day on the calendar of the Ephesian church, but the life and faith of any congregation is shaped not so much by special events as by faithful obedience. **Until I come, Paul writes, give yourself to the public reading of Scripture, to preaching and to teaching**. All three tasks center on the Word.

**Reading** scripture in public meant reading the Old Testament, which was the church's Bible in the apostolic age, and the writings of the apostles. To the Colossian church, Paul wrote, "After this letter has been read to you, see that it is also read in the church of the Laodiceans and that you in turn read the letter from Laodicea" (Col. 4:16; see also 2 Pet. 3:16, where Peter classifies Paul's letters as Scripture).

It is sometimes surprising how little Scripture is actually read in a typical worship service, even in churches that boast a high view of the Bible's inspiration and authority. Note the prominence that Paul gave to the use of Scripture in public worship.

**Preaching** has been identified with Christian worship since the church was born after Peter's stirring message on the Day of Pentecost (Acts 2:14–41). The sermon was an integral part of New Testament worship, not as a showcase for homiletical skill but as a way to open the Word of God and worship the God of the Word. The focus of preaching must be on God's revelation of Himself, and that's why biblical preaching is the best preaching. A good sermon digs deep, both into the text and into the hearts of the hearers.

**Teaching** is closely related to preaching. When Jesus delivered his "sermon" on the Mount, "His disciples came to him, and he began to *teach* them. . ." (Matt. 5:1–2, emphasis added). In 1 Tim. 5:17, Paul refers to elders "whose work is preaching and teaching." As pastor, Timothy had the same dual assignment. Given the competition from false teachers, Timothy's teaching ministry was especially important; teaching and teachers are mentioned more than thirty times in the Pastoral Epistles.

The church in the generation after Timothy's was firmly committed to *catechism*, the instruction required of all new converts prior to baptism. *Catechumens*, those under instruction, were not baptized until their instruction was complete, and they could not take communion until they were baptized. In fact, catechumens were dismissed from the worship services of the early church before the sacrament of the Lord's supper was celebrated. They were not considered ready to take their place in the church until they knew what and why they believed. We don't know as much about the church in Timothy's day, but the practice then would probably have been similar.

All three of these elements—reading, preaching, and teaching the Word—were borrowed from the Jewish synagogue. Unlike the Temple, which centered on sacrifice, synagogue worship emphasized instruction and prayer. We get a glimpse of that when Jesus enters His hometown synagogue of Nazareth on the Sabbath (Luke 4:16–30). He stands to read from the scroll of Isaiah, then hands it back to the attendant (who would return the scroll to the ark, the place of honor where it was kept), and sits down to teach. First-century Christian worship reflected the influence of the synagogue, particularly the centrality of the Scriptures.

Timothy's ministry of the Word is the **gift** to which Paul refers (1 Tim. 4:14). At Timothy's ordination, this gift was given **when the body of elders laid their hands on** him. Not every occasion of the laying on of hands in the New Testament denotes ordination; this practice was also associated with receiving the Holy Spirit (Acts 8:17), healing (Acts 9:17), and commissioning for special service (Acts 13:2–3). But the context here supports the view that Paul has Timothy's ordination in mind (see also 5:22). Paul indicates in 2 Tim. 1:6 that he was the one who laid hands on Timothy, but that passage is easily reconciled with this one. As an apostle, Paul would have presided over the ordination of Timothy, in which the body of elders also participated. These elders, perhaps including elders from the churches at Lystra and Derbe in Timothy's home region, would have formed a "council of ordination."[5]

Timothy dare not **neglect** his **gift**. Like the talents and pounds of Jesus' parables (Matt. 25:28–30; Luke 19:24–26), it is a case of "use it or lose it." The gift makes Timothy's ministry possible; to lose the gift is to lose the ministry.

## REMAIN COMMITTED TO THE CALLING

The task for this young minister is daunting: train to be godly (1 Tim. 4:7), teach the truth (v. 11), set an example (v. 12), and preach the Word (v. 13). To these imperatives Paul adds two more: **Be diligent in these matters; give yourself wholly to them.** In reality Paul is not assigning additional tasks; he is revealing the secret for accomplishing the tasks already given. If Timothy will give himself wholly to God and His work, God will give Himself in return. Not only that, but **everyone** will see Timothy's **progress** as well. His dedication to the ministry will build their confidence in him and in his authority.

**Watch your life** is good advice to anyone; others are watching it too (v. 12b). To watch your **doctrine** is just as important; keep it uncontaminated by the fantasies and fables of Satan. The purity of both Timothy's character and his faith are once again on Paul's heart. The apostle knows that before any preacher prepares his message, he must prepare himself.

Paul offers a final word to Timothy on the subject of ministry: **Persevere**. Paul's encouraging advice is this: keep on keeping on. Moffatt translates it, "Stick to your work."[6] That powerful phrase recalls the focused, resolute, single-minded determination of a Nehemiah who refuses to be distracted, discouraged, or dissuaded from the "good work" he was doing until the walls of Jerusalem were rebuilt. The road of obedience is long, but the destination makes the journey worthwhile: **you will save both yourself and your hearers.**

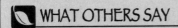 **WHAT OTHERS SAY**

It does not take great people to do great things. It only takes consecrated people.
—Phillips Brooks

It is God who saves, of course (v. 10). Paul is not suggesting self-salvation. These words must be read in light of Phil. 2:12, "Work out your salvation with fear and trembling, for it is God who works in you. . . ." Timothy can avoid every spiritual leader's fear—being lost himself after a lifetime of ministering to others (1 Cor. 9:27)—and experience the answer to every spiritual leader's prayer—the salvation of his people—by holding on to the faith with a sanctified stubbornness.

The promise is based on a condition: **if you do, you will.** Paul's clear implication is that if you do, *God* will. The God who is eager to save (2:4) will always do His part when we do ours.

That promise is a wonderful conclusion to a chapter that begins on a very different note. Paul starts with the problems in the church—deceit, hypocrisy, demonic influences, and spiritual defection (vv. 1–3). But he ends with the promise of God that there is salvation for both the pastor and his people if they will hold firm to faith (v. 16).

## ENDNOTES

1. Roy S. Nicholson, *I and II Timothy and Titus* (Grand Rapids, Mich.: William B. Eerdmans Publishing Company, 1965), p. 592.

2. Thomas Oden, *First and Second Timothy and Titus* (Louisville, Ky.: John Knox Press, 1989), p. 59.

3. Ibid.

4. James Moffatt, *The Bible: A New Translation,* Revised and Final Edition (New York: Harper and Brothers Publisher, 1950), p. 264.

5. D. Daube believes that Paul alone ordained Timothy and that the phrase "the laying on of hands of the eldership" is the Greek equivalent of a rabbinical idiom meaning "the laying on of hands *for ordination as an elder.*" Cited by J. N. D. Kelly, *The Pastoral Epistles* (Peabody, Mass.: Hendrickson Publishers, 1960), p. 108.

6. Moffatt, *The Bible: A New Translation,* p. 264.

# 8

# THE CONGREGATIONAL RELATIONSHIPS OF A MINISTER

## 1 Timothy 5:1–6:2

E very congregation is a mosaic. There is tremendous diversity in the pews on any given Sunday morning—a variety of people from different homes, backgrounds, age levels, vocations, and economic situations. Yet they are joined together, as Paul wrote in his earlier letter to these Ephesian Christians, in one body by one Spirit and with one hope, one Lord, one faith, one baptism, and one God and Father of all (Eph. 4:4–6).

In diversity, there is unity, utility, and even beauty. Construction materials that are all the same size, shape, and color make a tile floor, not a work of art. In the Church, the divine Artist has taken all of our differences and created a beautiful mosaic of grace to His glory.

Yet for church leaders, diversity within a congregation can be challenging. Beginning in 1 Timothy 5, Paul addresses the issue of a leader's relationship to various groups within a congregation: older men and younger men (5:1), older women and younger women (5:2), widows (5:3–16), slaves (6:1–2), and even other leaders (5:17–25).

Paul's approach is practical and, at one point, very personal as he speaks of Timothy's health and offers advice (5:23). The organization of this section is not precise; Paul doubles back to a previous thought once or twice, and he interrupts himself with the parenthetical remark to Timothy. Those characteristic touches only affirm the authenticity of the epistle. This is a real letter from a mentor to a pastor, and it has real value for leaders today.

# 1. PASTORAL CARE OF OLD AND YOUNG 5:1-2

Issues relating to age and gender top Paul's agenda as he offers advice on dealing with the various categories of people under Timothy's care. His instructions are, at the risk of using an oxymoron, profoundly simple.

First, Paul speaks of Timothy's relationship to **older [men]**. The Greek word used here is *presbuteros*, elder. In 1 Tim. 5:17 and Titus 1:5–6, that word is used to mean those who hold the office of elder in the church; here, the context makes it obvious that Paul means merely any older man. Paul's instruction is this: **Do not rebuke an older man harshly**. Chrysostom, writing in the fourth century, reasoned that a young pastor like Timothy would face three issues when trying to correct his seniors: (1) No one likes to be reprimanded, (2) especially those with seniority in the group, (3) and certainly not by someone considerably younger than himself. In a society where elders were afforded a great deal of respect, that would be especially true. **Exhort him**, Paul says, using a much kinder word, **as if he were your father**.

The same pattern should be used for dealing with people of other ages—treat them like family. **Treat younger men as brothers, older women as mothers, and younger women as sisters**. If Christians are indeed the family of God and are members of His household (3:15), then we are father, mother, brother, or sister to each other—leaders included. Paul thinks we should act like it.

That principle is given reinforcement with reference to younger women. To avoid any impropriety or even the hint of it, Timothy's relationship with these sisters in the faith should be marked by **absolute purity**.

Every person falls into one of these four inclusive age categories, but as Paul moves into the heart of the chapter, he offers more detailed instructions for dealing with some other groups within the church. Even so, this simple instruction applies to every relationship; widows, slaves, and leaders alike are family first of all.

# 2. WIDOWS IN THE CONGREGATION 5:3–16

Paul's instructions concerning widows are surprisingly lengthy, comprising over half of the chapter. The abundance of detail provides a window on widowhood in that era and shows the possible origin of an important lay ministry in the early church.

## MINISTRY TO WIDOWS

Christianity inherited its concern for widows from Judaism, which considers the care and well-being of widows to be the responsibility of the entire community. Since God is identified in the Old Testament as a defender of widows (Deut. 10:18; Ps. 68:5), His people must be also (Isa. 1:17). In the New Testament, James picks up that theme, going so far as to define "pure and faultless" religion as, in part, looking after widows in their distress (James 1:27). Jesus once stopped a funeral procession to restore a widow's only son to her (Luke 7:11–15). He made a widow the heroine of one of His parables (Luke 18:1–8), and He had high words of praise for a widow who gave all she had to God (Mark 12:41–44). By doing so, He put to shame the rich and the religious leaders standing by, who had a reputation for devouring the houses of widows (Mark 12:40). Is there any doubt that God cares about helpless people?

In the patriarchal system of the first century, widows had no inheritance rights and, along with orphans, were often forced to depend on charity for their survival. When Hellenistic Jews in the New Testament church felt that "their widows were being overlooked in the daily distribution of food" (Acts 6:1), the church created a ministry (the diaconate) to ensure that needs like that would be met. The phrase *widows and orphans* was verbal shorthand for the weak, the powerless, and the vulnerable. As such, these women and children deserved special care in the church. At the same time, the church recognized that widows could make a valuable contribution to the spiritual welfare of the congregation.

In 1 Timothy 5, Paul distinguishes between **widows who are really in need** and those who aren't. A "real widow" (as the New Revised Standard Version puts it)—one eligible for the church's financial support—was one who had no relatives to help her. She was **left all alone**, and, without the care of the church, would be desolate and destitute. At the same time, she was deserving; her circumstances led to stronger faith, and she **[put] her hope in God**, continuing **night and day to pray** (compare 1 Thess. 5:17), **[asking] God for help**. The church, Paul said, should give such a widow **proper recognition**, a term that is sometimes translated *honor* and which recalls the familiar phrasing of the Fifth Commandment.

**If a widow has children or grandchildren**, she is not a widow in the fullest sense—not a "real widow"—because she is not **really in need** of a share of the limited resources of the church. Presumably, her family members will take care of her. When they do so, they **put their religion** (the same word translated "godliness" in 1 Tim. 2:2) **into practice**, Paul says, by caring for those who once cared for them.

Paul has strong words, on the other hand, for families who refuse to help the widows among them. They have **denied the faith**, he says, and are worse than unbelievers (v. 8). Even nonbelievers take care of their own families; should a Christian live below pagan standards? (Compare 1 Cor. 5:1.) "A person of faith who acts in such a way as to deny that faith in practice," Manfred Brauch suggests, "is worse than those who never profess faith in the first place."[1]

In 1 Tim. 5:16, Paul returns to the subject of families caring for their own widows, which lightens the burden on the church, enabling it to help others. The separation of this thought from its natural context in vv. 4–8 is awkward. There is another problem with v. 16: why does it specify that **any woman** should help take care of the widows in her family, but does not extend the instruction to men? The King James and New King James Versions follow texts that read "man or woman," but the reading followed by the New International Version has the strongest support. It is possible that Paul's use of *woman* in v. 16 is meant to reinforce the fact that vv. 4 and 8 apply to women as well as men. However, since the Greek text literally reads, "If any woman who is a believer has widows" (and does not add "in her family"), J. N. D. Kelly suggests that Paul is referring to widows who are servants, dependents, or friends living in the household of a Christian woman but who are not members of her family. Unlike the subject of family obligations, this topic has not yet been addressed by Paul in this chapter, so the instruction would not be redundant. Given the social customs of the first century, even if the believing woman were married, the care of a widow living in her household would logically fall to her.[2]

Another type of widow is mentioned in this passage: **the widow who lives for pleasure**. This widow may or may not have family to look out for her, but she doesn't "put her hope in God." Instead, she pursues a sensual, self-indulgent lifestyle and is spiritually dead—"a religious corpse,"[3] **dead even while she lives**.

Timothy is to **give the people these instructions, too**. The verb used is the same one that is translated "teach" in 4:11. Combating the Devil's doctrines (1 Timothy 4) and caring for widows in the church (1 Timothy 5) are both part of knowing "how people ought to conduct themselves in God's household, which is the church of the living God" (3:15).

## MINISTRY BY WIDOWS

An order of widows assigned to Christian service flourished in the second century according to church fathers Ignatius and Polycarp. The order was distinct from deaconesses, although the two may have merged later, and it vigorously served the church. Tradition credits the female disciples of Jesus (see Luke 8:1–3, for example) as the inspiration for this order and sees 1 Timothy 5 as an early profile of its organization and duties. Is Paul speaking of such an order in 5:9–10? Or is he describing the roll of widows eligible for the charity of the church? It is an open question, but there are good reasons for supposing that an order of widows existed or was instituted in Ephesus at the time of Paul's writing.

The verb used in v. 9 for enrolling the widows carries a specialized meaning; it is commonly used to denote the enlistment of soldiers into the military. Ordination was not appropriate for ministry at this level, but widows might have been "enlisted" for service in the Kingdom.

The qualifications for being **on the list of widows** are both specific and strenuous.

- She must be **over sixty**, the age at which someone in that culture was considered elderly.[4]

- She must have been **faithful to her husband**. (For a comparison of this stipulation to the similar requirements for overseers and deacons, see the notes on 3:2 and 3:12.)

- She must be **well known for her good deeds**. Doing good is a recurring theme in the Pastoral Epistles; all believers should be active in good works (Titus 2:14, 3:8, 3:14), especially the wealthy (1 Tim. 6:18). Leaders are expected to set an example for others to follow (Titus 2:7). For widows, doing good is a major responsibility, and Paul offers a checklist of service opportunities. **Bringing up children** would logically include any children or grandchildren of her own, but the care of others' children or of orphans would be included as well. She must show **hospitality** (also required of overseers, 3:2), demonstrate an attitude of servanthood by **washing the feet of the saints**, and have a reputation for **helping those in trouble**. As Timothy was to "devote [himself] to the public reading of Scripture, to preaching and to teaching" (4:13), so she was to be known for **devoting herself to all kinds of good deeds**.

- She must be a woman of prayer (v. 5). This may be understood as a reference to public as well as private worship. Some have translated this phrase as "attends the prayers continually," meaning that she is present at public worship, like the widow Anna in Luke's account of the dedication of Jesus (Luke 2:36–38).

It is difficult to imagine that only widows who were spiritually active to this degree would be eligible for church relief funds, but such high expectations would be appropriate for enrollment in an order of lay ministry.

Another clue to the existence of such an order is found in the paragraph on **younger widows**. They don't qualify for **such a list** because they are likely to remarry, and that would mean that they had **broken their first pledge** (literally, faith). The marriage vow isn't the issue here, and neither, probably, is a vow to remain unmarried as a condition of eligibility for church aid (although that theory has some support). It is more likely that the vow was associated with membership in the order. Paul also is concerned that in the conduct of their charitable works, younger widows would be tempted to be idle and gossip. For these reasons, and contrary to the false teaching of the ascetics who forbade marriage, Paul advocates remarriage for younger widows. (See the notes on 3:2).

> ### QUALIFICATIONS FOR WIDOWS IN LAY MINISTRY IN EPHESUS
> - Must be over sixty
> - Must have been faithful to her husband
> - Must be well known for her good deeds
> - Must be a woman of prayer

The church provided relief for widows who were truly needy, but not for those with families who could support them or for those who were worldly, rather than spiritually, minded. Younger widows were encouraged to remarry. Older widows who qualified were given an opportunity to serve in a ministry designed for their spiritual gifts and social situation.

## 3. SELECTION AND CARE OF ELDERS 5:17–25

The discussion of widows serving the church leads naturally to a section of Paul's letter that deals with another level of leadership, the **elders**. Like the elders in a Jewish synagogue, elders in a Christian congregation were to **direct the affairs of the church**. Paul puts in a word for excellence in ministry when he singles out those who do it **well**.

### A CALL TO EXCELLENCE

The calling of God is always a call to excellence; could it be to anything less? Yet His work isn't always done well, for a variety of reasons. A Christian leader who assumes that good motives sanctify careless work misjudges God's standards. Elton Trueblood said it often: "Holy shoddy is still shoddy." The quality of ministry is important to Paul because of its importance to the church.

Elders who serve well **are worthy of double honor**. It is clear from the quotations in the following verse that Paul is thinking of ministerial remuneration. He himself is writing as a bivocational minister, working as a tentmaker to support his ministry (Acts 18:3; 20:34; 1 Cor. 9:3–18; 1 Thess. 2:9; 2 Thess. 3:8). But Paul sees his situation as the exception rather than the rule. It is appropriate, even essential, for ministers to be financially supported by the churches they serve, just as a **worker**

**deserves his wages** from an employer and **the ox** who treads the grain should get his dinner from the threshing floor.

Some commentators see the **double honor** as (1) respect and (2) remuneration. Others understand the phrase to imply quantity—twice as much as other elders receive, or perhaps twice the amount given the widows in the preceding section. It is possible that Paul is making an allusion to the Jewish birthright, by which the oldest son received the honor of a double portion of the inheritance. By that interpretation, Paul would be saying that the elder should be given the honor of a double portion, meaning ample wages, proportionate to his effective service.

This applies especially to **those whose work is preaching and teaching**. Just as all elders had responsibility for leadership in the congregation, all were to be "able to teach" (3:2). For some, though, teaching would be the primary assignment, and Paul's specific salute to preachers and teachers indicates that that work is of primary importance in the church.

Note that Paul introduces both of the quotations in v. 18 as **Scripture**. The example of the ox is from the Old Testament (Deut. 25:4; compare 1 Cor. 9:9), but it was Jesus who spoke of the workman and his wages (Luke 10:7). The New Testament was still being composed as Paul wrote these words, but parts of it were already accepted as authoritative Scripture.

## HANDLING ACCUSATIONS

Leadership has its liabilities, and in 1 Tim. 5:19–20, Timothy is given practical advice on situations he might have to face. It was easy to bring **an accusation against an elder**, or against any church leader. They are in the public eye, and their ministry will have opponents in the world— even in the church. To provide a measure of protection for anyone accused of wrongdoing, the Law of Moses demanded the testimony of **two or three witnesses**. Elders deserve no less protection in the church.

Sometimes, of course, the accusations will be true. **Those who sin—** that is, elders against whom charges have been proven—**are to be rebuked publicly** (literally, before all). That could mean in front of their fellow elders or in front of the entire church, but the latter seems more likely. This public reprimand would certainly follow private confrontation and counsel, but a public office requires a public accounting. The effect of that public display on **the others**, the rest of the elders, would be a **warning** that no one is above the possibility of sin.

In all of these matters, Paul expects Timothy to judge **without partiality** or **favoritism**. All of the elders are Timothy's colleagues; some of them were probably appointed by Timothy himself. But God deals with all of us impartially (Acts 10:34; Rom. 2:11; Eph. 6:9; Col. 3:25), and Timothy must do the same in the supervision of his fellow ministers. To make his point, Paul invokes **God, Christ Jesus, and the elect angels—** the officers of the court on Judgment Day (see Matt. 25:31; Mk. 8:38; 2 Tim. 4:1; and others)—in a solemn and awesome charge.[5] The point of that charge would not be lost on Timothy: don't take this matter lightly.

Since judgment is a terrible task and the sin that requires judgment is even more terrible, leaders must be chosen carefully. **Do not be hasty in the laying on of hands**, but take care whom you ordain. Ordination councils have a tough job, but they owe it to the church and to the candidates who come before them to ask tough questions and make tough choices. To be careless in the selection of Christian leaders is to **share in the sins of others** when those improperly or negligently ordained elders fall. In that event, Paul seems to think there's more than enough responsibility to go around.[6]

Above all, Timothy must **keep** himself **pure**. His life must be above reproach if he is to handle this kind of Kingdom business.

Perhaps to reassure him that the assignment is not overwhelming, Paul mentions an observation from his own experience (vv. 24–25). **The sins of some men are obvious**, and judgment is a simple matter. The sins of some others are hidden, but Paul has noticed that they **trail behind them** and will eventually come to light (Num. 32:23). It works **in the same way** with **good deeds** too.

## TIMOTHY'S HEALTH

In a parenthetical note dropped squarely into the middle of this section on elders, Paul pauses to make a comment on Timothy's health. **Stop drinking**

**only water**, he urges, **and use a little wine because of your stomach**. It is a digression, but not totally unconnected with Paul's train of thought. In keeping himself pure (v. 22), Timothy may have put his health at risk. It's evident that Timothy practiced total abstinence from alcohol. But given his **frequent illnesses**, which may have been related to the poor quality of available drinking water, Paul writes an apostolic prescription for medicinal wine. The prohibitions against "much wine" (3:8) and "drunkenness" (3:3) still stand, of course, and these instructions are not inconsistent with them.

# 4. SLAVES AND MASTERS 6:1–2

A good number of people in the New Testament church were slaves or former slaves. Critics of the church often referred to Christians in general as slaves by way of insult. Little did the critics know that they were right.

Christians are "slaves to righteousness" (Rom. 6:18) and "slaves to God" (Rom. 6:22). One of Paul's favorite self-descriptions was "a servant (literally, slave) of Christ Jesus" (Rom. 1:1, for example). That metaphor was a powerful one in the first century because of the incredible network of slavery that covered the Roman Empire.

One third of the population of the empire was enslaved. Including the large number of freedmen—most slaves in the Roman world could expect their freedom by age thirty—the number would be dramatically higher.

Slavery in the Roman world was not based on race. Most slaves in the generations prior to Paul had been captured in war. In Paul's day the children of women who were slaves, along with newborns who were *exposed* (abandoned by their parents, a wide-spread practice), accounted for the largest share of the slave population.

The New Testament does not explicitly condemn the institution of slavery, probably because of the chaos that would have resulted from immediate abolition and the repercussion for the church if Christians were thought to be inciting a slave rebellion. Paul addresses the issue of slavery by calling on slaves and masters alike to act like Christ (Eph. 6:5–9; Col. 3:22–4:1; Titus 2:9–10; and Philemon).

Here in 1 Timothy, Paul's word for those **under the yoke of slavery** is that they should give their masters **full respect**. That is the rule for slaves held by unbelieving masters, **so that God's name and our teaching may not be slandered** by reports of uncooperative Christian slaves. The same rule is applied to slaves owned by Christian masters (a situation we can hardly imagine). In those cases, **those who benefit from [the slaves'] service are believers** and **brothers** who are **dear to them**.

Some New Testament congregations included both slaves and their masters— Onesimus and Philemon, for example—and it would be understandably awkward for one Christian brother to own another.

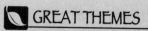

## GREAT THEMES

### OPPOSITION TO SLAVERY

The Christian witness against slavery has been strong and effective. John Wesley, William Wilberforce, English and American Quakers, and evangelical abolitionists such as the early Wesleyan Methodists in America had major roles in dismantling the European-American system of slavery over the past two hundred years. The roots of that successful crusade lie in the New Testament principles of Paul and others, who lived not in but above the slave-saturated society around them.

In Christ there is neither slave nor free (Gal. 3:28), but at the communion table, a free believer might break bread with a brother who was his slave.

Paul asks Christian slaves not to resent their believing masters on the one hand nor to take advantage of their kindness on the other. Instead, **serve them even better**, Paul advises, because of the spiritual bond between you, a tie that is stronger than the bonds of slavery. In his letter to Philemon, Paul urges a Christian master to accept his believing slave as a brother in Christ—in fact, to treat him as he would treat Paul himself! No Christian would make a slave of Paul. If Paul's plea were applied in the spirit of Gal. 3:28, the issue of Christians owning slaves would soon disappear.

Attitude is the key for both slave and master.

### ENDNOTES

1. Manfred Brauch, *Hard Sayings of Paul* (Downers Grove, Ill.: InterVarsity Press, 1989), p. 266.

2. J. N. D. Kelly, *The Pastoral Epistles* (Peabody, Mass.: Hendrickson Publishers, 1960), pp. 120–121.

3. E. K. Simpson, cited by Donald Guthrie, *The Pastoral Epistles* (Grand Rapids, Mich.: William B. Eerdmans Publishing Company, 1957), p. 101.

4. Kelly, *The Pastoral Epistles*, p. 115.

5. The elect angels are those who remained faithful, in contrast to the fallen angels who sinned (2 Pet. 2:4; compare Jude 6).

6. It is possible, but not probable, that the phrase *laying on of hands* here refers to the restoration of repentant elders following the rebuke of v. 20. No evidence exists for such a ceremony in the New Testament church, although one was in place by the third century. The term *laying on of hands* in 1 Timothy refers to what we call ordination.

# 9

# THE PERSONAL VALUES OF A LEADER

## 1 Timothy 6:3-10

The sixth chapter of 1 Timothy is the only place in Paul's epistles where money is discussed at some length. Paul was fond of using wealth and poverty as figures of speech, spiritual metaphors with reference both to God (Rom. 2:4, 9:23, 11:33; Eph. 2:4, 7; 3:8, 16) and to the church (1 Cor. 1:5; 2 Cor. 6:10, 9:11; Col. 2:2). However, the proper use of wealth and the inherent risk of riches receive comparatively little attention in Paul's writing. This passage goes a long way toward filling that void.

Once again false teachers are on Paul's mind. The passage begins with a description of their corruption (1 Tim. 6:3–5) and ends with the promise of their destruction (vv. 9–10). Although the faults and flaws of these teachers are numerous, the one that draws Paul's fire is greed— specifically, their attempt to use godliness for personal financial gain.

Godliness itself is gain enough for Paul (6:6). Material wealth is transitory (6:7), seductive (6:9–10a, b), and potentially destructive (6:10c), and believers are forewarned that it can be hazardous to their spiritual health.

## 1. FALSE DOCTRINE AND FINANCIAL GAIN 6:3-5

"These are the things you are to teach," Paul writes (again—see 4:11, 5:7) at the close of the previous paragraph. Teach that love is the goal and that it is linked to holy living (1:5). Teach that Christ Jesus came into the world to save sinners (1:15) because God wants all to be saved (2:3). Teach that prayer and worship are pleasing to God and needed by us (2:1–15). Teach that God is the giver of all good things (4:4–5). Teach leaders to give more thought to their character than to their gifts (3:1–13), teach families to care for their own who are in need (5:3–16), and teach slaves to act like Jesus in bonds (6:1–2). Teach all of these things because they are true, unlike the words of the false teachers.

## PORTRAIT OF A FALSE TEACHER

**If anyone teaches false doctrines**, contrary to **the sound instruction of our Lord Jesus Christ** (compare 1:10) **and to godly teaching**, he is unworthy to teach. Paul's psychological and spiritual profile of a false teacher in vv. 3–5 shows just how unworthy he was. It is an unflattering portrait, to say the least, and it completes the picture Paul began in 1:3–11 and continued in 4:1–3.

The false teacher is **conceited**, proud of his "learning" and his own brand of "truth," calling attention to himself in a display of self-aggrandizement and self-exaltation. When self is exalted, Jesus isn't. C. S. Lewis called pride the greatest of all sins,[1] and spiritual pride is the worst kind of pride. The false teacher of 1 Timothy 6 seems to worship himself; he has an "altar ego."

The false teacher **understands nothing**. What irony! The scholar is a dunce, a teacher who can't pass the test and, even worse, doesn't know it. About these false teachers, Paul marvels, "they want to be teachers of the law, but they do not know what they're talking about" (1:7). The New English Bible combines these first two characteristics and labels the false teacher a "pompous ignoramus."

The false teacher has **an unhealthy interest in controversies**, loving to debate just for the sake of argument. That is the same contentious attitude that fuels television and radio talk shows, and it does even more harm in the church than it does in the entertainment media (see 1:4). His specialty is **quarrels about words**, theological trivia that edify no one, confuse many, and usually miss the truth entirely. Like modern cultists who miss the clear witness to Christ in Scripture because they focus on minutia, the false teacher can't see the biblical forest for the trees. His pseudo-intellectualism is incompatible with the faith. His **unhealthy** fascination with these pursuits is, literally, "sick" or "diseased" and stands in stark contrast to the **sound** (healthy) **instruction** of Christ.

The false teacher's life is marked by **envy** because his conceit fears any rival. His life is marked also by **strife** and **malicious talk,** common companions of envy and jealousy (see Mark 7:22; Rom. 1:29, 13:13; Gal. 5:20, 21); **evil suspicions,** imagined threats that rise from his own evil motives; and **constant friction between men of corrupt mind** (the New English Bible reads, "their reasoning powers [have] become atrophied"). This teacher is depraved. **Robbed of the truth,** he would rob others of it too.

James Russell Lowell captures the question before the Ephesian church as Timothy defends the truth (2:4, 3:15, 4:3; compare 2 Tim. 2:15) and the false teachers attack it:

> Once to every man and nation
>   comes the moment to decide,
> In the strife of Truth with Falsehood,
>   for the good or evil side;
> Some great cause, God's new Messiah,
>   offering each the bloom or blight,
> Parts the goats upon the left hand,
>   and the sheep upon the right,
> And the choice goes by forever
>   'twixt that darkness and that light.[2]

Timothy must have felt at times that truth was losing the fight. Paul urged him to fight on.

## FLEECING THE SHEEP

Perhaps the most telling characteristic of the false teachers is their greed. They see **godliness** as **a means to financial gain.** Paul strongly defends the right of a minister to expect proper financial support from the congregation (1 Tim. 5:17–18), but the motives of the false teachers are very different. They're not seeking legitimate remuneration; they're looking to make a profit. Religion is a business for them, and the church is their meal ticket. Many commentators believe that they were charging high fees for their teaching, fleecing the flock and commercializing the faith. These false teachers were not in a non-profit ministry; their work is better described as non-*prophet*. No truthful teaching could come from such a corrupt source.

Financial gain aside, to treat godliness as a means to *anything*, even good things, is to use God for our own purposes. Godliness has many benefits: peace of heart and mind, a sense of purpose, healed relationships, even the improved financial situation that results from good stewardship. But these things are all secondary to God Himself, the ultimate benefit from our faith and the ultimate goal of our godliness. He is an end in Himself, and even the good things we become so focused on He gives us freely when we surrender ourselves.

Contrast the character of the false teachers with the character of the true Christian leaders at Ephesus, described in 1 Timothy 3. The false teacher is given to "controversies and quarrels" (6:4) while the true teacher is "not quarrelsome" (3:3). The false teacher thinks "godliness is a means to financial gain" (6:5), but the true teacher is "not a lover of money" (3:3) and does not pursue "dishonest gain" (3:8). The false teacher is beneath contempt; the true teacher is "above reproach" (3:2).

It is no wonder that Paul felt deceiving spirits were at work in the church. He saw their handiwork in the persons of the false teachers.

## 2. GODLINESS AND SPIRITUAL GAIN 6:6-10

Godliness must not be "a means to financial gain" (3:5), but **godliness with contentment is great gain**. Godliness is not a means—not even a means to spiritual gain, strictly speaking, as if godliness could lead to some other, more desirable goal. Rather, godliness itself is **great gain**; it is its own goal. According to 4:8, **godliness** is gain in not one but two worlds, for it has value for the present world and the world to come.

*Contentment* was a popular word among Stoic philosophers, whose ideal was self-sufficiency and independence, traits marked by indifference to any outside forces, events, or conditions, including sickness, poverty, or even death. Paul's immediate point is that neither money (v. 5) nor the lack of it should shake our inner world. But the application of his point could be extended to cover any external circumstance. When Paul tells the Philippian Christians that he has "learned to be content whatever the circumstances" (Phil. 4:11), he uses a form of the same word, *contentment.* The Stoics prized self-sufficiency, but Paul is after something more. His sufficiency, and ours, is in God.

Two well-known proverbs appear in this short section. The first deals with the transitory nature of wealth, the second with its spiritual perils.

**For we brought nothing into the world, and we can take nothing out of it**. That idea is mentioned also in Job (1:21) and Ecclesiastes (5:15), and it has parallels in Greek philosophy. Who can argue the point? Money becomes irrelevant when considered from the perspective of our entry into and exit from life on earth. **Food and clothing**—the basics—will be enough for anyone whose treasure is elsewhere (see Matt. 6:19–34). The term *contented Christian* ought to be a redundancy.

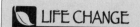

## LIFE CHANGE

### CONTENTMENT

John D. Rockefeller was once asked "How much money is enough?" He replied, "Some more." Contrast that attitude of acquisition with this entry in John Wesley's *Journal.* Speaking of a member of Oxford's Holy Club, he wrote, "One of them had thirty pounds a years. He lived on twenty-eight and gave away two. The next year, receiving sixty pounds, he still lived on twenty-eight and gave away thirty-two. The third year he received ninety pounds and gave away sixty-two. The fourth year he received one hundred and twenty pounds; still he lived as before, on twenty-eight, and gave to the poor all the rest."

That "one" was Wesley himself, and he carried the same attitude toward money throughout his life. He was content.

**People who want to get rich**, in Paul's view, are asking for trouble. The three-step road to their reward begins when they fall (1) **into temptation,** then (2) **into many foolish and harmful desires**, after which they are plunged (3) **into ruin**. (Compare that to the progression of temptation and sin in James 1:13–15.) The ruin that Paul speaks of has eternal consequences. The word for **destruction** is sometimes translated perdition or damnation. One who wishes for wealth risks a far more serious plunge than a drop in the stock market.

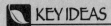

## KEY IDEAS

### STEWARDSHIP

Street-corner sages have had their own versions of the proverb in 1 Tim. 6:7. For example, "Shrouds have no pockets" and "There's no trailer hitch on a hearse." The man who was buried in his new Cadillac convertible succeeded only in ruining a nice car. When we leave, we leave it all. That awareness can make us content with less. It can also revolutionize our stewardship.

Paul's dire words are not necessarily for the rich but for any who want to get rich. Wealth has its perils, but they're associated with the desire for money (1 Tim. 6:9) or the love of it (v. 10). **For the love of money is a root of all kinds of evil**.

Verse 10 is often misquoted. Not money itself but the love of it is the problem. To have money without loving it must be difficult. One sign of the last days is that "people will be lovers of money" (2 Tim. 3:2); that prophecy has been fulfilled in every generation.

Paul echoes Jesus' teaching about money, which is that the rich are not lost simply because they are rich but because they succumb to the risks associated with wealth (Matt. 6:24; Luke 16:19–31, 18:18–30). Wealth seduces, and the love of it is **a** (not *the*) **root of all kinds of evil**.

It is probably the false teachers of 1 Tim. 3:5 Paul is thinking of when he writes of **some people, eager for money**, who **have wandered away from the faith**. Unlike the godly, who are content, these unhappy wanderers find **many griefs**. It is their own fault, of course; they **have . . . pierced themselves**. Serving mammon has its consequences.

### ENDNOTES

1. C. S. Lewis, *Mere Christianity* (New York: Scribners, 1943), pp. 94 and following.

2. James Russell Lowell, "The Present Crisis."

# FINAL INSTRUCTIONS

## 1 Timothy 6:11–21a

A stirring doxology is the centerpiece of Paul's charge to Timothy in the closing words of this epistle. It is a hymn in praise of the unimaginable majesty and might of God, **the only Ruler, the King of kings and Lord of lords,** in all of His power and glory (6:15–16).

It is this great God whom Timothy serves. He is a **man of God** (6:11) and has God's work to do (6:14), but Timothy must be careful to walk God's way (6:11). Paul's benediction contains the promise that will make it all possible: God's grace will be with the young man as he fights the good fight, and will be with his congregation as well (6:12, 21).

Before closing his letter, Paul has one final word for the wealthy. There's a place for them in the Kingdom if they remember that its headquarters are in heaven, not on earth, and live accordingly (6:17–19). Several major themes of the epistle are revisited in these final paragraphs—the dangers of the Ephesian heresy (6:20), the good fight of the faith (6:12), the virtues of a Christian (6:11), the proper attitude toward wealth (6:17–19), and the responsibilities of a Christian leader (6:13–14, 20). Modern communications experts tell us that we haven't said it until we've said it more than once. Paul was there ahead of them.

## 1. A CHARGE TO TIMOTHY 6:11–16, 20–21A

Timothy is a **man of God**. He may be young and a bit timid, but he is a man of God. What a great compliment from one's mentor! It's easy for us to imagine Timothy thinking of Paul as a man of God; Paul was on a par with the heroes of the Old Testament who bore the honor of that title, men like Moses (Josh. 14:6), Samuel (1 Sam. 9:6–14), Elijah (1 Kings 17:18), Elisha (2 Kings 4:7), and David (Neh. 12:24). Yet Paul honors Timothy with that same description and, in doing so, must have given Timothy's confidence a tremendous boost.

Any pastor can be a man or woman of God. In fact, every pastor should be. More to the point, every Christian should be.

## AVOIDING SIN

None of the giants of the Old Testament who were called men of God lived in a monastery. They all wrestled with sin in the real world, and so did Timothy. He wrestled with sin in the church too. **But you, man of God, flee from all this**. Paul's phrase **but you,** which appears several times in his second letter to Timothy (translated "you, however" in 2 Tim. 3:10; "but as for you" in 3:14; and "but you" in 4:5), creates a clear contrast. You are not like the hypocritical teachers, Paul says, with their disagreeable vices (1 Tim. 6:3–5) and foolish choices (6:9–10). They are far from being men of God. You're different. Like Joseph in Potiphar's house (Gen. 39:12), you must **flee from all this**. Timothy was to avoid participation in (but not confrontation of) the sins of the heretical party at Ephesus (1 Tim. 1:3).

Avoidance of sin is coupled with an attraction to sanctity: **pursue righteousness, godliness, faith, love, endurance, and gentleness**. The list resembles the fruit of the Spirit in Gal. 5:22–23. Paul repeats the flee/pursue instruction in 2 Tim. 2:22, mentioning faith and love in yet another such list.

## ADVANCING THE CAUSE

Fleeing sin is not running away from the field of action. To **fight the good fight of the faith** is still Timothy's assignment. This is the same idea Paul expressed in 1 Tim. 1:18, but not the same imagery. In chapter 1, Paul used "the good fight" as a military metaphor; the phrase there means literally the good warfare. In chapter 6, the allusion is to athletics— literally, the good contest. It is this phrase from the athletic arena that Paul uses in his famous farewell at the close of 2 Timothy (4:7).

Paul now speaks about the prize for victory in the contest: **take hold of the eternal life to which you were called.** Eternal life is not merely waiting for us at the end of this life; it is a present possession of the faithful (see John 3:36, 5:24, 10:28; 1 John 5:11–12).

The good confession that Timothy made **in the presence of many witnesses** may have been either at his baptism or his ordination. Since baptism is the event associated with the call to **eternal life**, it's probably baptism that Paul has in mind. At Timothy's baptism, he would have made the simple but life-changing **confession** that Jesus is Lord. That statement was the first creed of the church. It was, among other things, a denial of the notion that Caesar was Lord, and it cost many Christians their lives. Paul sees a connection between Timothy's confession and **the good confession** Christ made **while testifying before Pontius Pilate**. Standing in the Praetorium before the Roman governor, Christ did not deny His Lordship: "My kingdom is not of this world. . . . [but] I am a king" (John 18:33–37).

Just as Paul had earlier charged Timothy "in the sight of God and Christ Jesus and the elect angels" to be fair and impartial in his leadership (1 Tim. 5:21), so he charges him now **in the sight of God . . . and of Christ Jesus . . . to keep this command without spot or blame.** Some commentators think it is the message (**command**), and not Timothy himself, that is to be preserved **without spot or blame**, pure and undefiled in the midst of the lies of the false teachers. More likely,

## LIFE CHANGE

### The Cost of Discipleship

The Christians in Germany who stood up to Adolph Hitler before and during World War II were known as the Confessing Church. When leaders like Dietrich Bonhoeffer, Karl Barth, and Martin Niemoller made their "good confessions" of Christ (6:12), it cost them their jobs, their freedom, and—in some cases—their lives. Out of that struggle, Bonhoeffer wrote *The Cost of Discipleship*, in which he rejects the easy belief that he calls "cheap grace." Christ calls us to costly grace, Bonhoeffer says. Even in our open culture, a good confession can and probably will cost us something.

Look what it cost Christ.

though, the object of the charge is Timothy's own character. Like the elders he appoints (3:2), Timothy is to be blameless and above reproach while keeping **this command**—that is, while carrying out all of the instructions of the epistle.

From its opening verse, a *command theme* has run through this epistle. Timothy has been given orders. He is to execute them faithfully, and he need not expect them to change **until the appearing of our Lord Jesus Christ, which God will bring about in his own time**. Again, as in 2:6, God's own good time is *kairos*, not *chronos*. *Kairos* has to do with the quality of time; it indicates a strategic time and not a time on the clock or calendar. This means that God will give the signal for the Second Coming as He did for the first—when the time is right (Gal. 4:4).

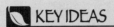

## KEY IDEAS

### THE SECOND COMING

The booklet *88 Reasons Why the Rapture Will Be in 1988* was rewritten as *89 Reasons Why the Rapture Will Be in 1989*, but both predictions were wrong. In the fall of 1994, another prognostication fell flat, and someone pointed out to the end-times prognosticator that Christ Himself has said no one except the Father knows the day or hour of the Son's Return (Mark 13:32). The incredible response: "He didn't say we couldn't know the month or year!"

Ever since the Great Disappointment left some Christians gazing heavenward to no avail in 1844—and, incidentally, spawned the Jehovah's Witnesses' penchant for date-setting later in the century—there has always been someone with a chart, book, or tape said to "reveal" the date of Christ's Return. C. S. Lewis's simple formula says it best: (1) Christ is coming back. (2) We don't know when. (3) So we'd better be ready.

Paul finds it hard to write about God without breaking into praise. The doxology that accompanies Timothy's charge is typical for Paul—a paean to God's power and majesty, creating a great parenthesis of worship in the final lines of his letter. As usual, Paul's hymn of praise is theologically filled to overflowing with truth about God.

*God Rules.* He is the King of kings and the Lord of lords, a superlative comparison meaning that He is the greatest King and the greatest Lord (just as the term *Holy of Holies* indicates the holiest of holy places and *Song of Songs* means the best of all songs). God is not only the greatest but also **the only Ruler**. He has no rival on earth, in heaven, or in hell. God is supreme. No one can stand above Him.

*He Rules in Power.* The word translated **Ruler** is *dunastes*, meaning potentate. It's a power word, derived from the Greek root *dunamis,* from which we get the English words *dynamic* and *dynamo*. No one can stand against God.

*He Rules Forever.* He and He **alone** is inherently **immortal**. No one will outlive or outlast Him, and He will have no successor.

*He Rules in Splendor.* God **lives in unapproachable light**, and **no one has seen or can see** Him. Moses was given a passing glance at His glory (Exod. 33:17–23), and Peter, James, and John were given a sneak preview of Christ's transcendent glory on the Mount of Transfiguration (Matt. 17:1–8), but no one has seen God in all of His splendor (see John 1:18, 6:46).

*He Is Worthy to Rule.* **To him be honor and might forever.** No one else is worthy of the throne.

## GUARDING THE DEPOSIT

Following a brief word to the wealthy of the Ephesian church (1 Tim. 6:17–19), Paul concludes his charge: **Timothy, guard what has been entrusted to your care.** The Greek word used here and in 2 Tim. 1:12, 14 means a deposit. God has placed the gospel in Timothy's safekeeping. Timothy is a trustee; the faith is his sacred trust. Vincent of Lerins, writing in the fifth century, speaks to the modern church as well.

> What is meant by *the deposit*? That which is committed to thee, not that which is invented by thee; that which thou hast received, not that which thou hast devised . . . a thing brought to thee, not brought forth out of thee; wherein thou must not be an author but a keeper; not a leader but a follower. Keep the deposit.[1]

Not only the truth but also the people of the truth are entrusted to a pastor's care (1 Tim. 6:20). Asking a pastor "How many souls are under your care?" is different from asking "How large is your church?" or "What's your average attendance?" Pastoral responsibility is at one and the same time a unique privilege and an awesome responsibility.

A final time Paul urges Timothy to **turn away from godless chatter,** the ramblings of the heretical teachers, and from **what is falsely called**

**knowledge** (*gnosis*, from which are derived the terms *Gnostics* and *Gnosticism*). Steer clear of these fatal fallacies; those who have fallen under their influence **have wandered away from the faith**.

And so Paul ends where he began, with a warning about "those who have wandered away and turned to meaningless talk" (1:6). Between these bookends (1:6 and 6:20–21) are stacked volumes of truth. Timothy's call, commission, and charge is to teach that truth, model it, and guard it so that he can pass it on to others, just as it was passed on to him.

## 2. A WORD TO THE RICH 6:17–19

Paul has a final word for rich Christians in Ephesus. This postscript is much more positive in tone than was his negative assessment of wealth seekers in vv. 3–10, but it is still plain truth plainly put.

**Command those who are rich in this present world** (v. 17) to **lay up treasure for themselves as a firm foundation for the coming age** (v. 19). Heavenly, not earthly, riches are of true value, Paul says. He advises wealthy Christians to transfer funds immediately. Paul is not mixing the metaphor when he introduces the image of a **firm foundation** to a discussion of wealth, because that term carries the idea of a fund or account as a financial foundation. Paul advises that good deeds and generosity form a solid foundation for eternal life. But how does one go about this

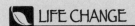

**LIFE CHANGE**

GUARDING THE FAITH

A little girl hesitantly approached her mother and said, "Mom, you know that vase that's been in our family for generations? Well, this generation just dropped it." We dare not be the generation that drops the banner of the faith, the holy deposit passed on to us by generations of faithful believers and entrusted to us by God Himself. Yet we may be on the verge of doing just that.

In our evangelistic zeal, we're not free to re-define the *evangel* to make it more palatable. As we earnestly try to win a hearing for the gospel within our culture, what will happen if the culture decides it doesn't like the content of our faith? We might be tempted to change that faith in order to win more adherents.

We are charged with guarding God's deposit and winning a world at the same time. We need not expect the world to guard it for us.

transfer of "funds"? Paul's answer is a four-point outline on Jesus' text in Matt. 6:19–24:

(1) Don't be **arrogant**. A Wall Street witticism holds that "the one with the most toys wins," but God doesn't keep score that way.

(2) **Don't put [your] hope in wealth . . . but put [your] hope in God**. Wealth is **so uncertain**; to Jesus' examples of moth, rust, and thieves (Matt. 6:19), we could add business failure, uninsured loss, and market crashes. Using a clever play on words, Paul points out that God **richly provides us with everything for our enjoyment**. And He has never lost a cent of His investors' spiritual capital.

(3) **Be rich in good deeds** (another word play by Paul). Financial management specialists advise: "Make your money work for you." God says, "Put your money to work for Me and for others."

(4) **Be generous and willing to share**. This sounds like John Wesley's dictum: "Earn all you can, save all you can, give all you can." Be a conduit, not a lockbox. Transmit to others that with which God has blessed you. William Barclay writes, "The whole teaching of the Christian ethic is, not that wealth is a sin, but that wealth is a very great responsibility."[2]

In the language of accounting, the bottom line, that which finally matters, is **the life that is truly life**—the one that lasts for eternity.

### ENDNOTES

1. Vincent of Lerins, quoted in William Barclay, *The Letters to Timothy, Titus, and Philemon* (Philadelphia: The Westminster Press, 1960), pp. 160–61.
2. Barclay, *Letters*, p. 159.

# 11

# AN APOSTOLIC BENEDICTION

## 1 Timothy 6:21b

**G**race be with you. The benediction is brevity itself, but it carries much meaning.

A benediction is a blessing, and grace, God's unmerited favor toward us, is the best blessing of all. In each of his letters, Paul closes "gracefully." Here is a sample.

- "The grace of our Lord Jesus be with you" (Rom. 16:20b, where Paul places the benediction several verses before his closing ascription of praise to God).

- "May the grace of the Lord Jesus Christ, and the love of God, and the fellowship of the Holy Spirit be with you all" (2 Cor. 13:14).

- "Grace to all who love our Lord Jesus Christ with an undying love" (Eph. 6:24).

- "The grace of our Lord Jesus Christ be with your spirit, brothers. Amen" (Gal. 6:18).

In 1 Tim. 6:21, the pronoun *you* is plural. Even though the letter is addressed to Timothy as the pastor, Paul meant for it to be read to the entire congregation. All of them—pastor and people alike—needed a gracious God, and they had one.

So do we.

# 2 TIMOTHY

# INTRODUCTION TO 2 TIMOTHY

"Come before winter," Paul urges Timothy (2 Tim. 4:21). But when he wrote those words, Paul had no way of knowing whether he would be alive at the onset of winter. As we read them, we, too, wonder if Timothy made it to Rome in time.

Second Timothy is the last New Testament letter Paul wrote. There is a sense of urgency about it, and understandably so. As a prisoner awaiting execution at the hands of the Roman Emperor Nero, Paul wastes no words and pleads with Timothy to waste no time. This letter gives us a glimpse of the man Paul, and draws us powerfully into his story. This is the most personal of all of Paul's epistles. Here we see his heart.

## AUTHORSHIP

In the opening verse of both 1 and 2 Timothy, the Apostle Paul is identified as the author, and, until comparatively recent times, that claim went unchallenged. Based on vocabulary and style, the known chronology of Paul's life and ministry, and several other factors, some scholars now question the authorship of these epistles. However, there is solid evidence for Pauline authorship, and support for it has been growing in recent years. It seems most probable that Paul did, in fact, author 1 and 2 Timothy. For a more extensive discussion of the authorship of these epistles, see the introduction to 1 Timothy.

## RECIPIENT

Timothy was Paul's co-worker and son in the faith (1 Tim. 1:2; 2 Tim. 1:2). A native of Lystra, Timothy was born to a Jewish mother and a Greek father. He was apparently converted on Paul's first missionary journey and joined Paul's team at a young age during the second missionary journey. (He is still considered young in the Pastoral Epistles, at which time he might have been in his mid-thirties.)

Timothy was ordained by Paul (2 Tim. 1:6) and "the body of elders" (1 Tim. 4:14) through the laying on of hands. He traveled with Paul and represented Paul on a number of special assignments. Out of Paul's ten letters besides the Pastoral Epistles, Timothy is listed as co-author (a largely honorary designation) in six, and he is mentioned in a seventh.

At the time of the writing of this second Pastoral, Timothy was in Ephesus as Paul's apostolic delegate or personal envoy, a position which carried considerable influence because of the authority of the appointing apostle. Timothy was pastoring the Ephesian congregation on temporary assignment. Ephesus, a city on the trade route that runs along the western coast of Asia Minor, could not have been an easy church to pastor. Paul had both extraordinary success and extraordinary opposition in Ephesus during his stay there (Acts 19). It was a center of the worship of Artemis (to the Romans, Diana), and her temple in Ephesus was one of the seven wonders of the ancient world. The Ephesian church was troubled, and Paul wanted Timothy there to bring stability and to ensure the triumph of orthodox theology and biblical beliefs.

## DATE OF WRITING

As he wrote 2 Timothy, Paul was a prisoner for the Lord's sake (2 Tim. 1:8, 16; 2:9) in Rome (1:17). Yet there are strong reasons to suppose that this is not the same imprisonment described in Acts 28. If Paul was released from the imprisonment mentioned in Acts and undertook a fourth missionary journey, as seems likely, then he wrote 2 Timothy after being re-arrested. Paul's circumstances were very different from his first imprisonment. He was longer under house arrest but was, according to Christian tradition, languishing in a dungeon near the Roman Forum. He expected death, not release. At his initial hearing, he was snatched from the jaws of the lion (4:17), but that lion still lurked.

Paul's circumstances had changed because there was a change in Rome's policy concerning Christianity. After a fire nearly destroyed the city of Rome in A.D. 64, the Emperor Nero placed blame on the Christian community in Rome, probably to divert suspicion from himself. Paul and Peter both became martyrs to the faith in this new and highly charged atmosphere of suspicion and hatred.

The precise date of Paul's death is uncertain, which makes the date of this letter uncertain as well. Some scholars believe Paul died in or around A.D. 64 in the immediate aftermath of the fire and the early stages of the Neronian persecution. That would have allowed little time for travel as extensive as would have been involved in a fourth missionary journey. A date of A.D. 67 or 68 is more likely for both the writing of 2 Timothy and the death of Paul.

## PURPOSE

Paul had three purposes in writing a second time to Timothy. The first was personal; he called for Timothy to come to Rome as quickly as possible (4:9, 21) and bring with him needed items, a cloak and scrolls (4:13). These things were important, but most of all Paul longed to see Timothy again (1:4). The second purpose was pastoral; Paul wrote to encourage Timothy and to steel him against the hardships that intensified persecution was sure to bring. The eventual report of Paul's martyrdom would be one of those hardships, and the apostle knew how difficult that news would be for his son-in-the-faith to hear. The third purpose was practical; Paul wrote to sound another alarm about the false teachers who sought to divide the Ephesian congregation. Their depravity was extreme, and Paul was intent on warning Timothy of the danger they posed. It would be up to Timothy to keep the church together both theologically and organizationally. The church's integrity (literally, oneness) was at stake.

There is a second way to understand the purpose of this letter. If Luke Timothy Johnson is correct, 2 Timothy is a *paraenetic epistle*. A paraenetic epistle is a letter from one who assumes the role of a father writing to a son on matters of morals. It follows a three-part formula: memory, model, and maxims. That is Paul's pattern, Johnson believes.

- *Memory.* Paul reminds Timothy of both his spiritual heritage (2 Tim. 1:5–6) and his congregational challenges (2 Tim. 2:14–3:9; 4:3–4).

- *Model*. Paul offers himself as a model (2 Tim. 1:13; 3:10–11), just as he had previously urged Timothy to model the faith for his congregation (1 Tim. 4:12).

- *Maxims*. Paul instructs Timothy (and, through him, his congregation) on the moral attitudes and actions that he should exhibit and avoid.

## HOLINESS THEMES

Paul's focus is not doctrinal in 2 Timothy, but he does clearly emphasize the contrast between certain false teachers, who are unholy (3:2), and the people of God, who are holy. God's people are pure in heart (2:22). They yield themselves to Him as holy vessels (2:20–21), fit for the noble work of the Kingdom. John Wesley incorporated 2 Tim. 2:20–21 into his Covenant Service, a litany of commitment for early Methodists, as a powerful reminder of the necessity of holy living. In 2 Timothy, the sanctifying Spirit (2:21) is the indwelling Spirit (1:14) who brings power, love, and self-discipline (1:7) to the Christian's life.

Paul's modeling and mentoring did not end when the courier took the scroll for delivery to Timothy. Paul was soon to model the way in which a Christian dies. Until death came, Paul remained obedient to the commission he had received on the Damascus Road. His last letter is not a portrait of a condemned man sinking in self-pity but of a faithful servant of God, still hard at work in the dying light.

### ENDNOTES

1. P. N. Harrison published an influential study in 1921 that employed statistical analysis of the vocabulary of the Pastoral Epistles to find evidence of authenticity. A number of respected scholars have demonstrated that Harrison overstated his case and drew unwarranted conclusions. See John R. W. Stott, *The Message of 1 Timothy & Titus, The Bible Speaks Today* (Downers Grove, Illinois: InterVarsity Press, 1996), p. 25. Counterstudies have found that analyzing Paul's other, more widely accepted letters yields similar results in

some categories. See Donald Guthrie, *The Pastoral Epistles*, Tyndale New Testament Commentaries (Grand Rapids, Mich.: William B. Eerdmans Publishing Company, 1957), pp. 212–228.

2. The term comes from John R. W. Stott, *The Message of 2 Timothy* (Downers Grove, Ill.: InterVarsity Press, 1973), p. 15. Stott doesn't subscribe to that view, however. He supports Pauline authorship.

3. J. N. D. Kelly, *The Pastoral Epistles* (Peabody, Mass.: Hendrickson Publishers, 1960), p. 30.

4. Robert E. Picirilli, *Paul the Apostle* (Chicago: Moody Press), p. 233.

5. Guthrie, *Pastoral Epistles*, p. 228.

6. Thomas Oden, *First and Second Timothy and Titus*, Interpretation Commentary Series (Louisville, Ky.: John Knox Press, 1989), p.15.

7. Kelly, *The Pastoral Epistles*, p. 25.

8. Stott, *The Message of 1 Timothy and Titus*, pp. 25–26.

9. Picirilli, *Paul the Apostle*, p. 232.

10. Oden, *First and Second Timothy and Titus*, p. 13.

11. F. F. Bruce, *Apostle of the Heart Set Free* (Grand Rapids, Mich.: William B. Eerdmans Publishing Co., 1977), pp. 408–409.

# OUTLINE OF 2 TIMOTHY

I. An Apostolic Greeting (1:1–2)
II. The Challenge of Ministry in Difficult Days (1:3–3:9)
  A. Faithful Ministry of the Good News (1:3–14)
    1. A Gift for Effective Service (1:3–7)
    2. A Gospel to Be Preached (1:8–14)
  B. The Cost of Faithful Ministry (1:15–2:13)
    1. True and False Friends (1:15–18)
    2. Three Examples of Endurance (2:1–7)
    3. A Royal Reward (2:8–13)
  C. The Opponents of a Faithful Ministry (2:14–3:9)
    1. God's Unwavering Church (2:14–19)
    2. The Unholy Opposition (2:20–26)
    3. Evil Times, Evil People (3:1–9)
III. The Continuity of Ministry for a New Day (3:10–4:21)
  A. The Close of a Faithful Ministry (3:10–4:8)
    1. Paul's Example (3:10–13)
    2. The Authority of Scripture (3:14–17)
    3. The Charge to Timothy (4:1–5)
    4. Paul's Epitaph (4:6–8)
  B. Final Words (4:9–21)
    1. The Human Face of Leadership (4:9–18)
    2. The Network of the Faithful (4:19–21)
IV. An Apostolic Benediction (4:22)

# AN APOSTOLIC GREETING

## 2 Timothy 1:1-2

Every apostle is a disciple of Christ, but not every disciple is an apostle. From among His large number of disciples, or followers, Jesus chose twelve to receive an apostolic appointment. They would be His "sent ones," His ambassadors having special responsibility, special empowerment, and special authority to build His church. Over time a few others were added to the Twelve, among them a converted Pharisee named Saul. In Acts 26:17, we read the actual words with which Christ commissioned Saul: *ego apostello*, literally translated "I apostle you."[1]

This same Saul, who had changed his name to its Roman form, Paul, now at the close of his apostolic service and imprisoned on Rome's version of death row, still refers to himself as **an apostle of Christ**, honored to be called **by the will of God, according to the promise of life that is in Christ Jesus**. Certain that he would face execution, Paul must have thought much about that promise of life. The first sentence from his pen records his anticipation of it.

The notion of being **in Christ** is one of Paul's favorite themes. The phrase *in Christ* and related phrases such as *in Him* and *in the Lord* occur more than 160 times in Paul's epistles. They are an eloquently simple expression of spiritual union with the Lord, a concept that has been popular with mystics but is always grounded by Paul in the everyday events of the real world. In 2 Timothy, grace (1:9, 2:1), faith (1:13), love (1:13), salvation (2:10), a godly life (3:12), and even life itself (1:1)—

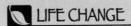

## LIFE CHANGE

### DWELLING IN CHRIST

G. K. Chesterton, a great Christian author and journalist of the early twentieth century, was notoriously absent minded. He once sent his wife a telegram that read: "Am in Brighton. Where should I be?"

Paul knows where we should be: "In Christ!" (See Eph. 1:1.) We may be in Ephesus or in Evansville, in Galatia or in Grand Rapids, but wherever we are, we must be *in Christ*. The realtors are right after all; spiritually speaking, the only thing that matters is location, location, location.

eternal life—are found "in Him," with no hint of the ecstasies of the mystic. Paul did have his rapturous moments (see 2 Cor. 12:1–10), but his chief interest was not out-of-body experiences but in-the-body obedience.

This letter, probably the last Paul wrote and certainly the last of his letters recorded in the New Testament, is addressed **to Timothy, [his] dear son** in the Lord, who was also Paul's apostolic delegate to the church at Ephesus. The salutation is repeated from his first letter to Timothy: **Grace, mercy, and peace from God the Father and Christ Jesus our Lord** (1 Tim. 1:2; see the discussion of that wording earlier in this book). This salutation includes the third mention of Christ in the first two verses of 2 Timothy. Even in a Roman prison awaiting trial on a capital charge, Paul's allegiance is clear. Jesus, not Caesar, is his Lord.

### ENDNOTES

1. John R. W. Stott, *The Message of 2 Timothy* (Downers Grove, Ill.: InterVarsity Press, 1973), p. 24.

# FAITHFUL MINISTRY OF THE GOOD NEWS

## 2 Timothy 1:3–14

From his Roman dungeon, Paul reminisces (1:3–7). He thinks of Timothy and longs to see him again. He remembers Timothy's mother and grandmother, which, in turn, reminds him of his own forefathers. He recalls the ordination service where he laid hands on Timothy. The great apostle realizes that most of his life now lies behind him.

Yet the future concerns Paul even more than the past. Timothy must be encouraged to continue developing his gift for ministry and to raise his level of confidence with the help of the Spirit (1:6–7). The future of the gospel is on Paul's mind too. He has guarded it—preserved it, maintained its purity, passed it on (1:11–12)—and now, as Paul's end is near, he sees it as essential that Timothy guard the true faith in the same way (1:14).

It is hardly surprising that in a letter from an apostle at the close of his life to a young minister in his prime, the subject is faithful ministry.

## 1. A GIFT FOR EFFECTIVE SERVICE 1:3–7

There is a saying from the Old West to the effect that the prospect of hanging "greatly concentrates the mind." Paul realizes that he is certain to be executed: "the time has come for my departure" (2 Tim. 4:6b). The apostle was living under the shadow of the headsman's sword, and everything he wrote in his last letter to Timothy must be read in that context.

## PAUL'S MEMORIES

In light of Paul's circumstances, even the epistle's traditional thanksgiving carries new significance. **I thank God . . . as night and day I constantly remember you in my prayers**. With these words, Paul models his own exhortation to the Thessalonians, written early in his ministry (1 Thess. 5:17–18): "Pray continually" and "give thanks in all circumstances." Jesus did much the same on the night of His arrest, only hours before His crucifixion. After the Last Supper, He and His apostles sang a hymn (Matt. 26:30). We know from Jewish religious customs surrounding the Passover that the hymn was probably the second half of the Egyptian Hallel, the traditional praise hymn of the seder.[1] Despite His understandable concern over what lay ahead, Jesus did not alter the ritual. He went to Gethsemane with praise and thanksgiving on His lips to spend His few remaining hours in prayer (Matt. 26:36–46).

Paul wraps a testimony inside his thanksgiving. He serves God **with a clear conscience**, a spiritual characteristic that he considers one of the graces of the believer (1 Tim. 1:5). That "the worst of sinners" (v. 15) could have a clear conscience is a tribute to God's mercy, as Paul readily acknowledges (v. 16). That an accused prisoner could have one is a rebuke to the case against him in the Roman court.

It is interesting that Paul believed that his **forefathers** served God with clear consciences as well, that they were faithful under the old covenant as he was faithful under the new. Paul respected and appreciated those who preceded him, recognizing the continuity between Law and gospel. Paul's mind was turned to his own heritage because he was thinking of Timothy's (2 Tim. 1:5).

With his memory stirred by his circumstances, Paul recalls three things and reminds Timothy of a fourth within the space of four verses. (1) In v. 3, Paul remembers Timothy in prayer. (2) In v. 4, Paul recalls Timothy's **tears**, perhaps at their last parting. When Paul left Ephesus at the conclusion of his third missionary journey, "they all wept as they embraced him and kissed him" (Acts 20:37), but that was six to eight years earlier. Paul is probably writing of a more recent occasion, especially if he had been released from his first imprisonment and spent time with Timothy before being re-arrested. (3) In v. 5, Paul is **reminded of** Timothy's **sincere faith** in contrast to the hypocrisy of the false teachers in his church (4:2). Finally (4), in v. 6, Paul reminds Timothy of something he had previously been encouraged to do—**fan into flame the gift of God**, which was in him **through the laying on of [Paul's] hands**. No doubt the apostle's mind revisited Timothy's ordination service as he wrote those words. A chapter later, Paul directs Timothy to the greatest memory of all: "Remember Jesus Christ."

## TIMOTHY'S HERITAGE

The affection for Timothy that prompted these memories is apparent in the verses surrounding them. **I long to see you**, Paul writes. At the letter's close he adds, "Do your best to come to me quickly" (4:9), "before winter" (4:21). If Timothy can come, Paul will be **filled with joy**, a counterpoint to the tears of separation. Their relationship was mutually warm and loving, the relationship of a father and his spiritual son (1:2).

We know little of Timothy's biological father. He was a Greek and evidently was neither a Jewish proselyte nor a Christian. In the two passages that speak of Timothy's mother's faith (1:5; Acts 16:1), the silence about his father's religious experience is significant.

In his **grandmother Lois** and his **mother Eunice**, however, Timothy had a great heritage. They were both believers, perhaps converted under Paul's ministry in their hometown of Lystra in central Asia Minor on his first missionary journey (Acts 14). Upon his return to Lystra on his

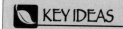

## KEY IDEAS

### SPIRITUAL HERITAGE

Not everyone can relate to the intergenerational discipleship that was so beneficial to Timothy, but those who can are eternally grateful for the legacy. "The lines are fallen unto me in pleasant places; yea, I have a goodly heritage" (Ps. 16:6, KJV). The task for the second-, third-, or fourth-generation Christian is to keep the legacy intact. The task for the first-generation Christian is to create a new legacy. All Christian families start with a first generation.

second journey two years later, Eunice and Timothy are specifically mentioned as disciples (Acts 16:1). Timothy's faith **first lived** in his mother and grandmother, a beautiful picture of intergenerational discipleship.

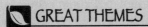

## GREAT THEMES

### THE HOLY SPIRIT

If the triad in 2 Tim.1:7—**spirit of power, of love and of self-discipline**—refers to the Holy Spirit, that is in keeping with the multiplicity of names associated with the Spirit in the New Testament. In addition to the standard and familiar designations Holy Spirit, Spirit of God, and Spirit of Christ (or Spirit of Jesus), the Spirit is also called the eternal Spirit (Heb. 9:14), the Spirit of truth (Jn. 14:17), the Spirit of glory (1 Pet. 4:14), the Spirit of wisdom (Eph. 1:17), the Spirit of life (Rom. 8:2), the Spirit of faith (2 Cor. 4:13), the Spirit of sonship or adoption (Rom. 8:15), the Spirit of holiness (Rom. 1:4), and the Spirit of grace (Heb. 10:29). Christ also offers the term *Paraclete* in John 14:16; it is variously translated Comforter, Counselor, Advocate, Helper, and Strengthener.

The triad in 2 Timothy 1 adds to that impressive and instructive list.

As a result of God's grace and their spiritual influence, Timothy became a faithful man of God. As a result of the grace of God and **the laying on of [Paul's] hands**, Timothy became a gifted minister of the gospel. (See the discussion of 1 Tim. 1:18 and 4:14.) Timothy was gifted in a literal sense. His ministerial leadership ability was given by God and affirmed by the church at what we would call his ordination. Paul's encouragement to **fan** that gift **into flame** does not imply that Timothy's fire had gone out or was about to do so. Even good fires need stoking, and spiritual gifts need development in order to increase their effectiveness.

God never calls without equipping, and Paul encourages Timothy to take care of his equipment.

## A SPIRIT OF POWER

**For God did not give us a spirit of timidity, but a spirit of power, of love and of self-discipline**. Because the Greek construction in both halves of this verse is identical and neither has a definite article, many understand Paul's reference to be to the human spirit. Others, however, see it as a reference to the Holy Spirit. Paul uses the past tense in combination with the plural pronoun **us**, suggesting that God's gift was given to His people on a definite occasion as distinct from His ongoing gifting of individuals. Jesus Himself predicted that such a gift would be given (Acts 1:4), and Peter reiterated the point in his famous sermon on the day of Pentecost (Acts 2:38). In any case, the most important of God's gifts is the Holy Spirit itself (Luke 11:13).

As the Spirit **of power**, the Holy Spirit, whose Pentecostal power launched the church in Acts 1:8, could certainly empower a hesitant Timothy. As the Spirit **of love**, He could bring the perfect love that drives out fear (1 John 4:18). As the Spirit **of self-discipline** (like love, a fruit of the Spirit, Gal. 5:22–23), He could provide the self-control Timothy would need in order to preach, teach, and act with boldness despite his tendency toward timidity.[2] The Spirit is all-sufficient.

Timothy seems to have had difficulty being assertive. Paul's first letter to the young minister is sprinkled with exhortations to confront the false teachers (1 Tim. 1:3, 4:11) and the wealthy within the congregation (6:17–18). Elsewhere, Paul asks the Corinthians to "see to it that [Timothy] has nothing to fear" while he is with them (1 Cor. 16:10). In a generous and tactful gesture, Paul refrains from saying that God's gifts are given directly to Timothy, thereby calling attention to his shortcomings. Instead, Paul says that God gives these gifts to us all. Paul's purpose is edification, not demolition. He's not out to tear Timothy down but to build him up. Paul has invested himself in Timothy, and now, on what might be his last occasion to mentor the young man, Paul urges Timothy to "stir up" his spiritual gifts (2 Tim. 1:6 KJV) and step out in the courage provided by God's greatest gift, the Holy Spirit (1:7).

## 2. A GOSPEL TO BE PREACHED 1:8–14

Timidity was hardly a problem for Paul. He was not ashamed of the gospel (1:12; see also Rom. 1:6), and he urged Timothy **not** to **be ashamed**, either of **our Lord or** of Paul, **his prisoner**. To be ashamed of the Lord is both foolish and potentially fatal spiritually (Mark 8:38). To be ashamed of Paul would be tantamount to being ashamed of the Lord, whose prisoner he was (2 Tim. 1:8). No matter how the court documents stated the matter, Paul was not really Caesar's prisoner. It was for Christ and the Kingdom that Paul was in chains, and Paul considered that status a high honor.

## A PRISONER OF CHRIST

Not everyone saw it the same way, of course. Paul was in prison and likely to be executed soon. No longer was he under house arrest, as he had been during his first imprisonment. Then he enjoyed plenty of visitors and few restrictions on his preaching and teaching (Acts 28:30–31). During this second imprisonment, Paul was in a Roman dungeon—dark, damp, cold, and sickeningly unsanitary, having none of the creature comforts that had made his previous two-year stay under Roman guard so tolerable. By this time, Paul was considered a dangerous man to know. Merely having one's name linked to his would have frightened some Christians into disavowing him. After all, some may have reasoned, Paul himself valued "a good reputation with outsiders" (1 Tim. 3:7). He didn't want the church to be disgraced or to "give the enemy . . . opportunity for slander" (1 Tim. 5:14; compare 1 Tim. 6:1). Paul's own words might have been unfairly used against him by some in order to rationalize keeping their distance from him. By the time he wrote to Timothy this second time, some of Paul's supporters had already deserted him (2 Tim. 1:15).

Onesiphorus, though, was not ashamed of Paul's chains (1:16), and Paul was intent on ensuring Timothy's continued support as well. Society could be expected to condemn a man in Paul's position. It was rejection by the church that cut far deeper; and if there should be any sign of rejection from Timothy, that would be, to borrow from Shakespeare, "the most unkindest cut of all."

Paul, in fact, goes so far as to offer Timothy this invitation: **join with me in suffering for the gospel**. Paul develops that prospect more fully in chapter 2. There would be no need for Timothy to muster the courage to embrace persecution from within himself; that courage comes **by the power of God** and is the result of God's gift: the Spirit of Power (1:7).

## HOLY LIVING AND HOLY DYING

Leaders aren't the only ones who may be called upon to suffer for Christ. Paul doesn't appeal to Timothy's call to the ministry as the grounds for his exposure to suffering; although, without question, ministers were prime targets (see 1:11–12a). Instead, Paul links his appeal to God's saving and sanctifying call. Not all followers of Christ were leaders, but all knew what it meant to be **saved** and **called to a holy life,** and any of them might be called upon to suffer.

The call to ministry is only one of God's calls. Most of them are common to all Christians. For example, He calls us to freedom (Gal. 5:13) and to fellowship with Christ (1 Cor. 1:9), and He calls us to holy living (see 1 Thess. 4:7; 1 Cor. 1:2). In the seventeenth century, an Anglican priest named Jeremy Taylor published a book that would later have a profound impact on a young man named John Wesley; the title was *The Rule and Exercises of Holy Living and Holy Dying.* Both holy living and holy dying are the privilege of a believer, and Paul wants to impress on Timothy the reality that under Roman persecution, the one may very well lead to the other. It had for Paul, and his mind was fixed on the One **who has destroyed death and has brought life and immortality to light through the gospel.**

Paul the soon-to-be-martyr was still Paul the theologian,

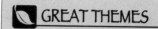

## GREAT THEMES

### GOD'S LOVE

Genesis 1 rivals 1 Corinthians 13 as the love chapter of the Bible. According to Paul, it was **before the beginning of time** that Christ provided for our salvation (2 Tim. 1:9). That means that before the Fall, even before creation, God knew—

- That the people He created in His own image would sin;
- That atonement would need to be made; and
- That only His Son would qualify as the necessary sinless sacrifice.

The marvel of it all is that in spite of the cost, He created us anyway. Genesis 1 is a love story.

and he didn't miss an opportunity to remind Timothy, and all who would read the letter, that our salvation is **not because of anything that we have done but because of his own purpose and grace** (as in Eph. 2:8–9).

## THE TIME OF OUR ATONEMENT

Saving grace was **given to us in Christ Jesus before the beginning of time.** Jesus died on Calvary at Passover in about A.D. 30. In the framework of human history, that's the date when redemption became a reality. Christ's death on Good Friday and His resurrection on the following third day are the hinges upon which salvation's door swings. But in a deeper sense, our atonement is dated from **before the beginning of time**, when in the timelessness of eternity, the Lamb slain "from the creation of the world" (Rev. 13:8) agreed to be our sacrifice. That event remained to be acted out on the stage of history—as Paul indicates with the words **it has now been revealed through the appearing of our Savior, Christ Jesus**—but in the mind of God, the atonement was accomplished before the beginning (see also Eph. 1:4 and 1 Pet. 1:20). **This grace was given us** at that time, not that we were chosen for salvation apart from our own freedom to accept it, but that God's plan to save the lost was made before the world was created.

If Christ **has destroyed death**, then why do people still die? It is true that death is a defeated enemy (1 Cor. 15:26)—the Resurrection of Christ was its deathblow—but its final end awaits the Judgment and the ultimate consummation of all things (Rev. 1:18, 20:14, 21:4). As John Donne puts it, "Death, thou shalt die"![3]

Echoing his self-description in 1 Tim. 2:7, Paul repeats his triple appointment as **a herald and an apostle and a teacher**. His wonder at the grace that makes that possible comes through in an emphatic Greek construction that J. N. D. Kelly translates, "I, even I. . . ."[4]

## WHAT OTHERS SAY

What is that bottom line doing there (1:12a)? It doesn't go with the rest of the paragraph.

Our bottom line would be: and therefore I proclaim as I do and succeed as I do and get all my prayers answered and once I missed a plane but God was in it because it crashed and I was spared . . . Thank God I was spared from suffering.

No. It doesn't end that way.

—Reuben Welch

Paul's spiritual journey—saved by grace, called to a holy life, appointed a herald, teacher, and even apostle—arrives at a jarring conclusion: **That is why I am suffering as I am**. Preachers of a prosperity gospel and proponents of a health-and-wealth theology stay far away from that text.

**Yet I am not ashamed**, Paul maintains, and that's a good reason for Timothy not to be ashamed of Paul (v. 8).

### KNOWING HIM

In one of his grandest declarations of faith, Paul expresses absolute confidence in the God who is absolutely able. **I know whom I have believed,** he begins. Knowing what we believe is vitally important, and knowing why we believe takes that faith a crucial step further. But there is a prior and greater need. We must know *whom* we believe. Christianity is not merely an abstract philosophy or enlightened moral code. At the heart of the faith is a relationship, and it's a relationship with Someone who is able. (Note the references to His power in 1:7–8.) In particular, Paul is confident that He is able **to guard what I have entrusted to him for that day,** the day when He will set all things right.

In 1 Tim. 6:20 and again in 2 Tim. 1:14, it is Timothy who is challenged to **guard the good deposit,** the gospel, that was entrusted to him by God. Significantly, it is God who helps us guard His own deposit by the indwelling power of His Holy Spirit. But there is another deposit, one that we leave with God: our hope, our faith, our life, our eternal destiny. This deposit is in God's hands. **I am convinced** that all is safe with Him, Paul affirms. Our stewardship of His resources is sometimes flawed, but His stewardship of our souls has never failed.[5]

All of what Paul has said is **sound teaching.** In contrast to the false teaching of some in his congregation, Timothy can rely on the truthfulness, doctrinal purity, and trustworthiness of the advice he has received from Paul. In his own teaching and preaching ministry, Timothy can make this his **pattern.**

Yet there will be a price to pay.

### ENDNOTES

1. The Egyptian Hallel (from the Hebrew word for *praise*) is Psalms 113–118, which celebrate the deliverance of Israel from bondage in Egypt. Customarily, Psalms 113–114 were sung before the meal and Psalms 115–118 after it.

2. *Self-discipline* is one of Paul's favorite terms in the Pastoral Epistles. Some form of the Greek root from which this term is derived appears ten times.

3. John Donne, "Death, Be Not Proud."

4. J. N. D. Kelly, *The Pastoral Epistles* (Peabody, Mass.: Hendrickson Publishers, 1960), p. 164.

5. Verse 12 literally reads, "He is able to guard my deposit." Does that mean Christ is able to guard the deposit He left with Timothy, as in 1 Tim. 6:20 and 2 Tim. 1:14? In that case, it could be called "my deposit" because Timothy holds if for Christ. Or is it a deposit Timothy has left with Christ (Timothy's life and faith) just as Christ has left one with Timothy (the gospel message)? Admittedly, the verse allows for ambiguity, but the most obvious interpretation is the concept of mutual deposits—ours in His keeping, His in ours.

# 3

# THE COST OF FAITHFUL MINISTRY

## 2 Timothy 1:15–2:13

On the subject of faithfulness, the opening theme of this letter, Paul has good news and bad news. The bad news is that some associates have proven unfaithful, and he feels their loss keenly. The good news is that he can point to one friend who was there for him, providing an example of faithfulness that he hopes will inspire Timothy. Like His Lord, Paul will not pretend that the Christian way is a walk in the park. It is a hard road at times, but it does lead home.

## 1. TRUE AND FALSE FRIENDS 1:15–18

Approximately one hundred individuals are identified in the book of Acts and in the Pauline epistles as associates of Paul. The current passage provides the only mention of **Phylegus** and **Hermogenes**; **Onesiphorus** appears again at the end of this letter (4:19). These men are all but unknown to us, yet to Paul they were very important—Phylegus and Hermogenes for their defection, Onesiphorus for his loyalty and faithful service.

### SPIRITUAL DEFECTION

Paul uses hyperbole when he writes that **everyone in the province of Asia has deserted me**. Onesiphorus had not; neither had Timothy, or, it may be presumed, a great many others. But some had, including more

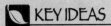

## KEY IDEAS

HUMILITY

Among the monuments in Washington, D. C., is a largely overlooked memorial to merchant marine sailors who fell in World War I. The inscription is gripping; it notes that the memorial is dedicated to those who were "Great without Glory."

That describes Onesiphorus perfectly, along with a multitude of other faithful Christians across the centuries who are better known in heaven than on earth. Few of us are counted among the movers and shakers of our society. (More often we're the moved and the shaken!) But in 1 Cor. 1:26, Paul writes of ordinary people who become world changers because of their extraordinary God.

than the two mentioned here. Ephesus was the capital of the Roman province of Asia (the western portion of Asia Minor), and Timothy would have known the details of the desertions and the people involved.

Some scholars deny that Phylegus and Hermogenes apostasized, arguing that they forsook only Paul and not the faith. The language closely resembles Paul's description of Demas in 4:9–10, however, and it seems clear that spiritual failure of some kind was involved. Again, how does one reject Paul the prisoner without rejecting Christ, whose prisoner he was (1:8)?

## A LOYAL ALLY

Onesiphorus was faithful to both Paul and Christ. In both Ephesus and Rome, **he helped** (1:18) and **often refreshed** Paul; and during the imprisonment, Onesiphorus was **not ashamed of [Paul's] chains.** In fact, when Paul proved hard to locate in Rome, Onesiphorus **searched hard** until he found him. The reference clearly indicates a change in Paul's status from his house arrest of Acts 28, where he would have been very easy to find, with visitors coming and going on a regular basis. The change in circumstances could have resulted simply from a change in the status of his case in court, but considering the clues that point to a release from Paul's first imprisonment, a later re-arrest and imprisonment under harsher conditions seem more likely.

One good find deserves another, Paul believes. Onesiphorus looked **until he found me,** Paul writes, so **may the Lord grant that he will find mercy from the Lord on that day**—the day of the Judgment.

The references to **the household of Onesiphorus** (1:16, 4:19) suggest that he might have been deceased at the time of Paul's writing. Taking that to be the case, Roman Catholic theologians have cited Onesiphorus as a New Testament example of the acceptability of prayers for the dead, based on 1:18a. (The classic text for the Catholic practice of prayers for the dead is found in 2 Maccabees, an apocryphal book not considered a part of the biblical canon by Protestants.) It is not certain that Onesiphorus was dead, however. He evidently wasn't in Rome, but he could have been elsewhere. Paul may have highlighted Onesiphorus's household not because they were his survivors but because they were in Ephesus with Timothy. Even if Onesiphorus was deceased, the supposed prayer is little more than a general expression of Paul's desire that his friend find favor from God and certainly is not grounds for a doctrine of prayer for the dead.

## 2. THREE EXAMPLES OF ENDURANCE 2:1–7

Paul has a word for Timothy: **You then, my son, be strong in the grace that is in Christ Jesus**. Paul urges Timothy to avoid the mistakes of those who failed under pressure and to imitate the loyalty and faithful service of Onesiphorus. Showing strength wasn't one of Timothy's strengths, but that's where **grace** comes in. Paul may have been thinking of what the Lord had said to him: "My grace is sufficient for you, for my power is made perfect in weakness," to which Paul added, "For when I am weak, then I am strong" (2 Cor. 2:9–10). Timothy would need strength for the perilous times ahead, and God has strength to spare for all who seek it.

### THE TRANSFER OF TRUTH

Paul knew that Timothy would especially need to be strong in the transmission of the gospel. The transfer of the faith through four generations is compactly packaged in just one verse. The chain begins with Paul (**the things you have heard me say**), who passed the legacy on to Timothy, and it continues with those whom Timothy would teach (**entrust to reliable men**), finally reaching a fourth generation through them (**who will also be qualified to teach others**). In fact, the chain did not end there; it remains unbroken to this day. Each of us learned the gospel from someone who had heard it from someone else. The chain might be traced all the way back to the apostles. This is not *apostolic succession*, the theory that ecclesiastical authority is handed from one bishop to the next in an unbroken chain of ordinations and consecrations leading back to the apostles. Rather it is a chain of evangelical truth based on the apostles' teaching, which is established in the New Testament.

It has been said that the church is always one generation from extinction. Logically, that is true, but God has promised that it will not happen (Matt. 16:18). He has not promised that every congregation will survive, or even every denomination. We must take care with our faith transfers, entrusting to others that which God, through others, has entrusted to us (1:14).

Paul mentions **many witnesses** to the transfer of truth. Unlike Gnosticism, whose adherents believed in a secret tradition transferred only to an elite few in strict privacy, the gospel is open to all.

## LIKE A SOLDIER

Timothy had to have known that it wouldn't be easy to maintain the true faith. "No cross, no crown," William Penn wrote three centuries ago, but long before that, Paul spelled out the cost of leadership just as Christ had spelled out the cost of discipleship. **Endure hardship with us, like a good soldier of Christ Jesus**, Paul wrote. Military analogies are common in Paul's letters, from the whole armor of God (Eph. 6:10–18) to the good fight of faith (1 Tim. 1:18). Here, he compares spiritual struggle to warfare, which includes all the deprivation and suffering associated with soldiering.

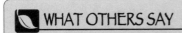

**WHAT OTHERS SAY**

One cannot enlist with a contractual stipulation that there be no conflict.
—Thomas Oden

Paul then expands the simile in the first of three examples that shed light on the rigors of Christian leadership.[1] Just as Jesus used many parables that make the same point (for example, the parables of the tares and the net; the hidden treasure and the pearl; the lost sheep, the lost coin, and the lost son), Paul uses several images that are likely to connect with his reader.

Being a Christian in general, and being a Christian leader in particular, is like being a soldier. **No one serving as a soldier gets involved in civilian affairs—he wants to please his commanding officer.** Paul's words are a lesson on the need for single-minded dedication to the assignment. Like a soldier, a Christian leader must resist the distractions that would make peripherals seem like priorities. The cost of leadership is full devotion to duty and full attention to the task at hand. This holy detachment does not make the Christian culturally, politically, or economically irrelevant. The idea is not to look away from the issues of the day but to look beyond them to Christ, who is eternally relevant.

## LIKE AN ATHLETE

Being a Christian in general, and being a Christian leader in particular, is also like being an athlete. **If anyone competes as an athlete, he does not receive the victor's crown unless he competes according to the rules.** More than fair play is involved here. In public contests, the rules of the day often required a certain level of preparation on the part of competitors. In the original Olympic games, for example, competitors had to swear that they had trained rigorously for a designated number of months.[2] Training, self-discipline, and preparation are required for the athletic arena; they are required also for the arena of faith.

## LIKE A FARMER

Being a Christian in general, and being a Christian leader in particular, is like being a farmer, **a hardworking farmer** who prepares fields, plants crops, gives them time and attention during the growing season, and harvests them at the right moment. Without hard work and perseverance, there is no harvest.

There's a price to pay for leadership in the church, but there are rewards also. "Beyond warfare is a victory, beyond athletic effort a prize, and beyond agricultural labor a crop," C. K. Barrett observes.[3]

In 2 Tim. 2:7, Paul, in effect, gives the formula for Bible study: **the Lord will give you insight into all this** provided that you, for your part,

**reflect on what I am saying**. This is not a promise of new revelation but the assurance that illumination and understanding of what has already been revealed will be given. In the study of the Word, by His design, our role and God's are interdependent.

# 3. A ROYAL REWARD 2:8–13

In the face of persecution, Paul urges Timothy to **remember Jesus Christ**. He is the heart of the faith. The short and simple phrases describing Christ here are doors that open to reveal profound truth.

When Paul writes that Christ is **descended from David**, he affirms Christ's humanity, asserts His incarnation, acknowledges His kingship, and attests to His mission as Messiah. When Paul reminds us that Christ has been **raised from the dead**, he both announces Christ's deity and alludes to the atoning death from which He was raised.

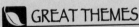

## GREAT THEMES
### THE TRAJECTORY OF GRACE

When Christ chose to leave heaven in order to come to earth, become a man, and be rejected, crucified, and buried, He followed the self-sacrificial path that we know as His Humiliation. That humiliation was immediately followed by Christ's resurrection and ascension to heaven—His Exaltation. If we were to diagram this salvation sequence, first downward and then upward, it might resemble the letter V, which is appropriate because we have spiritual "Victory in Jesus." That V-shaped pathway is the trajectory of grace.

**This is my gospel**, Paul proclaims, Jesus Christ, God in the flesh, who died for our sins and rose as the guarantor of our eternal life. Theologians call those events the Humiliation and Exaltation of Christ. This gospel is not a worldview, lifestyle, or system of belief, as important as each of those may be, but a Person—Jesus Christ, Savior and Lord.[4]

## SUFFERING FOR CHRIST AND HIS PEOPLE

The fact that Christ is central to the faith is reason enough for Timothy to remember Him, but there is another reason. Steeling his young charge against the suffering that is sure to come, Paul points out something

Timothy knows well but may not have related to his own situation: Jesus suffered. What is implicit in the shorthand creed of 2 Tim. 2:8 would later be made explicit in the Apostles' Creed: between His birth and resurrection, Jesus suffered, died, and was buried. Perhaps Timothy, in remembering Christ, would remember the Beatitude on persecution: "Blessed are you when people insult you, persecute you, and falsely say all kinds of evil against you

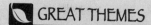

### GREAT THEMES

#### THE CENTRALITY OF JESUS

When the famous evangelist Sadhu Sundar Singh was first converted to Christianity, he faced a barrage of questions. Why did he leave the Sikh religion of his ancestors? He replied simply, "Jesus Christ." What did Christianity offer that Sikhism could not? Again, his answer was simple: "Jesus Christ." What Christian teaching did he find so compelling? "Jesus Christ." And what reward in Christianity could ever repay the loss of his family, his friends, and his future in Indian society? His answer again was "Jesus Christ."

because of me" (Matt. 5:10–11). More to the point, Timothy might remember that every detail of that teaching was fulfilled first in Christ Himself, who was insulted (John 8:48; Matt. 27:27–31), persecuted (Mark 15:22–26), and lied about (Matt. 26:59–60) to a greater degree than any of His followers.

Paul's suffering, too, is revealed in 2 Tim. 2:9. Paul often mentions his chains (for example, Eph. 6:20; Phil. 1:13–14; Col. 4:3, 18), but the expression used here contains an added element. Now Paul is **chained like a criminal**. The only other place in the New Testament in which this term appears is in reference to those crucified with Jesus.[5] But if Paul can **endure everything** by God's grace, so can Timothy. God's people, **the elect**, are looking to them for leadership in the arena of suffering.

What kind of world puts a monster like Nero on a throne and treats Paul like a criminal? A fallen world. But, as someone has said, the day would come when people would name their sons Paul and their dogs Nero.

Although Paul was in bondage, **God's word is not chained**. Over the centuries the Bible has been the target of more attacks than anyone can number, yet it still stands. It is an anvil that has worn out many a hammer. With God's Word at work in the world, God's goals will be achieved— even if God's workers sometimes languish in prison.

## REIGNING WITH CHRIST AND HIS PEOPLE

Bleak as the future seemed, Paul knew that suffering was not the end of the story. It never is. Beyond adversity lies eternity, and eternity in His Presence will make the worst suffering here seem inconsequential. C. S. Lewis closes his Chronicles of Narnia series with just that thought. "[the end] was only the beginning of the true story," he wrote. "All their life . . . had been only the cover and the title page: now at last they were beginning Chapter One of the Great Story, which no one on earth has read: which goes on forever: in which every chapter is better than the one before."[6]

Just as a modern writer might anchor this point by quoting from a hymn like *A Mighty Fortress is Our God*—

> Let goods and kindred go, this mortal life also;
> The body they may kill. God's truth abideth still.
> His kingdom is forever.

or *The Church's One Foundation*—

> 'Mid toil and tribulation and tumult of her war,
> She waits the consummation of peace forevermore,
> Till with the vision glorious her longing eyes are blest,
> And the great Church victorious shall be the Church at rest

so Paul appears to quote from a first-century hymn to make his point. The writer of this hymn fragment pairs the two positive statements at its beginning with two negative ones at its end, and the effect is powerful.

**If we died with him** is taken by some to be an allusion to martyrdom. William Barclay even entitles this section "The Song of the Martyr." That certainly fits the context—both the preceding paragraph and the reference to endurance in the verse that follows. But why wouldn't the verb be present tense, as it is in 2 Tim. 2:12a? The use of the past tense (died) suggests a previous death, such as the believer's death to sin and self. (Note the similarity of the wording to Rom. 6:8.) By that death, **we will also live with him.**

The second positive statement is undoubtedly the one that brought this hymn to Paul's mind: **If we endure, we will also reign with him.** That prospect must have sustained Paul in prison, and it could sustain Timothy in all that he was to face. When God sets all things right, either for the individual believer at his death or for all believers at Christ's return, those who belong to God will enjoy all that He is. Heaven with Him, not earth without pain, is our goal.

*If* is a conditional word, and the one who wants to realize the benefits it implies will have to meet the requirements it carries. Like the open heart in Rev. 3:20, the repentant heart in 2 Chron. 7:14, and the abiding heart in John 15:5–7— each one conditional, governed by the small but powerful *if*— the condition attached to the enduring heart in this hymn implies that some will not endure. That conclusion is

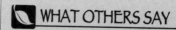

**WHAT OTHERS SAY**

Heaven offers nothing that a mercenary soul can desire. It is safe to tell the pure in heart that they shall see God, for only the pure in heart want to. There are rewards that do not sully motives.

—C. S. Lewis

reinforced by the negative line which follows. Some **disown him**. As a result, they will be disowned. Christ says exactly that in Matt. 10:32–33, even using the same word. Not every believer endures; cases in point include Phylegus and Hermogenes in chapter 1 and Demas in chapter 4. "It is the one who has endured to the end who will be saved" (Matt. 10:22, NASB)—and will reign.

The final lyric of the hymn breaks its poetic pattern but fits the character of Christ perfectly. He may be betrayed, but He will never betray. Christ, who is Truth (John 14:6), cannot be untrue to Himself or anyone else. This **trustworthy saying**, one of five in the Pastoral Epistles, declares that Christ is absolutely trustworthy. This is not an offer of what Dietrich Bonhoeffer dismissed as "cheap grace." A hymn warning that Christ will, in turn, disown those who disown Him does not suggest that Christ's faithfulness allows us to be faithless with impunity. He will judge, but even in judgment, He is faithful to His nature and His covenant. The saving relationship may be broken, but it will not be broken by Him.

Biographical information about Timothy is limited, so we don't know what persecution he may have experienced. Hebrews 13:23—"Timothy has been released"—indicates that he suffered imprisonment, but exactly when or where is unknown. One thing is certain: he would have taken to heart

Paul's exhortation to endurance. That need for endurance was a present reality, not a hypothetical possibility, for anyone in the early church.

## ENDNOTES

1. J. N. D. Kelly, *The Pastoral Epistles* (Peabody, Mass.: Hendrickson Publishers, 1960), p. 174.

2. Ibid., pp. 175–176. Some sources say the required training period was six months while others say ten. All agree that it was extensive.

3. C. K. Barrett, *The Pastoral Epistles in the New English Bible* (Oxford: Clarendon Press, 1963), p. 102.

4. Reuben Welch, *To Timothy and All Other Disciples* (Kansas City, Mo.: Beacon Hill Press, 1979), pp. 45–46.

5. Kelly, *Pastoral Epistles*, p. 177.

6. C. S. Lewis, *The Last Battle* (New York: Macmillan Publishing Company, 1956), p. 184.

# 4

# THE OPPONENTS OF A FAITHFUL MINISTRY

## 2 Timothy 2:14–3:9

Second Timothy is not Paul's most carefully crafted epistle, nor should we expect it to be. His time was growing short, and the issues before him were momentous. The intensity level of this letter is understandably high, and careful organization of thought was not Paul's priority. Still, themes emerge, and Paul's major concern in this section of the letter is the contagion spread by the false teachers in Ephesus. Paul sketches a profile of these opponents of truth and at the same time creates what John Stott calls a "composite portrait" of a Christian leader by adding three more illustrations to the similes of soldier, athlete, and farmer mentioned earlier.[1] The contrast between false and true Christian leaders is unmistakable, making the counterfeit easy to detect.

## 1. GOD'S UNWAVERING CHURCH 2:14–19

Timothy's adversaries in Ephesus were given to **quarreling about words,** as Paul had noted in his previous letter (1 Tim. 6:4–5; compare 1 Tim. 1:6). They were adept at creating controversies in the church and confusing gullible followers. Paul called it **godless chatter,** and said that **those who indulge in it will become more and more ungodly.** The words *more and more* show progression, but of the wrong kind; instead of growing in grace, these false teachers would grow in disgrace. Like some modern cults, the Ephesian heresy dealt in fiction and fable, not in fact. God's representatives dare not deal in worthless words; they must be those who **correctly** handle **the word of truth**. The contrast is striking. When Scripture is faithfully taught and preached, error suffers by comparison.

## LIKE A WORKMAN

Paul's next metoaphor for Timothy compares him to a skilled **workman**, whose craftsmanship is a credit to his profession. That would not be an easy description to live up to. The encouragement to **do your best** indicates that excellence in biblical teaching and preaching doesn't happen automatically, even for those who approach it with a heart for God. "Work hard," the New Living Translation reads; the New American Standard Bible says, "Be diligent." Those wordings sound odd to those familiar with the King James Version's "study to show thyself approved unto God." That translation seems

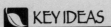

**KEY IDEAS**

THE AUTHORITY OF SCRIPTURE

Memo to the modern age: a loose-leaf Bible won't do. Adding to and taking away from God's Word are both out of the question. We do not have the freedom to toss away a commandment because it makes us feel guilty or to remove the account of a miracle because science can't explain it. "If you believe what you like in the gospel and reject what you like," St. Augustine wrote sixteen hundred years ago, "it is not the gospel you believe, but yourselves."

to imply that good leadership is all about hitting the books, or at least *the Book*. But when the King James Version was translated, the word *study* meant exactly what today's newer versions are saying. Study (as we understand the term) is an important part of doing our best, but Paul had something more in mind. Second Timothy 2:15 is not so much "the student's verse" as it is "the craftsman's verse."

The Greek words translated **correctly handles** mean, literally, "cuts a straight line." John Stott likens it to cutting a road across the countryside; C. K. Barrett sees it as cutting a stone to fit into place in a building. To St. Chrysostom, it was plowing a straight furrow.[2] All are helpful pictures, and each one makes Paul's point. Since the workman is **approved** by God, he **does not need to be ashamed.** The bottom line is that God expects, and is prepared to bless, our best. Our less-than-best effort is another matter. Elton Trueblood's warning should hang on the wall of every pastor's study and in every Christian teacher's office: "Holy shoddy is still shoddy."

The unorthodox teaching of men like **Hymenaeus and Philetus** was far worse than shoddy. The problem was not that they were simply unskilled in their handling of the truth; it was much more serious than that. They **[had] wandered away from the truth**. The road they cut through the countryside wasn't off by a degree or two; it swerved radically and recklessly into wastelands unfit for travel. Borrowing medical imagery, Paul fears their false doctrines **will spread like gangrene**. It's a particularly apt, if unpleasant, comparison. Gangrene rots the body, bringing decay to organs and tissues; if it enters the bloodstream, it can prove fatal. What a graphic picture of the damage that false teaching can do to the Body of Christ, the church! Paul notes that these men have **[destroyed] the faith of some**. As with gangrene, radical measures are called for. Hymenaeus had already been amputated; Paul mentions his expulsion from membership in 1 Tim. 1:20. Apparently, however, he continued to do damage, even outside the church. Philetus is mentioned only here, but given the serious charges against him, it's reasonable to assume that he faced similar discipline.

Paul singles out one aspect of the heresy: the false teachers claim **that the resurrection has already taken place**. If Timothy was dealing with an early form of Gnosticism in Ephesus (as seems most likely), then the false teachers would have downplayed the physical or material aspects of life in favor of a skewed emphasis on the human spirit. Since Gnosticism saw the physical body as sinful, a doctrine of physical resurrection made no sense in their system of thought. That devaluation of the physical creation caused them to reject Christ's resurrection too. In fact, they rejected even His incarnation because it meant that God had come "in the flesh." It is probable that Hymenaeus and Philetus were twisting Paul's doctrine of baptism as dying and rising with Christ (Rom. 6:3–4) in order to deny the physical resurrection in the last days. Your baptism was your resurrection, their followers would have been told; don't expect another.

## AN UNASSAILABLE BUILDING

**Nevertheless**, Paul continues, signaling a contrast to the damage done by insidious doctrines, **God's solid foundation stands firm**. In 1 Tim. 3:15, Paul calls the church "the pillar and foundation of the truth." Here it is **God's solid foundation**. In both cases he wants us to picture an entire building, not just its supporting structure. Paul uses a figure of speech called *synecdoche*, in which a part stands for the whole. The foundation is highlighted to represent the building's strength.[3]

How strong is God's foundation? It is strong enough to withstand the assault of error and evil. When Paul earlier wrote to these same Ephesian Christians, he compared false doctrines to waves that toss immature believers to and fro, and winds that blow them here and there (Eph. 4:14). Think of television footage of storm victims struggling to keep their feet against hurricane winds and pounding surf. That's how vulnerable an unstable Christian is to false teaching. But a massive building with a bedrock foundation and reinforced girders can take the brunt of a storm without effect. Waves may break on the church, but they will not break the church.

A closer look at this building reveals two inscriptions in the stone, both based on Scripture and both related to Paul's point. The first is from the story of Korah, who led a rebellion against Moses' leadership and threatened the unity of God's people: **The Lord knows those who are his.** (Compare Num. 16:5.) The second inscription seems to be gathered from several Old Testament passages: **Everyone who confesses the name of the Lord must turn away from wickedness.**[4] Not everyone within the community of faith is a man or woman of faith, sad to say; Korah and his supporters certainly weren't. God saw their sin, and in judgment He caused the earth to open up and swallow them (Num. 16:23–33).

Like Korah and company, the false teachers in Ephesus were not really people of faith. To paraphrase John 17, they were in the church but not of it. And like Korah, they were dividing God's people. They would finally be brought under God's judgment, just as Korah was.

For Timothy, the pastor of a troubled church facing Roman persecution from the outside and heresy from within, this vision of God's unassailable building with its reassuring inscriptions emblazoned on resplendent walls must have been most welcome.

## 2. THE UNHOLY OPPOSITION 2:20–26

To provide the setting for yet another comparison, Paul takes the solid foundation image a step further. Imagine that God's magnificent building is **a large house**. Naturally, that house would include **articles not only of gold and silver, but also of wood and clay; some are for noble purposes and some for ignoble.** In these household articles Paul sees another metaphor for Christian leadership, but modern interpreters don't agree on exactly what he saw.

### LIKE A NOBLE VESSEL

Does Paul mean that fine vessels (an exquisite vase, an expensive candlestick) and common ones (pots and pans, for instance) both have their place, as long as they honorably fulfill their function? If so, the lesson would be that God's true people are vessels of all kinds, but each one is honorable; the false teachers, however, are dishonorable.

The other possibility is that Paul identifies grand vessels as ones for **noble** purposes and common vessels as **ignoble.** If that is his point, then the difference between true and false leaders in Ephesus is the difference between a silver goblet and a garbage pail, in the words of Gary Demarest.[5]

> ### WHAT OTHERS SAY
>
> Lord Jesus, if Thou wilt receive me into Thy house, if Thou wilt but own me as Thy servant, I will not stand upon terms . . . Make me what Thou wilt, Lord, and set me where Thou wilt. Let me be a vessel of silver or gold, or a vessel of wood or stone; so I be a vessel of honor, I am content . . . Lord, put me to what Thou wilt; rank me with whom Thou wilt. Put me to doing; put me to suffering. Let me be employed for Thee, or laid aside for Thee, exalted for Thee, or trodden underfoot for Thee. Let me be full; let me be empty. Let me have all things; let me have nothing. I freely and heartily resign all to Thy pleasure and disposal.
>
> —John Wesley's Covenant Service

Walter Liefeld goes further; he thinks Paul associates the heretics with a chamber pot or a bed pan—a first-century toilet![6] Paul has just characterized the influence of these men as gangrenous, so he's not afraid to be plainspoken. Paul doesn't mince words, or word pictures.

Was there spiritual corruption in the Ephesian congregation? Yes, for even a great house produces its share of garbage. But to focus on the waste is to miss the splendor and grandeur of the mansion. In addition, there's something unusual about this house. The owner wants only noble vessels, clean and beautiful. The good news for ordinary people is that even vessels that don't meet this standard can be cleansed.

The analogy is not perfect, for even the lowest furnishings are necessary for the functioning of a real household. They don't need to change into something they are not, and how could they if they wanted to? But Paul is not talking about everyday life here. In God's great house, to be spiritually clean and noble is the norm. The word for it in 2 Tim. 2:21 is **holy**.

Chrysostom, the prince of preachers in the early church, used Paul as an illustration of Paul's own point. "Paul was an earthen vessel," Chrysostom said, "and became a golden one. Judas was a golden vessel and became an earthen one."[7] Nothing would have pleased Paul more than to hear that the false teachers had followed his example and had become golden vessels too.

If Timothy were to remain the right kind of vessel in God's great house, he would have to

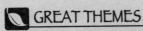

## GREAT THEMES

HOLINESS

The Wesleyan theological tradition asserts that Christian holiness embraces not only *power* for effective service but also *purity* of heart and life. Power is the Spirit at work through us; purity is the work of the Spirit in us. Paul told the Thessalonians, "It is God's will that you should be sanctified. . . . For God did not call us to be impure, but to live a holy life" (1 Thess. 4:3a, 7). Holiness and purity are interrelated, and when His Holy Spirit purifies our hearts by faith (Acts 15:8–9), His holiness is imparted to us. Sin-bent lives aren't simply counted pure and left in their pollution; they are made pure and cleansed. Charles Wesley captures that concept in his magnificent hymn "Love Divine, All Loves Excelling":

Finish then Thy new creation;
Pure and spotless let us be.

**flee the evil desires of youth and pursue righteousness, faith, love, and peace.** By running away from some things and toward others, he could be among those with a **pure heart**. Purity is everything the vessels of vv. 20–21 should be—cleansed, holy, and noble. **The evil desires of youth** are sensual sins. Like Joseph in Potiphar's house, the best recourse when facing those temptations is flight (Gen. 39:11–12; compare 1 Tim. 6:11).

Paul's other warnings concern temptations to sins of the spirit. The pure heart is not argumentative because **foolish and stupid arguments . . . produce quarrels.** It follows,

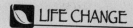

## LIFE CHANGE

### PERFECT LOVE

John Fletcher was an acclaimed theologian who defended Wesley's doctrine of free will from its critics within Christianity. In the process, he himself became the target of attacks that were sometimes bitter and angry.

On one occasion a clergyman who opposed Fletcher traveled to his home at Madeley, determined to do theological battle. But that opponent was totally disarmed by the warmth of Fletcher's greeting, and the men spent the afternoon worshiping God rather than warring with each other. Fletcher's new friend compared the visit to heaven.

The theological disagreement was real, and it remained when the afternoon was over. But greater than the controversy was the Spirit of Christ in the life of John Fletcher.

then, that Timothy **must not quarrel**, nor should he be **resentful**. Instead, he **must be kind to everyone**. To say that Timothy must be **able to teach** does not impose a proficiency requirement but a purity test. This statement doesn't appear in a list of gifts but in a list of graces. Notice the context; it is positioned between being kind and not being resentful. The next sentence shows Paul's meaning clearly: Timothy **must gently instruct** even **those who oppose him**, and that will take grace.

A person with that kind of character can be used by God to bring sinners **to their senses**. After all, Satan and not sinners is the enemy; he has **taken them captive to do his will**. In this spiritual warfare, sinful people may act like enemy combatants, but they're actually POWs.

## LIKE A SERVANT

Hidden within this description of Christian holiness is Paul's final illustration; the Christian leader is the Lord's **servant**. All six metaphors for leadership take on richer texture when they are seen as descriptions of servanthood. Doesn't the soldier have a commander (2:4)? Doesn't the farmer get only "a share of the crops" (2:6) because the field belongs to the Lord of the harvest? Doesn't the mansion filled with noble vessels have a master (2:20–21)? It's certainly not for himself that the workman cuts a straight road; he seeks the approval of another (2:15). Even the athlete is not his own master, free to make his own rules; he competes in a contest whose rules were established by the governor of the games (2:5).

The Christian leader is the servant of the Lord and of the Lord's people.

# 3. EVIL TIMES, EVIL PEOPLE 3:1–9

We may be excused for thinking that Paul's description of the **last days** sounds a bit like someone forecasting rain while standing in a downpour. Everything he foresees about the future can be seen already in the world around him. As a result, Paul can shift almost imperceptibly to the present tense (vv. 5b-8) without altering his meaning.

## READY IN THE LAST DAYS

Christians have always been fascinated by the last days. When Christ was asked about them, He said to expect wars and rumors of war, earthquakes, famines, and false messiahs (Matt. 24). By that description, we are living in the last days, and so were our parents and their parents before them. Every age has fit that description of the end, which was precisely Christ's point. Since any days could be the last, we must be always ready (Matt. 25:1–13).

Paul gave to Timothy a general description of a godless age. More to the point, Paul described what our godless age looks like. Every reader for two thousand years has seen this laundry list of sins and vices as a description of his generation.

Since neither Jesus nor Paul gave a specific date for the end, taking their teachings seriously should discourage us from setting a date for the Second Coming. Unfortunately, date setters tend to be hard to discourage. Not even Jesus' explicit denial of the validity of that practice can dissuade them (Matt. 24:36).

## SINS AS SIGNS

In 2 Tim. 3:2–4, Paul lists eighteen sins, but his tally isn't meant to be exhaustive. Many sins are missing, and their omission doesn't carry hidden meaning. The list is open-ended. Yet without overanalyzing this partial picture, it is possible to find patterns in Paul's catalog of sins. The list begins with two words based on the root *philos*, a Greek term for love, and it ends in the same way. **People will be lovers of themselves and lovers of money**, Paul observes in v. 2; in v. 4, they will be **lovers of pleasure rather than lovers of God**. In between are two related phrases (v. 3): **without love** and **not lovers of the good**. The Great Commandment (Matt. 22:34–40) fares poorly with the folk Paul describes; fully a third of the list describes misdirected love.

Another pattern here involves a series of words that, in Greek, carry the negative prefix *a-*, similar to the English *un-* or *non-*. Some of this pattern emerges in English translation, but the full impact of the Greek wording, which creates a drumbeat of similar sounding negatives, is lost.

Selfishness dominates the list (**boastful, proud . . . conceited**). Those whom Paul describes treat others badly (notice the force of words like **abusive** and **brutal**), and God is disregarded in a particularly hypocritical way; these people are guilty of **having a form of godliness but denying its power**. John Stott calls them "religious sinners."[8]

## FRAUD AND FOLLY

When Paul warns Timothy to **have nothing to do with [these people]**, it becomes apparent that he has been describing the false teachers in Timothy's church. Their strategy is devious. **They are the kind who worm their way into homes and gain control over weak-willed women**. Paul is not dismissive of women; he knows the prominent role women played in Jesus' ministry, and he values the contribution women such as Priscilla (Acts 18:24–26, Rom. 16:3–4), Lydia (Acts 16:13–15), and Phoebe (Rom. 16:1–2). But women were typically deprived of educational opportunities in that day, which made some of them easy marks for spiritual con artists. In addition, the particular women to whom Paul alludes seem spiritually deficient as well (2 Tim. 3:6b). Verse 7 suggests that they were into the latest spiritual fads,[9] a characterization that sounds as much like our era as does the list of sins in vv. 2–4. For a spiritual faddist, the contrast is not between truth and error but between what's hot and what's not among the trendsetters they follow. The description **always learning but never able to acknowledge the truth** is a devastating critique of too many first-century church members, and of many twenty-first-century church members as well.

If a number of women were especially susceptible to the persuasive cult in Ephesus, it's not surprising that Paul decided against using women as teachers in that church (see 1 Tim. 2:12).

The moral depravity of the false teachers in Ephesus reminds Paul of **Jannes and Jambres**, who, according to Jewish tradition, were Pharaoh's magicians at the time of the Exodus (Exod. 7:11). Their names don't appear in the Old Testament, but legends later developed about them in Jewish writings. The court magicians of Egypt had been exposed as frauds, and the same prospect awaits the false teachers of Ephesus. **They will not get very far because . . . their folly will be clear to everyone**.

In the presence of the genuine, the counterfeit is easily detected. Heresies rise and fall, but God's truth endures. As yesterday's pseudo-Christian teachers have faded into oblivion, so too will today's. The tuth will stand; their perversion of it will not.

## ENDNOTES

1. John R. W. Stott, *The Message of 2 Timothy* (Downers Grove, Ill.: InterVarsity Press, 1973), p. 80.

2. Ibid., p. 67; C. K. Barrett, *The Pastoral Epistles in the New English Bible* (Oxford: Clarendon Press, 1963), p. 105; Chrysostom, cited in J. N. D. Kelly, *The Pastoral Epistles* (Peabody, Mass.: Hendrickson Publishers, 1960), p. 183.

The Greek word *orthomein* is related to English words with the prefix *ortho*, which connote the straightness of things from teeth (orthodontia) to doctrine (orthodoxy).

3. Some believe the *foundation* refers to Christ (1 Cor. 3:10–17), while others see it as a reference to the apostles and prophets (Eph. 2:20). See Walter Liefield, *1 & 2 Timothy, Titus*, The NIV Application Commentary (Grand Rapids, Mich.: Zondervan Publishing House, 1999), p. 259. In either case, the basic point is the same.

4. Combining the thoughts of Isa. 26:13 and 52:11 produces wording similar to 2 Tim. 2:19b. Others think Num. 16:26, part of the Korah narrative, may be the source, loosely paraphrased here.

5. Gary Demarest, *1& 2 Thessalonians, 1 & 2 Timothy, Titus*, The Communicator's Commentary (Dallas, Tex: Word Publishing, 1984), p. 267.

6. Liefield, *1 & 2 Timothy*, p. 260.

7. Cited by Thomas Oden, *First and Second Timothy and Titus*, Interpretation Commentary Series (Louisville, Ky.: John Knox Press, 1989), p. 72.

8. Stott, *Message of 2 Timothy*, p. 88.

9. Kelly calls them "religious dilettantes" (*Pastoral Epistles*, p. 196).

# 5

# THE CLOSE OF A FAITHFUL MINISTRY

## 2 Timothy 3:10–4:8

A t the 1976 Summer Olympics in Montreal, I watched as runners brought the Olympic torch up the broad boulevard toward the stadium that was the centerpiece of the Games. Thousands crowded the sidewalks and cheered the completion of the traditional relay, which had begun weeks before in Olympia, Greece. As I looked on, the flame was passed one last time, and a fresh runner, torch held high, raced down the stadium ramp amid the pageantry of the opening ceremonies.

It is the privilege and responsibility of every generation to pass its faith along to the next. At some times in the history of the church, this transfer has been especially critical. Paul wrote to Timothy at such a time.

It is important to pass also the torch of leadership. When Elisha struck the waters of the Jordan with Elijah's mantle, he cried, "Where now is the LORD, the God of Elijah?" (2 Kings 2:13–14) The answer, of course, is that the Lord was there, raising up an Elisha to carry on the work, just as He had provided a Joshua to follow Moses. In the same way, God had raised up Timothy—and Titus (2 Tim. 4:10) and Luke (v. 11a) and Mark (v. 11b) and a host of others—to take the torch of leadership from Paul, who had finished his race (v. 7).

It is true, as C. S. Lewis observed, that the church is always only one generation away from extinction. We dare not grow complacent. But it is true also that God, despite the failures of an individual here or a local congregation there, is building a church that will prevail against the very gates of hell (Matt. 16:18), and He will raise up leaders for His church in every generation.

# 1. PAUL'S EXAMPLE 3:10–13

Having given a scathing description of the opponents of truth, Paul offers a contrast—in fact, two of them. First, he contrasts Timothy with the false teachers. **You, however** is the New International Version rendering of a Greek phrase that may be literally translated "but you." Paul uses the same expression in v. 14. There, as here, it comes hard on the heels of a condemnation of Timothy's enemies. You're not like them, Paul is saying. The difference is clear; it is the difference between death and eternal life.

Paul draws a second contrast, this one between himself and the false teachers. Against the catalog of vices in 3:1–9 Paul holds up his own record of virtue—**my teaching, my way of life, my purpose, faith, patience, love, endurance**. Paul is not boasting. He determined long before that he would boast only in the cross of Christ (Gal. 6:14). Instead, he is demonstrating the difference between those who market error and those who model truth. Timothy knew Paul's teaching well. He knew also that his mentor's life backed up what he taught.[1]

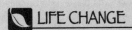

## LIFE CHANGE

### INTEGRITY

Francis of Assisi once invited a young priest to join him on a preaching tour. Through the city streets they walked, meeting and mingling with people, until finally they returned to their starting point.

The novice was puzzled. "I thought we were going to preach," he protested.

"We have preached," Francis replied. "We preached as we walked."

We all do, and the result is sometimes unfortunate. Columnist David Broder coined the term *integrity deficit* to describe moral breakdowns in the political arena. An integrity deficit in Christian leadership is an even greater tragedy.

There was no integrity deficit with Paul (2 Tim. 3:10). He walked the talk. Do we?

The last two items in Paul's list, **persecutions** and **sufferings**, are not virtues in themselves, but Paul's willingness to endure them for Christ's sake certainly is. Paul doesn't enumerate his sufferings here as he did in his second letter to the Corinthians (2 Cor. 6:3–10, 11:23–33), but he does refer to the persecution he suffered in a cluster of Galatian towns—**Antioch, Iconium, and Lystra**. Timothy really did **know all about** what Paul endured there because Timothy lived in that region; Lystra was his home (Acts 16:1).[2]

Acts 13–14 provides the background for Paul's autobiographical reference. Paul was unceremoniously evicted from Pisidian Antioch (Acts 13:50) and was forced to flee a plot against his life in Iconium (Acts 14:5). In Lystra he was stoned and left for dead (Acts 14:19–20). In 2 Timothy 3, Paul recalls these battlefield memories, which were intense and painful. Yet Paul was willing to revisit them because they verified his allegiance to Christ. In fact, Paul points out, **everyone who wants to live a godly life in Christ Jesus will be persecuted**.

"It is taken for granted throughout the New Testament, and nowhere more so than in Paul's letters, that suffering is inevitably incurred by Christian existence in the present world," writes F. F. Bruce. "There was nothing surprising in this: Christ had suffered, and his followers—those who were 'in Christ'—could expect nothing less."[3]

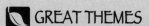

## GREAT THEMES

### SUFFERING FOR CHRIST

In February 1844, David Livingstone was mauled by a lion in the African jungle. His thick jacket and the quick response of his companions prevented the loss of the missionary's arm and perhaps his life, but his shoulder was shattered. When Livingstone died almost thirty years later, his body was returned home for burial with honor. His identity had to be authenticated before he could be buried among England's greats in Westminster Abbey. The circumstances of his isolated death in the African interior could have made identification difficult, but it wasn't. The evidence of his injury was the proof of his identity.

Is it possible that evidence of suffering for Christ's sake is the authenticating mark for the Christian in his quest for heaven? It may not be *physical* suffering; for most Christians in the western world, it won't be. But if no one reigns with Him who hasn't suffered for Him (Rom. 8:17; 2 Tim. 2:12), perhaps we should check ourselves for scars.

If we haven't suffered, have we served?

Paul's recollection goes further; he asserts, **The Lord rescued me from all of them**, that is, from the persecutions he endured. That is a stirring witness, one that every Christian can depend on. It is important that we not read Paul's testimony as a guarantee of physical safety, however. Paul would not be delivered from his present persecution except in death, and he knew that even as he wrote to Timothy. His final deliverance from evil was his safe entrance into the heavenly Kingdom (4:18). Christ is exalted when we exhibit the faith of the three Hebrew youths in Dan. 3:16–18, believing that our God can deliver us but that even when He does not, He is still our God. (The same idea is expressed poetically in Hab. 3:17–18 and explored in Heb. 11:32–40.)

Those who are faithful under persecution soar above their surroundings spiritually, but **evil men and impostors** (the false teachers) travel in a different direction. They **will go from bad to worse** in the same spiritual free fall that Paul alludes to in 2 Tim. 2:16. It is not apparent in the New International Version, but Paul uses the same verb, meaning to advance or make progres, with a negative spin in both 2:16 and 3:13. The spiritual frauds are advancing to the rear. Like lost motorists, they are making good time in the wrong direction.

The word translated *impostors* literally means sorcerers or magicians. It provides another link to Jannes and Jambres (3:8), which Paul meant to be obvious to the reader but which is lost in some English translations. These fakers **deceive**, but they are also **being deceived**. The old saying holds that you can't con a con man, but these shysters have been duped by the ultimate liar, Satan.

## 2. THE AUTHORITY OF SCRIPTURE 3:14–17

Woven like a thread through 2 Timothy is Paul's reliance on God's Word. Paul may be chained, but God's Word isn't (2:9). Paul has already emphasized the importance of handling God's Word correctly (2:15), and before the letter closes he will urge Timothy to preach that Word, even though many in his congregation will not want to hear it (4:2). When error runs rampant, there is no better corrective than the truth of God's Word.

### KEEP ON KEEPING ON

The false teachers at Ephesus are on the wrong road (3:13), but Timothy is on the right one. His task, then, is to keep on keeping on. Paul urges him, **Continue in what you have learned and have become convinced of.** Others may change with the seasons or turn with the tide, but Timothy must hold his course. It is the right one.

Timothy knew he was on the right track for two reasons. First, he knew **those from whom he learned it.**[4] As a third-generation Christian, Timothy had a great heritage of faith. He could rely on the instruction he received from trustworthy teachers like his mother and his grandmother; the false teachers at Ephesus couldn't match their integrity. Timothy had also learned from Paul, a point the apostle makes repeatedly (1:13; 2:2; 3:10). In this school of faith, Timothy has studied under a first-class faculty.

Second, Timothy knew he was in the right because he knew **the holy Scriptures.**[5] Paul refers to the Hebrew Scriptures, which Christians know as the Old Testament. Timothy knew these Scriptures **from infancy**. In the first century, a Jewish father was supposed to begin teaching his son as soon as he was able to learn, and the principal text was the Scriptures. Acts 16:1 indicates that Timothy's Greek father was neither a convert to Judaism nor a Christian, so Timothy's mother and grandmother assumed responsibility for his religious education. At age five he would have been enrolled in a synagogue school for Scripture study, and at age ten he would have studied the Mishnah, Jewish commentary on the Law. But Timothy's religious education began long before that, in his own home.

The New Testament was still in the process of formulation as Paul wrote to Timothy. Some New Testament books had yet to be written. It was already clear, however, that there would be Christian Scriptures, a New

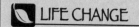

## LIFE CHANGE

FAITHFULNESS

Eugene Peterson's study of the songs of ascent in the Psalms is a classic text in Christian discipleship. One of the great things about the book is its title: *A Long Obedience in the Same Direction*. That idea goes against the grain of a society that believes change is the only constant. People change addresses, jobs, styles, diets, phone companies, spouses, and churches quickly and often. For our age, continuing in anything is asking almost too much, yet that's the discipleship principle Paul presents to Timothy. Step one is to find the truth; step two is to continue in it.

Testament alongside the Old. Peter refers to Paul's letters as Scripture (2 Pet. 3:15), and Paul quotes Christ's words from Luke 10:7 as Scripture (1 Tim. 5:18). Therefore what Paul says about Scripture in this passage is true of the entirety of God's Word, both the part that had already been formed (the Old Testament) and the part that was still being composed (the New Testament). The authority of God's Word needs to be emphasized in every age.

Paul's five-fold view of Scripture is encapsulated in 2 Tim. 3:16–17.

First, **the Scriptures . . . are able to make you wise for salvation.** This book from God, which is inspired by God, shows the way to God.

Second, Scripture offers salvation that is available **through faith in Christ Jesus.** Even though Paul's primary emphasis here is on the Old Testament, he asserts that Christ stands at the center of the story. From the promise of redemption (which is given immediately after the first sin) to the Israelite sacrificial system (which is rich with symbols pointing to Christ) to the detailed prophecies of the Incarnation, the Christ of the New Testament is anticipated in the Old.

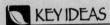

## KEY IDEAS
### CHRIST IN THE OLD TESTAMENT

In the Library of Congress there is a copy of the Emancipation Proclamation that is unlike any other. The calligrapher shaded certain letters so that a viewer, looking not at specific phrases or lines but at the document as a whole, can see the profile of Abraham Lincoln. It may not be immediately apparent, but Christ's image is on every page of the Old Testament.

Third, **all Scripture is God-breathed.** This phrase is the basis for the Christian doctrine of divine inspiration. *Inspired* is an overused word, applied to everyone from Renaissance artists to interior decorators. But when it is used of Scripture, that word denotes much more than a work of genius. It signifies that the work originated with God, who prompted its human authors to record divinely revealed truth.[6] The image of God breathing Scripture makes a brilliant analogy. Not only is breath integrally associated with life (as in Gen. 2:7), but the Greek word for breath also means spirit. And it is by the agency of the Holy Spirit that all Scripture is given (2 Pet. 1:21; Acts 1:16).

Paul's statement in 2 Tim. 3:16 can be alternatively translated "every God-breathed Scripture," as in the New English Bible. But those who render it that way are forced to translate the *and* that follows as "also." That is technically legitimate, but it produces a decidedly more awkward grammatical construction. More to the point, it seriously compromises the doctrine of inspiration, implying that some parts of the Bible are not divinely inspired. A partially inspired Bible is little better than no Bible at all, for who would determine which parts of it are from God and which are not? The Bible would become a human invention, no more authoritative than any other man-made thing. That is not the Bible Paul speaks of here and elsewhere. He testifies in tenor with the entire witness of the Scripture that its source is God. As the poet John Dryden wrote, "Majestic and divine, it speaks no less than God in every line."[7] Paul doesn't clarify all the issues related to inspiration or their implications, but he does give us a place to stand in defense of the full and complete inspiration of the Bible.

Fourth, Paul asserts the purpose of Scripture. **All Scripture . . . is useful for teaching, rebuking, correcting, and training in righteousness.**[8] For the Christian, both creed and conduct are grounded in the Word. Scripture directs both our beliefs and our behavior, our theology and our ethics. This purpose statement is a double-edged sword, having both positive and negative applications. For Scripture gives us not only God's *Yes* but also His *No*. Both are given for our benefit.

Fifth, the end result of Scripture is **that the man of God may be thoroughly equipped for every good work.** *Man of God* is the title Paul gives Timothy in 1 Tim. 6:11. Almost certainly, his use of it here is intended to personalize this teaching. Scripture is for the whole church, of course, but Paul's present point is that it is indispensable in the preparation of a Christian leader.

Walter Liefield calls 2 Tim. 3:16–17 "the strongest statement in the Bible about itself"[9] This tribute to the Word is a wonderful parting gift from Paul to Timothy, and to us.

## 3. THE CHARGE TO TIMOTHY 4:1–5

Charles Wesley captures the spirit of Paul's final charge to Timothy in one of the poet's most famous hymns, "A Charge to Keep I Have."

To serve the present age, my calling to fulfill;

O may it all my powers engage to do my Master's will!

With words very much like those, Paul gave a solemn commission to his son in the faith.

## PREAMBLE

Paul prefaces his charge to Timothy with words of nearly ceremonial dignity. No English term precisely captures his tone. In Latin, it is *gravitas*, most solemn and of momentous importance. Paul's words have the impressive feel of an oath of office or courtroom declaration; in fact, some translators build on the judicial imagery by offering as the main phrase in Paul's sentence "I adjure you." For a minister, Paul's preamble may recall the weighty words of an ordination vow.

Paul has addressed Timothy is similar language twice before (1 Tim. 5:21; 6:13–14), but this charge will be his final one. The apostle intends to make sure that the gravity of these words will not be lost on the one who reads them.

Paul invokes the awe-filled majesty of God to impress upon Timothy the eternal significance of the moment. Paul is transferring the torch of leadership to Timothy **in the presence of God and of Christ Jesus.** To a believer such as Timothy, Paul hardly needed to say more, but he does. One day Timothy will stand before the divine judgment seat to answer for his faithfulness to this charge, and those to whom he ministers will be among **the living and the dead** who stand there too. Paul concludes his preamble in anticipation of Christ's **appearing** and the consummation of **his kingdom**, which lends even greater urgency to what he is about to write.

Heaven leans forward at Paul's words and awaits Timothy's response, as it does the response of every Christian leader who hears and answers a similar summons.

## MANY DUTIES, ONE MISSION

Paul's solemn charge is given in five commands, each one brief and to the point. Thomas Oden calls them "death cell imperatives."[10] Sensing that the hour of his execution is near, Paul had neither the time nor the inclination to dress his words in elaborate language.

Timothy's task will not be easy, but it is at least simple. Principally, he is to **preach the Word**. This ministry of proclamation will link him not only to His Lord, who "came . . . preaching" (Mark 1:14–15 KJV; see also Mark 1:38; Matt. 4:17, 23), but also to the Twelve, who received that assignment from Christ (Mark 3:14), and to Paul, his mentor, for whom preaching was of primary importance (1 Cor. 9:16; Rom. 1:15; 10:14–15).

In a recent survey, a majority of pastors identified preaching as their most important assignment. In terms of the time invested, however, those same pastors admitted that administrative duties and other ministerial responsibilities received the lion's share of their attention. To Paul, ministerial leadership was more spiritual than managerial, and preaching heads his list of spiritual responsibilities.

Paul states emphatically that it is the Word that is to be preached. He places no premium on preaching anything else. A study of the direct objects of the verb *to preach* in Paul's letters reveals remarkable consistency and a single-minded purpose; he repeatedly writes that he preaches *the gospel*, and when he uses another word or phrase as his object, it is almost always either *Christ* or *the Word*. "We do not preach ourselves" (2 Cor. 4:5), Paul reminds us.

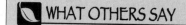

## WHAT OTHERS SAY

The supreme work of the Christian minister is the work of preaching. One of our greatest perils is that of doing a thousand little things instead of the one thing, which is preaching.

—G. Campbell Morgan

Personal opinions, pop psychology, and political agendas are not proper subjects for a preacher of the Word. Preaching God's Word was Paul's first priority; it must be ours as well.

That commitment to proclamation was to be an ongoing obligation for Timothy. He needed to **be prepared in season and out of season**. That means he was to proclaim the Word when it was "convenient or inconvenient" (New English Bible), "welcome or unwelcome" (Jerusalem Bible). Opposition is to be expected. Someone has paraphrased Paul by saying that for the preacher, it can be in season, out of season, or open season! But the preacher answers to a higher authority than earthly critics. Hugh Latimer, preparing a sermon to be preached in the court of Henry VIII, seemed to hear a voice that said, "Be careful what you preach today. You preach before the King of England." An answering voice replied, "Be careful what you preach today. You preach before the King of Kings."

Paul's admonition to be ever ready suggests the image of a physician on call, never knowing when his life-saving services will be needed.[11] Timothy, to borrow a phrase from the discipline of pastoral care, was on call for the cure of souls.

The final three imperatives of Paul's charge apparently relate to the variety of avenues preaching can take. *To **correct*** involves the intellect and the world of the mind, *to **rebuke*** concerns moral persuasion, and *to **encourage*** connects with others on a relational and emotional level. Today's preachers would do well to serve such a balanced diet to their people. In the discussion of 1 Tim. 1:3–7, four basic homiletical "food groups" were mentioned: doctrinal preaching (propagation of sound belief), moral or ethical preaching (instruction on behavior), pastoral preaching (suggestion for dealing with felt needs), and evangelistic preaching (invitation to salvation). Interestingly, the first three categories are found here in 2 Tim. 4:2, and the fourth is found in v. 5.

All must be done **with great patience and careful instruction**. Timothy was to preach with a pastor's heart. He would need one, because his task would not easy.

When Paul says **the time will come**, he is speaking in the prophetic *now* of 2 Tim. 3:1. Those who **will not put up with sound doctrine** were already in the Ephesian congregation, and Timothy knew it all too well. Sound doctrine is essential in a healthy church (which makes our current tendency to devalue theology a risky practice), and Timothy's problems in Ephesus were directly related to the unsound teaching of his opponents.

The result was a cluster of counterfeit Christians within the church who had **[gathered] around them** (the New Revised Standard Version says "accumulate") **a great number of teachers to say what their itching ears [wanted] to hear.** Like the Red Queen in *Alice in Wonderland*, who declared that words meant what she wanted them to mean, these counterfeit Christians had redefined the gospel to suit themselves. Truth is never determined by an opinion poll, but truth wasn't their concern. Timothy could watch them **turn their ears**—their itching ears—**away from the truth** he preached as they **[turned] aside to myths** (1 Tim. 1:4). Truth doesn't always attract; sometimes it repels.

Trading truth for myths is a bad bargain, but Paul had seen the pattern before. In his epistle to the Romans, he shook his head over those who had traded God for idols (Rom. 1:22–23), natural desires for unnatural ones (1:26–27), and the truth of God for a lie (1:25).

Timothy was charged with championing the truth despite opposition from defectors. Above all, he was not to fall for their lies himself. **But you**, Paul admonishes him, **keep your head in all situations**. Don't overreact to these cultists, Paul was saying, and don't be seduced by their fantasies. To lead a divided church may be hard, but Timothy's assignment was to **endure hardship** (see also 2 Tim. 2:3).

This crisis could easily have consumed all of Timothy's time and energy, but as a pastor, he had other responsibilities. Paul incorporates them into his charge. His admonition to **do the work of an evangelist** is not a reassignment of Timothy to the New Testament office of evangelist (Acts 21:8; Eph. 4:11). It is a reference to the evangelistic outreach every pastor is expected to pursue. Evangelizing the counterfeit Christians would have been the logical place for Timothy to start. Paul goes on to urge Timothy to **discharge all the duties of [his] ministry**. The Greek word for *discharge* carries the idea of fulfilling or finishing, an idea Paul has written about before. In Col. 4:17, for example, Paul sent this cryptic message to a church member named Archippus: "See to it that you complete the work you have received in the Lord." We don't know who Archippus was, and we have no idea what his spiritual work may have been, but we do know that Paul wanted him to finish it. (The Colossian church undoubtedly became an instant accountability group for Archippus!) In a similar way, Paul tacitly gives the Ephesian Christians who have not followed the false teachers permission to hold their pastor accountable for discharging all the duties of a minister.

The idea of completion provides Paul with a bridge to his own closing witness. He, too, is finishing the work he has received in the Lord. In Paul's conversation with the elders of this same Ephesian church at the end of his third missionary journey, Paul said, "I consider my life worth nothing to me, if only I may finish the race and complete the task the Lord Jesus has given me—the task of testifying to the gospel of God's grace" (Acts 20:24). At that time, Paul still had many laps to run; as he writes to Timothy, Paul can see the finish line.

## 4. PAUL'S EPITAPH 4:6–8

This section of 2 Timothy is one of the most familiar passages in the New Testament. In its context, it provides a counterpoint to the charge given to Timothy.[12] It is as if Paul is saying, "I give you this charge because I myself have finished the race" (4:1, 6–7). **The time has come for my departure,** Paul writes, using a term often applied to striking a tent or loosing the lines on a ship. Moffatt's translation is succinct: "My time to go has come."[13]

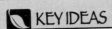

### KEY IDEAS

#### COMPLETION

Author Dorothy Sayers imagines that at the carpentry shop in Nazareth, young Jesus would emerge with His latest handiwork—a table, a shelf, a yoke for the oxen—to be inspected by His earthly father, Joseph. "I have finished the work you gave me to do," Jesus might have said.

Years later, on the night of His betrayal, we know that Jesus did say to His heavenly Father, "I have brought you glory on earth by completing the work you gave me to do" (John 17:4). A day later, from the cross, He announced to the world, "It is finished" (John 19:30).

Paul's life after his Damascus Road conversion led to the moment when, like his Lord, he could testify, "I have finished . . ." (2 Tim. 4:7).

### DEATH OF A LIVING SACRIFICE

Drawing a compelling word picture, Paul compares his life to a **drink offering**. A drink offering, or libation, in the Jewish sacrificial system was not a sacrifice in itself but was a ritual associated with the meal offering that accompanies burnt offerings and peace offerings (Exod. 29:40–41; Lev. 23:13; Num. 15:4–10). Paul must have seen many drink offerings given. Wine from a ceremonial cup was poured on the altar, probably on the sacrifice itself. Paul knew what it was to be a living sacrifice (Rom. 12:1), and why should a living sacrifice flinch at the prospect of death? "Ever since his conversion," William Barclay writes, "Paul had offered everything to God—his money, his scholarship, his strength, his time, the vigour of his body, the acuteness of his mind, the devotion of his passionate heart. Only life itself was left to offer, and gladly Paul was going to lay life down."[14]

The prospect of losing his life was no longer a distant one for Paul. It had already occurred to him that his life was a drink offering. During his first imprisonment, he had reflected on his death in those very terms. But then he wrote, "Even if I am being poured out" (Phil. 2:17), indicating his belief that he might survive that imprisonment. To Timothy, he writes **I am already being poured out**, indicating his belief that he was about to die. He is in a frozen moment between the tipping of the cup and its return, now empty, to its place. In a sense, Paul's death has already begun. Tom Oden puts it this way: "He sees himself as having lived a purposeful life, now living out a purposeful death."[15]

Paul's testimony makes a marvelous epitaph for a magnificent life. **I have fought the good fight, I have finished the race, I have kept the faith**. The good fight (see also 1 Tim. 6:12) may be a military allusion but probably is not. Because the reward is a crown (2 Tim.4:8), it's likely that Paul is using an athletic metaphor, just like the race metaphor that follows it. Winners in athletic competitions were awarded a laurel crown. In a strikingly parallel passage (1 Cor. 9:25–26), Paul not only refers to a winner's crown, as he does here, but also specifies the competitors who win it as a runner and a fighter, the same images he uses in 2 Timothy 4. Since the fighter in 1 Corinthians is clearly a boxer and not a soldier, it's reasonable to assume that that was Paul's intent in 2 Timothy 4 as well.

Some commentators think keeping the faith, the third expression in Paul's confession of faith, is like keeping the rules in an athletic contest, but that seems forced. It is more probable that Paul is abandoning figures of speech here to make a clearer witness to his spiritual principles. The faith is the deposit he has successfully guarded, just as he urged Timothy to do (1 Tim. 6:20; 2 Tim. 1:14). It is also *his* faith.

## CORONATION DAY

The **crown** (or garland) **of righteousness** is a reward for righteousness, which is already Paul's through faith, and not a conferment of righteousness. Paul will treasure that crown, perhaps, until even it will be laid along with others at Jesus' feet (Rev. 4:10). **That day** seems to refer to the day of Christ's **appearing**. If so, the Second Coming, rather than the day of Paul's martyrdom, will be his coronation day.

The reward is not Paul's alone (v. 8b), nor is it reserved only for God's most visible or celebrated servants. It is for **all** of God's faithful ones.

Nero may find Paul guilty, and he realized that. In fact, Paul assumed that he would be condemned. Yet he knew that **the Lord, the righteous Judge,** would reverse that unjust verdict.[16]

Peter Marshall, once chaplain of the U. S. Senate, said, "The message of a life is not in its duration but in its donation." Paul's donation to the world at large and to the church in particular is immeasurable.

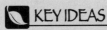

### KEY IDEAS

#### MARTYRDOM

The early church father Tertullian wrote, "The blood of the martyrs is seed." Paul was one of those martyrs, and their number is multiplying in our day.

Ask Betty Bitterman about martyrdom, and she won't talk to you about Roman arenas filled with gladiators and wild beasts. She'll tell you about Colombia, South America, and her husband Chet, who was a missionary linguist kidnapped by terrorists and held for forty-eight days. The ransom demand—withdrawal of all missionaries connected with Wycliffe Bible translators—was unacceptable, and Chet's body was found in a bus on a Bogota Street. He had been shot once through the heart.

More than a hundred translators associated with the mission were offered reassignment in the aftermath of Chet's murder, but all remained at their posts. In fact, more than two hundred applications were received from individuals volunteering to take Chet's place. Out of martyrdom comes new life for the church.

Those whom the world considers victims, God calls victors.

## ENDNOTES

1. When Paul says Timothy knows these things, he uses a verb that carries the idea of following, as a disciple would follow a master. See J. N. D. Kelly, *The Pastoral Epistles* (Peabody, Mass.: Hendrickson Publishers, 1960), p.198. Timothy knows Paul's history in part because Timothy has followed Paul's ministry with interest much greater than that of a casual onlooker. As a disciple and protégé, Timothy was expected to learn from Paul's example and imitate it in his own ministry.

2. Some consider this an anachronism because Paul suffered the Galatian persecution before Timothy joined his missionary team. But the text doesn't claim that Timothy was an eyewitness, simply that he has knowledge of these events. Still, as a young resident of Lystra, where the worst attack took place, Timothy may well have been an eyewitness. It is an indication of Paul's courage that he immediately re-entered Lystra (Acts 14:20), that he passed through the same towns again later in the same journey, and that he came back to all of these Galatian towns on his second and third missionary journeys. It is the only region Paul visited on all three of his journeys.

3. F. F. Bruce, *Philippians*, A Good News Commentary (San Francisco: Harper and Row, 1983), p. 32. There is no shortage of biblical texts making this point. See Matt. 10:22; Acts 14:22; Phil. 1:29; and 1 Pet. 4:12.

4. The Greek text actually reads "you know from whom you learned it." In some early manuscripts, the pronoun *whom* is plural, which produces translations like the New International Version's "those from whom you learned it." In other manuscripts, the pronoun is singular. If that reading were correct, the reference would obviously be to Paul alone. Compare C. K. Barrett, *The Pastoral Epistles in the New English Bible* (Oxford: Clarendon Press, 1963), p. 113 and John R. W. Stott, *The Message of 2 Timothy* (Downers Grove, Ill.: InterVarsity Press, 1973), pp. 98–99.

5. The Greek term translated "holy Scriptures" in 2 Tim. 3:15 is not the commonly used *graphe* but the unusual *hiera grammata*. This text contains the singular occurrence of this Greek term in the Bible. Kelly, *Pastoral Epistles*, 201.

6. That Scripture is divinely inspired does preclude human instrumentality in its writing. Peter clearly indicates that "men spoke," but they spoke "from God as they were carried along by the Holy Spirit" (2 Pet. 1:21). Each biblical book reflects the vocabulary, style, and even personality of its human author.

7. John Dryden, "Religio Laici," line 140.

8. The literary form Paul uses here is called *chiasm*, an A-B-B-A arrangement that, when diagrammed, resembles the X-shaped Greek letter, *chi*. In this case, the progression is (A) Teaching, (B) Rebuking, (B) Correcting, and (A) Training.

9. Walter Liefield, *1 & 2 Timothy, Titus,* The NIV Application Commentary (Grand Rapids, Mich.: Zondervan, 1999), p. 279.

10. Thomas Oden, *First and Second Timothy and Titus*, Interpretation Commentary Series (Louisville, Ky.: John Knox Press, 1989), p. 135.

11. Philip H. Towner, *1–2 Timothy & Titus,* The IVP New Testament Commentary Series (Downers Grove, Ill.: InterVarsity Press, 1994), p. 204.

12. Stott, *2 Timothy*, 113.

13. James Moffatt, *The Bible: A New Translation,* Revised and Final Edition (New York: Harper and Brothers Publishers, 1950), p. 269.

14. William Barclay, *The Letters of Timothy, Titus, and Philemon*, The Daily Study Bible (Philadelphia: The Westminster Press, 1960), p. 240.

15. Oden, *First and Second Timothy*, p. 171.

16. Kelly, *Pastoral Epistles*, p. 210.

# 6

# FINAL WORDS

## 2 Timothy 4:9–21

John Stott sets the stage perfectly for the closing section of 2 Timothy: "From his majestic survey of the past ('I have fought the good fight . . .') and his confident anticipation of the future ('henceforth there is laid up for me the crown . . .'), Paul returns in thought to the present and to his present predicament."[1]

Paul's predicament, of course, was his imprisonment, but several other challenges had combined to complicate his situation even more. One of his coworkers had deserted him (v. 10), he was dealing with a powerful personal enemy (vv. 14–15), no one was there to support him at his court hearing (v. 16), and most of his remaining colleagues were scattered elsewhere in ministry (vv. 9–13). **Only Luke** was with Paul. The Roman Christians who send greetings to Timothy in v. 21b were evidently in contact with Paul, but were not members of his team. Paul's circle of friends, which had been so important to him in so many situations, was broken, and Paul felt the loss of companionship keenly.

## 1. THE HUMAN FACE OF LEADERSHIP 4:9–18

William Barclay has called this section a "roll of honor and dishonor."[2] The only one able to answer Paul's roll call at that dark hour was Luke. Let's examine the roster of Paul's associates.

## ROLL CALL OF THE FAITHFUL

**Luke**, a Gentile Christian, joined Paul on his second missionary journey, soon after Timothy had signed on. The rest, as they say, is history—the history of the apostolic church penned by Luke and known to us as The Acts of the Apostles. Luke was a Renaissance man long before the Renaissance. In addition to being a historian and the author of the third Gospel, he was also a physician (Col. 4:14). It is possible that he was attending Paul during his imprisonment because the apostle needed medical attention. More important to Paul, Luke was a "fellow worker" (Philem. 24) and a "dear friend" (Col. 4:14). Luke may have been serving as Paul's amanuensis (secretary), writing down this epistle as Paul dictated it.

**Crescens** is all but unknown to us. This is the only reference to him in the New Testament. He was on assignment **to Galatia**, perhaps sent there earlier by Paul. By Galatia, Paul means the province by that name in Asia Minor (modern Turkey), which was the site of church plants by Paul and the home of Timothy. European Gaul was also called Galatia at times, and there is an ancient tradition that credits Crescens with being an early missionary to the West and the founder of the church in Vienne, near Lyons, France.[3] It is most likely, though, that Paul refers to the province in Asia Minor.

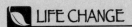

**LIFE CHANGE**

FELLOWSHIP

Evangelicals have so stressed the importance of a personal relationship with Christ that we tend to neglect the role that others play in our spiritual lives. It's true that we come to Jesus one by one, but by God's design, we travel to heaven together.

Deprived of his freedom, Paul was hungry for Christian fellowship and particularly the fellowship of his associates in ministry.

True Christian fellowship can be very costly. It means investing ourselves in each others' lives, encouraging each other (1 Thess. 4:18), serving each other (Gal. 5:13), bearing each other's burdens (Gal. 6:2), and submitting to each other (Eph. 5:21).

Dietrich Bonhoeffer wrote a classic study of Christian community entitled *Life Together*. Paul's life was almost over; that's the time when the words *life together* take on new meaning.

Lord, show us what fellowship truly means.

**Titus** had gone **to Dalmatia**, which is in modern Albania and Bosnia-Herzegovina, the former Yugoslavia, on the Adriatic Sea. In the New Testament era, Dalmatia was part of Illyricum, which Paul visited (Rom. 15:19). On the basis on this verse in 2 Timothy and the tradition springing from it, however, Titus rather than Paul is credited with introducing Christianity to Dalmatia. Titus had served as a troubleshooter for Paul previously, both in Corinth (2 Cor. 2:13; 7:6, 13; 8:16–24; 12:18) and in Crete, where he was the recipient of Paul's third Pastoral Epistle. Apparently, Titus's work on Crete was complete. He, like Timothy, was a son in the faith to Paul (Titus 1:4).

**Mark** was needed by Paul, and he ordered Timothy, **bring him with you because he is helpful in my ministry**. What a reversal! Years earlier, Paul had been disappointed in Mark and had had a low opinion of his ministry potential. As a young man, Mark had abandoned his cousin, Barnabas, and Paul on their first missionary journey and returned home. Paul vetoed Mark's involvement in a second missionary journey, prompting Barnabas and Paul to part company and lead separate missionary teams, Mark joining Barnabas (Acts 15:36–41). From that inauspicious beginning, Mark matured into an effective leader in the New Testament church, becoming the spiritual protégé of Peter (1 Pet. 5:13), author of the second Gospel, and partner with the apostle he had once disappointed (Col. 4:14; Philem. 24).

**Tychicus** is less known to us but was not less important to Paul. He had accompanied Paul to Jerusalem (Acts 20:4) on the trip that ended in Paul's first arrest, and he had served as the trusted courier for Paul's letters to the Ephesians, to the Colossians, and to Titus. It is possible that Tychicus was the courier for 2 Timothy, even though Paul mentions that he has **sent Tychicus to Ephesus**. On the surface that would seem to rule him out as the deliverer of this letter. However, the Greek verb, though in the past tense, may be interpreted to indicate action that had not yet taken place but that would have happened by the time the letter was read.[4] Whether Tychicus delivered this epistle to Timothy or not, it seems probable that he was sent to Ephesus to release Timothy to go to Rome, filling in for him in his absence.

**Carpus** is not mentioned anywhere else in the New Testament. He was a resident of Troas in northwestern Asia Minor, a city visited by Paul on more than one occasion.

That leaves **Demas**, who accounts for one of the most haunting references in all of Paul's letters. Demas was once at the heart of Paul's missionary enterprise, listed as a "fellow worker" in the company of notables such as Luke and Mark (see Philem. 24; Col. 4:10, 14). But Demas **deserted** Paul **and [went] to Thessalonica**, which was perhaps his home (his name is Greek). Paul knew the reason for Demas's departure: it was **because he loved this world**. He may have found life in Rome too risky and association with Paul too dangerous for his liking. Displaying the opposite of Moses' character in Heb. 11:25–26, Demas may have chosen *not* to be mistreated along with the people of God, regarding disgrace for the sake of Christ of *lesser* value than the treasures of the world. If so, Demas's reward also would be different from Moses' (Heb. 11:26b). At any rate, Paul was profoundly disappointed by the failure of one for whom he had had high hopes.

There is debate over Demas. Some wonder whether he fell from faith or simply retreated to a safer field of Christian service, thereby disappointing Paul but not forsaking Christ. Sadly, Demas seems to be a case of apostasy. Paul's reference to Demas's love for this world (literally, this present age) in 2 Tim. 4:10 is placed in stark contrast to the believers' love of Christ's appearing in v. 8. The same word for love, *agapao*, is used in both verses.[5] Demas loved the wrong things, and the result was apostasy.

---

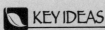

## KEY IDEAS

### FAITHFULNESS

Faithfulness is a major theme in 2 Timothy. We see God's faithfulness ("If we are faithless, he will remain faithful," 2:13), Paul's faithfulness ("I have kept the faith," 4:7), and Timothy's faithfulness ("I have been reminded of your sincere faith," 1:5).

But we see others who are memorable for their faithlessness. That certainly describes the false teachers, who "destroy the faith of some" (2:18) and were themselves rejected because of it (3:8). Their opposition to orthodoxy was longstanding. When we meet them for the first time in Paul's first letter to Timothy, it's very clear whose side they were on. They were flying a banner of rebellion against the truth.

Demas was different. The tragedy of Demas is that he changed banners, moving to the faithless crowd from the community of the faithful. He came to love this world, and so far as we know, he never returned to his first love.

This roll call of honor and dishonor ends where Paul begins, with Timothy himself. **Do your best to come to me quickly**, Paul urges. The visit may already have been planned, because the emphasis of the command seems to fall on the word *quickly* rather than the word *come.*[6] Imploring Timothy to hurry to Rome is one of Paul's principal reasons for writing. "I long to see you," he began the letter (1:4); he ends it, "Come to me quickly." In between, Paul encourages Timothy to pastor his people with patience and love, to preach the Word boldly, to block the schemes of the false teachers, and to endure suffering for Christ's sake, all assignments that pertain to Ephesus, by and large. But an assignment to Rome must take precedence, at least temporarily. Paul pleads with Timothy, in effect saying, "Come to me before I die." The poignant language and the father-son intimacy of this plea are deeply moving.

Some scholars think of the personal remarks that follow 4:6–8 as anticlimactic, but they aren't—and they weren't for Paul. These comments are the true climax of the letter because they are a primary motive for its writing. And Paul does not show weakness in this highly personal section; he shows strength under siege, great resolve in a time of testing. He shows the human face of church leadership.

## CLOAK, SCROLLS, AND PARCHMENTS

Paul needed Timothy, but that was not all he needed. **When you come**, Paul wrote, **bring the cloak that I left with Carpus in Troas.** The cloak would have been a heavy, woolen, sleeveless outer coat with a hole in the middle, somewhat like a poncho. Given the Spartan accommodations in Caesar's dungeon and with winter approaching (v. 21), Paul needed the warmth his cloak would bring.[7]

Also, Timothy was to bring Paul's **scrolls, especially the parchments**. The scrolls were made of papyrus, an early form of paper. Parchment was made from sheep- or goatskins and was much more expensive than papyrus. Whatever their form, Paul was asking for his books. Almost certainly, copies of the Scripture were among them, along with other works. Paul's own notebooks and copies of his correspondence would likely have been among the scrolls, too,

## WHAT OTHERS SAY

I entreat your lordship, and that by the Lord Jesus, that if I must remain here for the winter you would beg the Commissary to be so kind as to send me, from the things of mine which he has, a warmer cap; I feel the cold painfully in my head. Also a warmer cloak, for the cloak I have is very thin. He has a woolen shirt of mine, if he will send it. But most of all, my Hebrew Bible, Grammar, and Vocabulary, that I may spend my time in that pursuit.

—Letter from Bible translator William Tyndale to his jailer, 1535

and it is possible that legal documents, such as proof of his Roman citizenship, were included as well.

In this brief glimpse behind the curtain of Paul's life and ministry, we see Paul from another angle. Paul the world changer we know very well—apostle, missionary, martyr-in-the-making. But here is Paul the man. He needs "people to keep him company . . . a cloak to keep him warm . . . [and] books and parchments to keep him occupied."[8] We can relate.

### A POWERFUL ENEMY

**Alexander the metalworker** (some translations read "coppersmith") was an enemy against whom Timothy needed to be on guard. His identity is uncertain, but Paul probably refers to the former church member in Ephesus mentioned in 1 Tim. 1:20. Having "shipwrecked" his faith, that Alexander, along with Hymenaeus, was excommunicated, or removed from the church, in an act of redemptive discipline. If the enemy in 2 Timothy 4 is in fact the same Alexander, the discipline did not have its intended effect.

It is not clear what Alexander's offense was, but it was most likely connected with Paul's trial. Donald Guthrie believes that Alexander may have testified for the prosecution. Other scholars point out that the word translated "did me harm" is the word commonly used of an informant, which raises the possibility that Alexander engineered Paul's arrest.[9] Whatever the nature of his attack, Alexander remained a powerful enemy to Paul and a present threat to Timothy.

Beyond the warning, Paul's response is instructive: **The Lord will repay him for what he has done**. Paul follows his own prescription from Rom. 12:17–19: "Do not repay anyone evil for evil. Be careful to do what is right in the eyes of everybody. If it is possible, as far as it depends on you, live at peace with everyone. Do not take revenge, my friends, but leave room for God's wrath, for it is written: 'It is mine to avenge; I will repay,' says the Lord."

## DELIVERANCE FROM THE LION'S MOUTH

More painful to Paul than Alexander's opposition must have been the frightened silence of Rome's substantial Christian population at the outset of Paul's court case. Paul reports: **at my first defense, no one came to my support, but everyone deserted me**. That first defense would have been a preliminary hearing in Paul's present case and not the trial associated with his first imprisonment.

The parallels between Paul's account and Psalm 22 are remarkable, as many commentators have noted. Paul must have leaned on that psalm for the support he did not receive from his fellow Christians. Paul felt forsaken (Ps. 22:1; 2 Tim, 4:16a) but knew that he had delivered **from the lion's mouth** (Ps. 22:21; 2 Tim. 4:17c) so that a universal witness could be given for God (Ps. 22:27; 2 Tim. 4:17b), with His **kingdom** in view (Ps. 22:28; 2 Tim. 4:18b). Paul's words to Timothy are rooted in the psalm Christ quoted from the cross: "My God, my God, why have you forsaken me?" As Christ's death fulfilled David's prophetic psalm, so Paul's trial echoed both its personal threats and its positive trust in God's provision.

The absence of Christian supporters at Paul's hearing,

 **LIFE CHANGE**

PERSEVERANCE

Athanasius was the champion of biblical truth at the historic Council of Nicea in A.D. 325. Thanks largely to him, the church officially committed itself to full belief in Christ's deity. But palace intrigue combined with the Roman emperor's shallow theological understanding to threaten Nicea's landmark declaration of faith. Incredibly, Athanasius was discredited in the halls of power and exiled far from home. He was later recalled, only to be exiled again and then again. His refusal to play politics with the truth led to a popular epithet, *Athanasius contra mundum—* Athanasius against the world.

Sometimes loneliness is the price of principle. But the Lord stands by the faithful, as Paul testifies in 2 Tim. 4:17, and He will not let their sacrifice be forgotten.

though disheartening, was more than compensated for by the Lord's presence. **The Lord stood at my side and gave me strength**, Paul exults . . . **and I was delivered from the lion's mouth**. *Lion* is a figure of speech and does not refer to the lions of the arena. As a Roman citizen, Paul would have been exempted from the blood games in which lions literally devoured many Christians. It may be that Nero, a considerably more powerful enemy than Alexander the metalworker, is the lion to whom Paul refers. Or it may be Satan (see 1 Pet. 5:8). Neither is a match for Paul's Master, who will **rescue [him] from every evil attack and will bring [him] safely to [the] heavenly kingdom**, even though that rescue might be, as Paul's was, a spiritual rather than a physical one.

Paul's response to his situation also has striking similarities to Christ's. Paul not only was tried unfairly, feeling lonely, and strengthened by heaven's resources, just as Christ was, but he also imitated Christ in praying for those who caused his pain.[10]

For Paul, a doxology was in order, and he included one: **To him be glory for ever and ever. Amen.**

## 2. THE NETWORK OF THE FAITHFUL 4:19–21

Paul usually closed his letters with a transfer of greetings, and he saw no reason to discard the practice even under difficult circumstances. Many of the names are familiar.

He would not miss a chance to send greetings to **Priscilla and Aquila**, with whom Paul had worked both in ministry and in tentmaking, and to whom he owed a great deal. They had risked their lives for him (Rom. 16:3–5). Priscilla and Aquila appear and reappear throughout the New Testament—at Corinth (Acts 18:2), at Rome (Rom. 16:3–5), and at Ephesus (Acts 18:18–26). (See the notes on 1 Timothy 2 for a discussion of Priscilla's contribution to the church.)

**Onesiphorus** was faithful to both Paul and Christ (see 2 Tim. 2:16–19). The reference to **the household of Onesiphorus** (see also 1:16) suggests that he might have been deceased at the time of Paul's writing and has been taken as scriptural support for the practice of offering prayers for the dead. That is unwarranted; see the notes on 2 Tim. 1:16–18 for a full discussion.

**Erastus** is described in Rom. 16:23 as the city treasurer at Corinth, and archaeological evidence has confirmed the identification. Paul informs Timothy that Erastus **stayed in Corinth**, perhaps having accompanied Paul that far on his journey to Rome. Paul had earlier sent Timothy to Macedonia with a Christian named Erastus (Acts 19:22), perhaps the same man.

Timothy would have been interested to know that Paul **left Trophimus sick in Miletus.** Ephesus was Trophimus's hometown. He had accompanied Paul on part of his third missionary journey. It was the false rumor that Paul had taken the Gentile Trophimus into the Jewish courts of the Temple that had resulted in Paul's first arrest, years earlier.

Finally, four Roman Christians sent their salutations to Timothy: **Eubulus, Pudens, Linus, and Claudia.** Linus may have become the first Bishop of Rome later in the first century.

While writing these greeting, Paul can't help intensifying his plea: **Do your best to get here before winter.** Not only was he anxious to see Timothy, and the sooner the better, but winter would close the Adriatic to shipping, blocking Timothy's route to Rome. If his spiritual son were unable to come soon, Paul knew, he might never see him again.

### ENDNOTES

1. John R. W. Stott, *The Message of 2 Timothy* (Downers Grove, Ill.: InterVarsity Press, 1973), p. 117.

2. William Barclay, *The Letters of Timothy, Titus, and Philemon*, The Daily Study Bible (Philadelphia: The Westminster Press, 1960), p. 244.

3. J. N. D. Kelly, *The Pastoral Epistles* (Peabody, Mass.: Hendrickson Publishers, 1960), p. 213.

4. The Greek tense used here is *epistolary aorist*, and it is to be understood from the perspective of the recipient of a letter. Paul may not have sent Tychicus by the time the words were written, but by the time Timothy reads them, Tychicus will have been sent. See Kelly, *Pastoral Epistles*, 214.

5. *Agape* is not always holy love. See Guthrie, Donald. *The Pastoral Epistles*, The Tyndale New Testament Commentaries, vol. 14. Grand Rapids,

Michigan: Wm. B. Eerdmans Publishing Company, 1957), p.172.

6. Kelly, *Pastoral Epistles*, 211.

7. By *cloak*, Paul could mean a covering for the scrolls and parchments he has also requested. It seems more likely, however, that he refers to a personal outer garment.

8. Stott, *Message of 2 Timothy*, p. 119.

9. Guthrie, *Pastoral Epistles*, pp. 173–174; Stott, *Message of 2 Timothy*, p. 122; Barclay, *Letters of Timothy*, p. 252.

10. Oden, *First and Second Timothy*, p. 181.

# 7

# AN APOSTOLIC BENEDICTION

## 2 Timothy 4:22

P aul's final prayer is benedictory but not perfunctory. He intends to do far more than end the letter with a formulaic closing, a Christian version of "Sincerely Yours."

Paul's prayer for Timothy (the pronoun, *you*, is singular in Greek) is, **The Lord be with your spirit**. The Lord who stood with Paul so wonderfully at his first hearing, the Lord who supported him when no one else would, the Lord who opened a door for the message to be fully proclaimed in the city that prided itself as being the center of the world, may that Lord be with you, Paul wrote, and do for you what He has done for me.

Paul's prayer for the Ephesian Christians (here the *you* is plural) is that God's grace will sustain them. Underneath all that Paul has written is the grace of God. For Paul, grace is always foremost, never an afterthought. As he opened the letter with a salutation of "grace, mercy, and peace," so he closes it on a grace note: **Grace be with you**.

Those are the last recorded words of the Apostle Paul.

# PREFACE TO TITUS & PHILEMON

To write a commentary on any part of God's Word is both a great privilege and a daunting responsibility. Most Christians have an opinion on the meaning of Scripture, but if that opinion is to be grounded in truth, based on careful research, and faithful to the traditions of the church, one must approach the task of commenting on the Bible very cautiously.

The aim of this commentary is to assist laypersons and ministers in the various teaching ministries of the church. Consequently, I have kept this question in mind while writing this commentary: Will these words be helpful to those who are preparing sermons or lessons based on this passage? The reader will have to judge whether I have been successful in meeting this standard.

After thirty years of pastoral ministry and a few years in church administration, I am struck afresh with the relevance of the Apostle Paul's words, uttered nearly two millennia ago. My current assignment as a district superintendent has provided a laboratory for testing the very principles Paul has written. Although we live in a technologically complicated world, human nature hasn't changed much over the centuries. As was the case when Paul wrote to Titus, the church continues to need qualified leaders, must still confront error, and must continually emphasize the vital connection between conduct and character. While we seldom deal directly with slavery in present-day North America, we still need to receive one another as brothers and sisters in Christ—as Paul urged Philemon to do—regardless of age, race, social status, or ethnic background.

I would like to thank Donald D. Cady, general publisher for The Wesleyan Church, for offering this assignment to me. Since I am one of those people who can't not write, I welcomed the opportunity. Gratitude goes also to Stephen J. Lennox, my theological editor, for his many helpful insights and suggestions, and to Lawrence Wilson, for his editorial advice and encouragement. Further, I wish to thank Carol, my wife, for her constant encouragement. I appreciate the sacrifices she made during those times when I was absorbed by this project. I am grateful for her helpful suggestions, and I dedicate this project to her, with affection and appreciation.

RONALD C. MCCLUNG

Charles City, Iowa
December 2003

# TITUS

# INTRODUCTION
# TO TITUS

t would be easy to overlook the book of Titus. At first glance, one might be tempted to see it simply a smaller version of 1 Timothy. There are many points of comparison between the two letters. Only the introduction to Titus (1:1–4), the conclusion (3:12–15), and two other passages (2:11–14 and 3:3–7) have no points of correspondence with Paul's better-known pastoral letter.

Although it is similar to 1 Timothy in some ways, Titus is unique. It is shorter than 1 Timothy, and it contains fewer personal references. While the first letter to Timothy stresses sound doctrine, the letter to Titus emphasizes the Christian behavior that rises from sound doctrine. The author insists that Christian behavior is directly affected by Christian belief; solid truth and pure conduct go hand in hand. In fact, D. Edmond Hiebert asserts, "Nowhere else does Paul more forcefully urge the essential connection between evangelical truth and the purest morality than in this brief letter."[1] The letter to Titus also strongly emphasizes the regenerating work of the Holy Spirit and the importance of heart purity (1:15; 2:5, 14).

## AUTHORSHIP

In the early years of the church and for many centuries afterward, Bible scholars and readers alike commonly accepted Paul as the author of the letter to Titus. After all, he is identified as the author in the letter's opening line.

However, in 1835 F. C. Baur rejected Paul's authorship of all three Pastoral Epistles (1 Timothy, 2 Timothy, and Titus), and many scholars since then have echoed that sentiment. One of the objections to Pauline authorship of Titus is based on historical grounds. Nowhere in the book of Acts does Luke tell us that Paul ever visited Crete, as Titus 1:5 implies. A simple response to this objection is that Paul was likely released from prison following the events recorded in the book of Acts, after which he embarked on various missions, perhaps including a visit to Crete.

A second objection centers on the vocabulary used in Titus. The author of this letter uses a number of words not found in Paul's other epistles; critics argue, therefore, that the letter doesn't sound like Paul. It is possible, though, that Paul used an amanuensis, or secretary, when writing to Titus. This amanuensis may have been given the freedom to express Paul's thoughts in other words, subject to the apostle's final approval. John R. W. Stott writes, "We expect that the amanuensis contributed enough to explain the variations in style and language, but not enough to take over from Paul either the authorship or the authority of the letters."[2]

There are similarities between the vocabulary used in the Pastoral Epistles and the books of Luke and Acts, suggesting that Luke may have been Paul's amanuensis when he wrote this letter. That may be the case; however, even without the use of a secretary, the communication style of a preacher or teacher often changes over time. There is no reason to think that Paul could not have written in a different style toward the end of his ministry than he did near the beginning.

A third objection to Paul's authorship centers on the church polity implied in this letter. The reference to elders and overseers (1:5–7) seems to indicate the existence of a hierarchy that was not present in the church until decades after this letter is supposed to have been written. Thus, critics assert, Paul could not have written it. Other scholars answer this objection by pointing out that in the Pastoral Epistles, Paul used the terms *elder*, *bishop*, and *overseer* interchangeably; therefore, they do not necessarily imply a highly organized form of church government. Paul wrote to stipulate the qualifications for church leaders, regardless of what they may have been called at that early stage of church development.

A fourth and final objection to Pauline authorship of Titus focuses on the theology of the letter. Critics cite its supposedly inferior emphasis on the gospel, its purportedly low sense of Christian ethics, and its less-than-hopeful reference to the end times. Some assert that the emphasis on the gospel in this letter is weak compared to that in Romans, Galatians,

Colossians, and Philippians. However, in Titus 2:11–13 and 3:3–7, the author refers to salvation, rebirth, justification, and eternal life, linking all to Jesus Christ and His sacrificial death on our behalf.

Some say that this writer's view of Christian ethics is on a much lower plane than would be typical of the Apostle Paul. For instance, the instructions to overseers in 1:6–9 and the admonition to say no to ungodly passions in 2:12 sound more like the teaching of Stoics than Pauline instructions for leaders. But if these admonitions seem weaker than those written elsewhere by Paul, that may be because Titus had worked closely with Paul, and the apostle did not feel that he needed to spell these matters out in detail. The younger man may have been quite capable of elaborating on his mentor's teaching, giving them fuller expression to the Cretan leaders.

Regarding the eschatology of this letter, it is brief, but nonetheless hopeful. While eschatology is not a major emphasis, the writer does communicate hopeful anticipation about the Second Coming of Christ (2:12–14).

With respect for those who disagree, this commentary maintains a strong belief that the Apostle Paul wrote the letter to Titus.

## RECIPIENT

Even a mighty Christian soldier such as the Apostle Paul could not wage battles on all fronts at the same time. When he needed to dispatch a trusted lieutenant to a troubled church in a distant location, he selected Titus for the job. Commissioned under Paul's own authority, Titus represented the apostle, conveying his instructions and enforcing Christian doctrine in a difficult setting. Apparently, Titus was not plagued with Timothy's timidity (2 Tim. 1:7) nor his physical weakness (1 Tim. 5:23), as Paul does not refer to such personal issues in this letter. Gifted with a sturdy temperament and stalwart faith, Titus represented Paul admirably in both Corinth and Crete.

Titus is not mentioned at all in the book of Acts. To find his story, we must search the few references to him in Paul's letters: Galatians, 2 Corinthians, 2 Timothy, and, of course, Titus itself.

## BIOGRAPHY OF TITUS

| Event | Reference |
|---|---|
| Probably converted at Antioch | Acts 11:19–30 |
| A Greek by birth | Gal. 2:3 |
| Accompanied Paul and Barnabas to Jerusalem | Gal. 2:1–3 |
| Twice served as Paul's ambassador to Corinth | 2 Cor. 7:5–15; 8:6, 16–24 |
| Served as church leader in Crete | Titus 1:5 |
| Presumably spent the winter with Paul in Nicopolis | Titus 3:12 |
| Went to Dalmatia, probably at Paul's direction | 2 Tim. 4:10 |

Titus first appears, chronologically, in Galatians 2, where Paul reveals that Titus accompanied him and Barnabas to Jerusalem (vv. 1–3), where they delivered the gift from the believers in Antioch for the relief of suffering Judean Christians (Acts 11:29–30). Some scholars believe that Titus, a Greek by birth (Gal. 2:3), was converted in Antioch under Paul's ministry, because the apostle refers to him as a "true son in our common faith" (Titus 1:4).[3] Paul uses similarly affectionate terms referring to other converts (1 Cor. 4:14–15; Philem. 10). Paul and Barnabas had an extensive ministry in Antioch, where a great number of people came to know the Lord (Acts 11:19–26). This occurred just prior to their Jerusalem trip, upon which Titus accompanied them (Acts 11:27–30; Gal. 2:3). Titus was probably older than Timothy (see comments on 2:15).

Prior to this visit to Jerusalem, Paul had been evangelizing Gentiles. There was some question about whether the leaders of the church in Jerusalem would validate or condemn such ministry. Paul took Titus along as a flesh-and-blood example of a Gentile saved by grace. He knew it would be much more difficult to reject a Gentile convert than question or condemn the practice of evangelizing Gentiles. The church leaders in Jerusalem accepted Titus into their fellowship, even though he was not circumcised. They not only refused to require that Titus be circumcised but also accepted and endorsed Paul's ministry to the Gentiles (Gal. 2:9).

Some scholars think Titus accompanied Paul on at least some of his missionary ventures, although we read no more of him until the apostle's first visit to Ephesus during his third missionary journey.[4] While at Ephesus, Paul had several assistants, and Titus was likely among them (Acts 19:22).[5] It was probably from Ephesus that Paul dispatched Titus to Corinth with a letter to the Christians there. It is unclear whether that epistle was 1 Corinthians or some other letter (2 Cor. 2:3–4; 7:8).

When Paul left Ephesus, he went to Troas to evangelize. Although he found an open door for ministry, his heart was heavy because Titus had not arrived from Corinth as expected (2 Cor. 2:12–13). Continuing into Macedonia, Paul was restless until Titus, returning from Corinth, encountered the apostle with good news. Adding to the joy of the reunion was the younger man's report on the good reception he had received from the Corinthians. He told Paul how the Corinthians longed for him and had "ardent concern" for him. Titus was pleased that the Corinthians were amenable to Paul's instruction, even though they had earlier shown a disobedient spirit. These reports brought great joy to Paul's heart (2 Cor. 7:5–7, 13–15).

At some later date, the apostle sent Titus again to Corinth, with a two-fold mission. One was to carry the letter we know as 2 Corinthians, and the other was to collect the offering for the poor believers in Judea. Titus had grown to love the Corinthians. Paul said the younger man's concern for them was the same as his own (2 Cor. 8:16). Although Titus, whom Paul calls a "partner and fellow worker" (v. 23), went at the apostle's bidding, the younger man undertook the mission with great enthusiasm and, Paul adds, even "on his own initiative" (v. 17). Lest Paul should be accused of exploiting the Corinthians through the collection of this offering, he sent two others with Titus (2 Cor. 8:18–22; 12:17–18). Paul was not worried about how Titus would handle the money; he had absolute faith in the young man's ability and integrity. But to remove any question about his own handling of the offering, Paul created a system of checks and balances for himself, a wise procedure for anyone who handles the church's money.

Still later, presumably after Paul was released from his first Roman imprisonment, he traveled to various places, apparently leaving Timothy at Ephesus and Titus on the island of Crete (Titus 1:5). Paul made only one recorded visit to Crete prior to this, which came while he was under arrest and being transported to Rome for trial (Acts 27:7–16). When the wind blew his ship off course, it was forced to sail around the south side of Crete. With much difficulty, the sailors eased along the coast of Crete, arriving at Fair Havens, near the town of Lasea. Paul warned the centurion in charge, along with the pilot and the owner of the ship, not to proceed. They ignored his warning and attempted to make the harbor of Phoenix, a city on the southwest coast of Crete. That too proved impossible as the wind drove them away from the island.

At some point following his second visit to Crete, this one made while free and accompanied by Titus, Paul wrote a letter to his young associate, instructing him to appoint elders, complete what had not yet been done (Titus 1:6), teach appropriate Christian behavior (2:1), and remind the people of their civic responsibilities (3:1).

Paul urged Titus to join him for the winter at Nicopolis, a city on the Adriatic coast (3:12). We assume Titus did so. Then from Nicopolis, or perhaps from some other location, Paul sent his trusted lieutenant on still another mission, this one to Dalmatia (modern-day Croatia), farther north on the Adriatic coast (2 Tim. 4:10).

There is no further record in Scripture of Titus or his activities. According to Christian tradition, he later revisited Crete, became the first bishop of the church on that island, and lived for many years. Piecing together the brief references we have, it is easy to see that Paul held Titus in high esteem, not only as a son in the faith, but as a trustworthy ambassador, faithful teacher, and effective Christian leader.

## DATE OF WRITING

The date of this letter cannot be named with absolute certainty. It seems likely that Paul's first imprisonment in Rome occurred sometime between A.D. 59 and 63, and Titus appears to have been written after that. Reports from the early church indicate that Paul's death occurred at the hands of the emperor Nero, who himself committed suicide in A.D. 68. So Titus must have been written before that date. Most scholars believe Paul wrote Titus between the two letters to Timothy. If 2 Timothy was written no later than A.D. 67, and if Paul traveled to Crete after release from his first imprisonment, it seems likely that Titus was written sometime between A.D. 63 and 66.

## PURPOSE

Paul wrote to Titus for two reasons. One was that Zenas the lawyer and Apollos were on their way through Crete, and it was convenient for Paul to send a letter to his protégé along with them (Titus 3:13). The second and more important reason was that Paul wanted to strengthen Titus for dealing with problems in the churches on Crete. Along with appointing leaders in each of the churches on the island, Titus was to straighten out problems that the apostle had observed but was unable to deal with adequately in his apparently brief visit (Titus 1:5).

The island of Crete lies in the Mediterranean Sea, about eighty miles southeast of Greece. (See the map on page 36.) Crete was thickly populated; historians estimate that it held up to a million residents in ancient times, and Roman scholar Pliny said there were a hundred famous cities on the island. The inhabitants of Crete were also well known; they had a reputation for being liars. To say that someone was "Cretising" meant that he was lying. The expression "playing the Cretan with a Cretan" meant trying to out-trick a trickster. Cretans were considered greedy and dishonest, and they did not seem ashamed of that reputation.

It is not certain how the churches on Crete were established, but Paul's brief tour of the island convinced him that the inhabitants lived up to their negative reputation. Against that degraded culture, Paul wanted Titus to call believers to a true Christian lifestyle. This letter gave Titus the standing to teach with the full authority of the apostle behind him.

## MAJOR THEMES

A few major themes emerge from this brief letter. One is the qualification for church leadership. Paul's list (Titus 1:6–9), along with 1 Tim. 3:1–13, has served as a sort of handbook on the qualities of a Christian leader.

Another major emphasis is the rebuking of false teachers and rebellious people. In Titus 1:10–16, Paul gives Titus full authority to chastise such persons.

Also, Paul stresses the importance of instruction for all age groups and social classes, specifying what Titus is to teach to each group (Titus 2:1–10). Paul's concern for practical Christian living is evident in this letter as well. No fewer than five time, he challenges believers to "do what is good" (2:7, 14; 3:1, 8, 14). Along with instructions for good behavior, Paul gives the theological basis for such teaching. He makes it clear that the reason we are to be eager to do what is good is that our Lord Jesus Christ "gave himself for us to redeem us from all wickedness and to purify for himself a people that are his very own, eager to do what is good" (2:14). The theology of this letter includes a strong emphasis on salvation and on renewal by the Holy Spirit (2:11–14; 3:4–7). Paul stresses that our relationship with God comes not through our own good works, but through God's grace, manifested in Jesus Christ (2:11; 3:5, 7).

Holy living emerges also as a strong theme in this letter. The advice to church leaders contains specific instructions to be blameless, self-controlled, holy, upright, and disciplined (1:6–8). Paul urges Titus to instruct all people to live self-controlled lives (2:2, 5, 6, 12); purity is what every believer must pursue (2:5, 14).

### ENDNOTES

1. D. Edmond Hiebert, *Titus,* The Expositor's Bible Commentary: Ephesians through Philemon (Grand Rapids, Mich.: Zondervan, 1981), p. 424.

2. John R.W. Stott, *Guard the Truth: The Message of 1 Timothy and Titus* (Downers Grove, Ill.: InterVarsity Press, 1996), p. 32.

3. Hiebert, *Titus*, p. 421.

4. Stott, *Guard the Truth*, p. 171.

5. Hiebert, *Titus*, p. 422.

# OUTLINE OF TITUS

**I. Address and Greeting (1:1–4)**
   A. The Writer and His Ministry (1:1–3)
      1. Faith of God's Elect (1:1a)
      2. Knowledge of the Truth (1:1b)
      3. Hope of Eternal Life (1:2–3)
   B. The Reader (1:4a)
   C. The Greeting (1:4b)

**II. Character and Conduct of Leaders (1:5–16)**
   A. Understanding the Two-Fold Challenge (1:5)
   B. Appointing Qualified Leaders (1:6–9)
      1. Family Matters (1:6)
      2. Vices to Avoid (1:7)
      3. Virtues to Pursue (1:8)
      4. A Firm Grip on the Truth (1:9)
   C. Correcting False Teachers (1:10–16)
      1. Their Behavior (1:10–11)
      2. Their Reputation (1:12)
      3. Their Rebuke (1:13–14)
      4. Their Motivation (1:15)
      5. Their Hypocrisy (1:16)

**III. Character and Conduct of Various Groups (2:1–10)**
   A. Titus' Two-fold Assignment (2:1)
   B. The Various Groups (2:2–10)
      1. Older Men (2:2)
      2. Older Women (2:3)
      3. Younger Women (2:4–5)
      4. Young Men (2:6)
      5. Titus Himself (2:7–8)
      6. Slaves (2:9–10)

## IV. Doctrinal Basis for Moral Behavior (2:11–15)

A. The Grace of God (2:11–12)

    1. What Grace Brings (2:11)

    2. What Grace Teaches (2:12)

B. The Blessed Hope (2:13)

C. The Redeeming Christ (2:14)

    1. Redeeming (2:14a)

    2. Purifying (2:14b)

    3. Instilling Eagerness to Do Good (2:14c)

D. Restatement of Titus's Responsibility (2:15)

## V. Character and Conduct in the Marketplace (3:1–11)

A. How We Ought to Live (3:1–2)

B. How We Used to Live (3:3)

C. Why We Changed (3:4–6)

    1. He Saved Us (3:4–5a)

    2. He Gave Us a Rebirth (3:5b)

    3. He Renewed Us (3:5c–6)

D. What We Become (3:7–8)

E. What We Must Avoid (3:9–11)

## VI. Closing Remarks (3:12–15)

A. Appeal to Titus (3:12)

B. Reminder to Help Others (3:13)

C. Rationale for Doing Good (3:14)

D. Final Greetings (3:15)

# ADDRESS AND GREETING

## Titus 1:1-4

P aul begins his letter to Titus, in the custom of the day, by stating three things: the identity of the writer, the identity of the reader, and a greeting. Paul's introduction, however, is different from most of his letters in that it is relatively long, especially for a letter as brief as this one. Only Paul's letter to the Romans has a longer address and greeting. Most commentators, after acknowledging that this prologue is unusually lengthy, agree with Gordon Fee, who writes, "What is less clear is the reason for such an elaboration in this letter."[1]

The reason might be something as simple as Paul's mood at the time of writing. It may be that the apostle simply felt inspired to elaborate on the **faith**, **knowledge**, and **hope** we enjoy in **Jesus Christ** (1:1–2). Or perhaps Paul felt that weightier introductory remarks would emphasize his authority as an apostle, an emphasis that would strengthen Titus's hand for dealing with the false teachers on Crete.

### 1. THE WRITER AND HIS MINISTRY 1:1-3

Paul introduces himself in the first line of this letter, describing himself as **a servant of God and an apostle of Jesus Christ** (1:1). This is the only place in Paul's writings where he calls himself a servant of God. Elsewhere, he identifies himself as a servant of Jesus Christ (Rom. 1:1; Gal. 1:10; Phil. 1:1).

The Greek word Paul uses for *servant* means slave. Far from being a derogatory term, it places Paul in great company. The Old Testament refers to several of its prominent prophets and leaders as the servants of God (Josh. 1:2; 24:29; Amos 3:7; Jer. 7:25). This is the first of five references to God in Paul's introduction.

While Paul was a humble servant of God, he was also an apostle of Jesus Christ. Humanly speaking, Paul may have been content with the role of servant, but the situation on Crete made it necessary to emphasize his authority as an apostle. An apostle is a messenger or ambassador, someone who has been commissioned by a ruler. Paul wrote to Titus under the authority of Jesus Christ and was not afraid to exercise that authority when needed.

These were Paul's credentials: servant and apostle. Just as an ambassador might present his credentials upon arriving at a new assignment, so Paul declares his identity at the outset of his letter to Titus, a letter that Paul knew would be read by others. He was a humble servant of God, but one who would boldly declare God's truth.

Along with his credentials, Paul states the purpose of his ministry. He was called for **the faith of God's elect** (v. 1), **the knowledge of the truth that leads to godliness** (v. 1), and **the hope of eternal life** (v. 2). In other letters, Paul refers to the well-known triad of Christian graces: faith, hope, and love (1 Cor. 13:13; Col. 1:5; 1 Thess. 1:3; 5:8). Here he emphasizes faith, hope, and knowledge. The reason for Paul's subtle change is not that love was an unimportant virtue for the Cretans but that they needed the knowledge of God to combat the false teachings being propagated among them.

## FAITH OF GOD'S ELECT

Faith, to Paul, is trust in God's way of salvation. This is not faith in ourselves or in our own effort. It is faith in God's plan and in God's Son, whom He sent to be our Savior. True believers know that they are "justified by faith" (Rom. 3:28) and "not because of righteous things [they have] done" (Titus 3:5). Paul later reminds Titus that we are "justified by his grace" (3:7). When God extends his unmerited favor, we respond by putting our trust in Christ alone and are saved.

Paul further specifies that this faith is for **God's elect**. The term *elect,* meaning chosen ones, recalls ancient Israel, the nation whom God chose to be His people (Deut. 7:6; 14:2; Exod. 19:5). By calling the followers of Christ God's elect, Paul is saying that those who put their trust in Jesus are the people of God. This point may have been especially important for some Cretan churches where there was a strong Jewish element (note "the circumcision group" in Titus 1:10 and a reference to "Jewish myths" in v. 14). Paul hints at the outset of his letter that any who believe in Jesus Christ are God's chosen people, regardless of whether or not they are Jews.

## KNOWLEDGE OF THE TRUTH

Our understanding of God is not a matter of faith only but also of **knowledge** (v. 1); it is a concern of the mind as well as of the heart. Paul knew that believers cannot ride forever on a wave of emotion; they must come to grips with the truths of Christianity.

Paul's reference to knowledge implies that we know certain facts about spiritual things. We know these things because of our understanding of the Word of God. At various times, Christians have tended to ground their faith on spiritual experience rather than on knowledge of God through Scripture. Balance is always important here. A wonderful experience of God comes when we surrender our lives to Him by faith and are filled with joy and peace. There is also a growth in Christ that comes only when our minds are filled with His Word. Knowledge must be added to the experience of faith.

The knowledge of **truth** that Paul speaks of has an end: it **leads to godliness** (v. 1). We do not seek knowledge for its own sake; the goal of truth is to produce godly character in everyday life. The fruit of the Spirit—love, joy, peace, patience, kindness, goodness, faithfulness, gentleness, and self-control (Gal. 5:22–23)—are the godlike qualities that are evident in the lives of those who know the truth.

## HOPE OF ETERNAL LIFE

Our knowledge is not without foundation, Paul asserts. It rests on **the hope of eternal life** (Titus 1:2). And that hope is not merely a vague aspiration; it is solidly grounded in the trustworthiness of God. Eternal life is both our future hope and present possession. The Apostle John assures us that if we are in Christ, we have eternal life (1 John 5:12). This is not something we are uncertain about; we may *know* that we have eternal life (1 John 5:13).

To Titus, Paul makes three similar assurances about our hope of eternal life. First, God **promised [it] before the beginning of time** (Titus 1:2). What we now experience in Christ was in the mind of God before the creation of the world (Rom. 16:25–26; 1 Cor. 2:7–10; Eph. 1:4; Col. 1:25–26; 2 Tim. 1:9–10).

Second, Paul assures his reader that we can rely upon God's character, for He **does not lie** (Titus 1:2). In Greek mythology, the gods often deceived humans, and the Cretans themselves were known as dishonest (1:12). Not so with the eternal God. His character is without blemish; He always tells the truth. If God promises our ultimate salvation, and He does (see Gen. 3:15), we may be sure that it will be accomplished.

Third, Paul affirms that God has finally revealed our hope. **At his appointed season he brought his word to light** (Titus 1:3). Designed in eternity, this great hope was manifested in time. Eugene Peterson puts it this way: "When the time was ripe, he went public with his truth" (Titus 1:3 The Message).

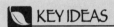

## KEY IDEAS

### GOD'S TIMING

Paul told the Galatians that "when the time had fully come, God sent his Son, born of a woman, born under law" (Gal. 4:4). The Roman world of the first century was ready for the gospel of Christ. Because of the earlier conquests of Alexander the Great, almost the whole world around the Mediterranean spoke Greek. There were few borders or hindrances to travel; no one needed a passport. The Romans had built roads which made travel easier. The world was largely at peace, thanks to the Romans. Furthermore, people were hungry for meaning in their lives. It was God's appointed season, and through Jesus Christ He brought His word to light (Titus 1:3).

That word, God's revelation, was further disseminated **through the preaching entrusted to me** (1:3), Paul asserts. The eternal One had entrusted His timeless message to a finite human being. Paul seems awed by that realization, for he mentions this trust in each of the three Pastoral Epistles (see also 1 Tim. 1:11; 2 Tim. 1:11). When any preacher or teacher stands before a congregation, he or she holds a trust from God. Those who communicate God's message must never lose their sense of wonder over this sacred responsibility.

Paul's commission to preach the Word came **by the command of God our Savior** (Titus 1:3). The strength of the word *command* underlines the authority by which Paul wrote to Titus. The phrase God our

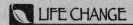

### LIFE CHANGE

#### THE GOAL OF MINISTRY

If every preacher, teacher, and Bible study leader adopted Paul's instructions to Titus as the purpose of his or her ministry, what a difference it would make for the church! When we make it our goal to build stronger faith in the hearts of our listeners, increase their knowledge of the truth, and instill the hope of eternal life within them, the church will thrive!

Savior is not used by Paul outside the Pastoral Epistles. Its use here seems to refer to God the Father, although the term *savior* is more often applied to the Son (as in v. 4).

When Paul uses unique terms such as *servant of God* and *God our Savior*, we may assume that these variations from his usual manner of speech are not accidental. Paul may have been sensitive to his audience and purposely chose terms that would resonate better with them. If so, he sets a good example for all who endeavor to communicate God's Word.

## THE READER 1:4A

Paul addressed his letter to **Titus,** calling him **my true son in our common faith** (1:4). The endearing term indicates an intimate relationship between the two. The Greek word translated *son* literally means child. It was not uncommon for rabbis and philosophers of that time to refer to their students as their children. Paul's use of that term here implies that Titus was converted under Paul's ministry.

The word *true* implies the legitimacy of Titus's spiritual heritage; he was a true son because he faithfully followed the true faith that had been passed on to him. Paul's reference to **our common faith** is a reminder that although Paul was a Jew and Titus a Greek, there was no distinction between them (see Gal 3:28). Faith is the common possession of all believers (Jude 3).

# THE GREETING 1:4B

Paul's greeting to Titus is brief but significant, invoking a blessing that was characteristic to his letters, **grace and peace** (1:4). The apostle employs this duet in all known epistles except 1 and 2 Timothy, where he adds one virtue to make the triad "grace, mercy and peace" (1 Tim. 1:2; 2 Tim. 1:2).

**Grace** refers to the unmerited favor of God, and **peace** indicates the harmony and well-being that result from a right relationship with Him.

Paul declares that the source of these blessings is **God the Father and Christ Jesus our Savior** (1:4). In v. 3 Paul refers to God our Savior. Here in v. 4, he calls Jesus our Savior. Both statements are accurate. God is the source of our salvation, and He graciously bestows it through His Son, our Savior, Jesus Christ.

### ENDNOTES

1. Gordon D. Fee, *1 and 2 Timothy, Titus,* New International Biblical Commentary (Peabody, Mass.: Hendrickson Publishers, Inc., 1988), p. 167.

# 2

# CHARACTER AND CONDUCT OF LEADERS

## Titus 1:5–16

Titus was the appointed leader of the churches on Crete. But the real measure of his leadership would be his performance, not the position Paul had given him. Titus faced a two-fold challenge as a leader. Paul wrote to his protégé in order to strengthen his hands for dealing with that challenge.

## 1. UNDERSTANDING THE TWO-FOLD CHALLENGE 1:5

When Paul left **Crete** so he could attend to other responsibilities, he **left** Titus there (v. 5), and he did so with a specific purpose. Titus was instructed to **straighten out what was left unfinished and appoint elders in every town** (v. 5). The second task, appointing elders, indicates that churches were already in existence on the island at the time of Paul's visit; but how had they come to be established?

Cretans were present in Jerusalem on the day of Pentecost (see Acts 2:11). It is reasonable to assume that some of them were among the three thousand souls who accepted Peter's message and were baptized that day (Acts 2:41). Presumably, Cretan Christians returned home after Pentecost, bearing with them the message of salvation through Jesus Christ.

Paul's later visit to the island was apparently brief, for he had to leave some business **unfinished**. Titus was to remain and **straighten [it] out** (Titus

1:5). The letter reveals several problems that needed attention. Organization was lacking because the churches did not have adequate leadership (v. 5), there were false teachers who needed to be corrected (1:10, 11; 3:10, 11), and the believers needed both doctrinal and moral instruction (2:1–10; 3:1–2).

The first task for Titus would be the appointment of elders in every town. The term *elder* appears to be used interchangeably with *overseer* in the Pastoral Epistles (see Introduction). Paul says much about the qualifications for elders but little about their responsibilities. We do know that elders were leaders in the church. Without leadership, both people and organizations lose their sense of purpose. In the church, new believers are easily led astray by false teaching if there is no one to oversee their spiritual condition. Given the false teaching afoot on Crete, the task of appointing leaders was especially urgent.

## 2. APPOINTING QUALIFIED LEADERS 1:6–9

Paul lists for Titus several qualifications for church leaders. This passage is similar to 1 Tim. 3:1–7. Both name fifteen characteristics for church leaders; some of the characteristics listed in Titus are identical to those in 1 Timothy, some are similar, and some are different. It is interesting, too, that Paul **directed** Titus to appoint elders (Titus 1:5), whereas for Timothy, Paul simply listed the required qualities of an elder. Also, the list in Titus seems better organized in that family matters are mentioned first, followed by five vices to be avoided, and then six virtues to be pursued. In Titus, Paul calls the leaders **elders** (1:6). In 1 Timothy, Paul uses the term *overseers*, which also appears in Titus (1:7).

The office of elder has its roots in the Old Testament. The word *elder* means, literally, bearded one. Even today in some cultures, older men typically wear beards, and a man with a gray beard is treated with great respect. In Old Testament times, every town had its group of elders who sat at the city gate, where important decisions were made. Elders were distinguished for their maturity and wisdom. Paul urges Titus to find the most mature, wisest men to lead the churches **in every town** (v. 5). Larger cities on the island may have had more than one congregation, all of them meeting in homes.

The first qualification for an elder is that he **must be blameless** (1:6). That does not mean perfect or faultless, for that would have eliminated all candidates. Rather, an elder was to be a person of, "unquestioned integrity," as J. B. Phillips puts it.[1] Leaders in God's church were to be people who had a lifestyle and reputation that were beyond reproach. Blameless character would be indicated by four things: an orderly family life, the avoidance of vice, the pursuit of virtue, and a firm adherence to the truth.

## FAMILY MATTERS

Paul directed Titus to appoint elders who were commendable as husbands and fathers.[2] The phrase **husband of but one wife** (v. 6) has given rise to five interpretations. It may be that Paul withheld leadership from

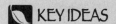

## KEY IDEAS

### CHRISTIAN LEADERSHIP

We first encounter elders in the New Testament in Acts 11:30, where they are leaders in the Jerusalem church. In Acts 14:23, we see that Paul and Barnabas appointed elders in each church they founded. The responsibilities of these elders included directing the affairs of the church (1 Tim. 5:17), shepherding and guarding the church (Acts 20:28–31; 1 Pet. 5:1–4), anointing the sick with oil (James 5:14), and teaching and preaching (1 Tim. 5:17).

Church leaders have been chosen by a variety of means. In the early church, apostles or their fellow workers, such as Timothy and Titus, appointed elders. Deacons were chosen by the church (Acts 6). The Holy Spirit selected Paul and Barnabas (Acts 13:1–3), and the church confirmed them by the laying on of hands. The church even selected one leader, Matthias the successor to Judas, by casting lots (Acts 1:23–26).

Churches continue to use various methods of appointing leaders. Some churches elect them; others appoint them. The Bible does not stipulate a single *method* for choosing leaders but does list the *qualifications* of Christian leaders.

(1) those who had never been married, (2) those who were widowed and had remarried, (3) those who were married but had been unfaithful, (4) those who practiced polygamy, or (5) those who had been married and divorced. Given the cultural context of the first century, it is most likely that Paul meant to exclude from leadership those who practiced polygamy. In any age, those entrusted with the care of God's elect must demonstrate integrity in their moral character.

Furthermore, a Christian leader was to give appropriate oversight to his **children** (1:6). If an elder's own children do not **believe**, Paul seems to reason, how could he hope to influence others for Christ? It was important, too, that an elder's children not be seen as **wild and disobedient** (v. 6). The Greek word translated *wild* is the same one used to describe the prodigal son, who "squandered his wealth in wild living" (Luke 15:13). Fairly or unfairly, the behavior of a profligate child is often taken as an indictment of his or her parents. Paul knew that reckless behavior by children of elders would cast aspersions also on the church.

For how long is a parent responsible for the behavior of his or her offspring? Would the unchristian behavior of adult children disqualify a person for church leadership? In the Roman world, sons were obliged to respect their fathers, who had legal authority over them as long as they lived. However, while the Greek word translated here as *children* is occasionally used to indicate adult offspring, it usually refers to minors who are still under the supervision of their parents. Paul was concerned that a parent's ability to properly discipline his children would affect his reputation both within the church and in the world. It is still a valid concern.

## VICES TO AVOID

Next, Paul lists several vices that a Christian leader must avoid. At the head of this list, Paul uses the term **overseer** (v. 7) in place of *elder* (v. 6). He seems to use these terms interchangeably; however, they are different words and refer to different aspects of the leader's work. *Elder* speaks of the leader's maturity and dignity while *overseer* indicates his role as a shepherd over the flock of God.

Paul reminds Titus that overseers are **entrusted with God's work** (v. 7). The phrase evokes a comparison between an overseer in the church and a steward. A steward was the manager of an estate that belonged to someone else. The comparison reminds us that the church is not the personal property of its leaders; their management of its affairs must be carried out under the lordship of Jesus Christ.

In addition to being **blameless**, an overseer must avoid being **overbearing** (v. 7). This negative trait is found in the leader who disregards the needs of others. Contemptuous of those entrusted to his care, he obstinately pushes his own agenda, taking little heed of the viewpoints of others. That is no way for a leader in God's church to behave, Paul reminds Titus.

Another potential pitfall is the tendency among some leaders to be **quick-tempered** (v. 7). There are two Greek words for anger. One indicates a flash of anger—anger that flares up quickly and then dies down. The other word, the one used here, indicates a slow burn—anger that, once kindled, remains hot for a long time. It is a seething, ongoing type of anger. Leaders in the church should be even tempered, Paul says, not easily moved to anger.

The leader must not be **given to drunkenness** (v. 7). Again Paul shows concern for the reputation of the church. Leaders with a reputation for overindulging in alcohol would set a poor example both to the church and the world. Imagine how much more volatile any of the other vices named by Paul would be if fueled by the consumption of alcohol.

According to some ancient documents, a few church leaders were so zealous that they resorted to violence in an effort to make people comply with the truth. Paul reminds Titus that the Christian leader must not be **violent** (v. 7). Our example is Jesus, who, when struck, did not strike back.

Leaders must avoid the pursuit of **dishonest gain** (v. 7). Plutarch, an ancient Greek writer, said that the Cretans "stuck to money like bees to honey."[3] Paul adamantly defended the right of those who serve the church to draw their livelihood from it (see 1 Tim. 5:17–18). However, a leader must never use a position in the church for personal advantage. Paul might have been writing about the church in any age; his advice is certainly appropriate for our day.

## VIRTUES TO PURSUE

Next, Paul next recommends six virtues for a Christian leader to pursue. First, he **must be hospitable** (v. 8). The Greek word used here means, literally, a lover of strangers. In the ancient world, inns were dirty and immoral. Even if they had been clean, the average itinerant person probably could not have afforded them, as they were expensive. The Christian world needed hospitable persons who were willing to befriend travelers—especially believers who were fleeing persecution.

Also, a church leader must be someone **who loves what is good** (v. 8). Paul is urging leaders to cherish both good things and good people. A Christian leader will not only reject what is unwholesome but also embrace what is good. Here Paul echoes his advice to the Philippian church, "Whatever is true, whatever is noble, whatever is right, whatever is pure, whatever is lovely, whatever is admirable—if anything is excellent or praiseworthy—think about such things" (Phi. 4:8–9).

The leader must also be one who is **self-controlled** (Titus 1:8). To be self-controlled means to be sober and sensible, keeping one's head. Paul stipulates self-control as a requirement for overseers also in 1 Tim. 3:2; however, the apostle must have believed that self-control was especially needed among the Cretans, for he mentions it five times in this brief letter (see also Titus 2:2, 5, 6, 12).

The Christian leader must be **upright** (1:8). That means his behavior toward others must be above reproach. He is one who behaves according to the right standard; he practices what he preaches.

Paul insists that the church leaders on Crete be **holy** (v. 8). In Scripture, things that are holy are both set apart for God and pure. The Christian is set apart, or different, from the world around him because of his desire for God. He is motivated by a strong inner desire to please God, to be pure in heart. Leaders in God's church must never be appointed or elected merely to fill positions. They must be living examples of holiness, people whose lives are dedicated to God and whose hearts have been cleansed by Him.

Finally, the leader must be **disciplined** (v. 8); he must have inner strength to resist the wrong and embrace the right. The word translated *discipline* here is the same one translated *self-control* in Gal. 5:23, Paul's list of the fruit of the Spirit. Discipline, or the ability to control our own actions, is one of the qualities produced in us when the Holy Spirit is given the freedom to work in our lives.

Each of these last three qualities in Paul's list of virtues looks in a different direction: **upright** looks toward others, **holy** looks toward God, and **disciplined** looks toward self. A Christian leader must be a well-rounded person, one who exhibits the character of Christ in all aspects of life.

## A FIRM GRIP ON THE TRUTH

In addition to maintaining correct behavior (avoiding vice and pursuing virtue), a Christian leader must maintain correct belief by **[holding] firmly to the trustworthy message as it has been taught** (Titus 1:9). Paul characterizes the message as trustworthy, or reliable. That means it is true and can be depended upon with confidence.

Paul insists that a leader hold to the message **as it has been taught**. J. B. Phillips refers to this message as "the orthodox faith."[4] Although the New Testament had not yet been assembled in its final form, it appears that there was in the early church an identifiable body of truth, communicated by the apostles, that was considered authoritative. Church leaders were expected to adhere to this teaching exactly as received, not being swayed by new doctrines or novel interpretations. By having a firm grip on the truth, a church leader proves him- or herself to be a person of stability, capable of leading God's flock.

When a leader has a firm grip on the truth, there are two results. First, he is enabled to **encourage others by sound doctrine** (v. 9). Scholars have noted that the word translated *doctrine* indicates ideas that are not merely taught but also become part of the teacher's life.[5] Holding firmly to sound doctrine causes us to live differently from those who do not know the truth or who simply know about it. What we believe affects the way we live.

The Greek word translated *sound* (v. 9) literally means healthy; it is the root of our word *hygiene*. The Gospel writers use the word to describe people who were once ill but have been made well, including the man with the withered hand (Matt. 12:13), the lame man by the pool of Bethesda (John 5:9), and the woman who had been plagued by bleeding for twelve years (Mark 5:34). Sound doctrine produces a healthy church.

The second positive result that comes from having a firm grip on the truth is that it enables leaders to **refute those who oppose it** (Titus 1:9). The word translated *refute* is variously translated as *reprove*, *rebuke*, and *convince* elsewhere in the New Testament. Clear, consistent teaching is the best antidote to false doctrine. When a leader can convincingly speak the truth, error will not stand for long.

## QUALIFICATIONS FOR CHURCH LEADERS

| Characteristic | Reference |
| --- | --- |
| Blameless (above reproach) | Titus 1:6, 7; 1 Tim. 3:2 |
| Husband of one wife | Titus 1:6; 1 Tim. 3:2, 12 |
| Children who believe (obey) | Titus 1:6; 1 Tim. 3:4–5, 12 |
| Not overbearing | Titus 1:7 |
| Not quick-tempered | Titus 1:7 |
| Not given to drunkenness | Titus 1:7; 1 Tim. 3:3, 8 |
| Not violent | Titus 1:7; 1 Tim. 3:3 |
| Not pursuing dishonest gain | Titus 1:7, 1 Tim. 3:8 |
| Hospitable | Titus 1:8; 1 Tim. 3:2 |
| Loves what is good | Titus 1:8 |
| Self-controlled | Titus 1:8; 1 Tim. 3:2 |
| Upright | Titus 1:8 |
| Holy | Titus 1:8 |
| Disciplined | Titus 1:8 |
| Holds firmly to the truth | Titus 1:9; 1 Tim. 3:9 |

Paul insisted that a Christian leader, whether known as an elder or an overseer, have a family that joined him in following Christ, avoid the vices that would sidetrack his ministry, and pursue the virtues that would enrich it. In addition to displaying a blameless lifestyle, he must keep a firm grip on the historic faith so that he could both encourage and convince others.

Paul's advice has held up well. After nearly twenty centuries, it continues to provide relevant criteria for selecting the leaders who will oversee God's church.

## 3. CORRECTING FALSE TEACHERS 1:10–16

Paul had left some business unfinished on his brief visit to Crete, and it was Titus's responsibility to "straighten [it] out" (see notes on 1:5). The most urgent task was to refute the false teachers who were propagating error on the island. Who were these false teachers? Though Paul does not name them, his comments to Titus clearly reveal both their flawed character and their false message.

## THEIR BEHAVIOR

Paul has harsh words for the false teachers of Crete. He begins his instructions to Titus concerning them by making an impressive list of their wrong behaviors. There are **many [of these] people**, Paul says (v. 10), and **they must be silenced** (v. 11).

Paul first characterizes the false teachers as **rebellious** (v. 10), using the same word translated *disobedient* in v. 6. These people, in other words, displayed the opposite character of a good elder. They were like soldiers who refused to follow orders.

Paul further describes them as **mere talkers and deceivers** (v. 10). His portrait is of people who were fluent in speech but whose speech was shallow. Further, they were bent on deception; they had the ability to fascinate others and lead them astray. Now it becomes clear why Titus was to take such care in appointing elders. Great harm might have been done if those **deceivers** had managed to gain appointment as leaders in the church.

Paul identifies the false teachers as **those of the circumcision group** (v. 10). The reference is to Jewish Christians who insisted that Gentile converts to Christianity must observe the Jewish law; in particular, they required that Gentile converts be circumcised.

The apostle emphatically declares, **They must be silenced because they are ruining whole households** (v. 11). The word picture in the original language is of using a bridle or a muzzle like those that might be used to control a horse or a barking dog. But how does one silence a false teacher? That is done by teaching the truth. Elsewhere, Paul refers to the Word of God as a weapon, "the sword of the Spirit" (Eph. 6:17).

There are three possible meanings of **household** in this passage. Paul may have been referring to individual households, or he may have meant house churches. A third possibility is that the false teaching may have been upsetting family life. Perhaps all three meanings apply. In any case, these teachers were corrupting entire groups of people, not just a few individuals.

And the motive of these teachers was materialistic. They taught **for the sake of dishonest gain** (Titus 1:11). These false teachers enriched themselves at the expense of sincere Christians, using their ministry "for the shameful purpose of making money" (TEV). One need not look far in the modern church to see that this motive continues to drive some religious leaders.

## THEIR REPUTATION

Paul's indictment of the Cretans in v. 12 seems at first to be a case of ethnic prejudice, and, as John Stott points out, "the Christian conscience is very uncomfortable with ethnic stereotypes of this kind."[6] Paul, however, is actually quoting one of the Cretans' own poets. Epimenides, who lived about 600 B.C., was a poet, prophet, and reformer highly honored by the people of Crete. He is credited with the statement that **"Cretans are always liars, evil brutes, lazy gluttons"** (v. 12).

The Cretans were so notorious for lying that the Greeks coined the word *kretizo*, which means to lie or to cheat. Some people joked that there were no wild animals on Crete because the people themselves, whom the poet described as **evil brutes** (v.12), were so wild.

We don't know what motivated Epimenides to make this judgment about his fellow Cretans, but Paul obviously agreed with the assessment. **This testimony is true**, he affirms (v. 13). And Paul had had the opportunity to verify their character by his own observation. Given the predisposition of some Cretans to be **lazy gluttons** (v. 12), it is not surprising that some among them would use the guise of religion to dupe others, both spiritually and materially.

## THEIR REBUKE

Paul's counsel on dealing with these false prophets is that Titus should **rebuke them sharply** (v. 3). The word *rebuke* is the same one translated *refute* in v. 9, where Paul says that a leader must be able to refute those who oppose sound doctrine. It is as if Paul is saying, "Titus, not only must a good leader be capable of refuting error, but you yourself must actually do so."

The rationale for the strong rebuke is **so that they will be sound in the faith** (v. 13). The goal is not simply to quiet these false teachers but to turn them away from error, to deliver them from the evil one, and, ultimately, to save their souls. Paul uses the word **sound** again in v. 9, speaking of sound doctrine; here Paul hopes that those who are rebuked may become **sound in the faith** (v. 13). A great deal of false teaching truly is sick, and it will make those who embrace it sick as well. When sick teaching is refuted with sound doctrine, spiritual health results.

Here is an example of the wonderful optimism of Christian ministry: After thoroughly discrediting the false teachers on Crete, Paul urges Titus to convert them. There is no case too hard for God; therefore, we teach, preach, and minister with confidence, believing that God's grace can deliver even the worst offenders from their sin.

Paul does not say exactly what the false teaching was either on Crete or in Ephesus (see 1 Tim. 1:4; 4:7; 2 Tim. 4:4). He does mention **Jewish myths** (Titus 1:14), which seemed to be a part of the heresy. Four times in the Pastoral Epistles, Paul mentions the fascination with myths that marks the false teachers. (See also 1 Tim. 1:4, 4:7; and 2 Tim. 4:4. The only other reference to myths in the New Testament is 2 Pet. 1:16.) Paul believed that when given sound instruction, the Cretans would turn away from these fables, which appear to have been speculative teachings based on the Old Testament. Paul did not intend to dispense with the Old Testament itself, only the fanciful conjectures that were being propagated.

Further, Paul hoped believers would ignore **the commands of those who [rejected] the truth** (Titus 1:14). It appears that some of the false teachers were promoting certain rituals, which they claimed Christians were bound to observe. These needed to be rejected because they were not truly Scripture but were based on "commandments of merely human origin" (1:14 NEB). Earlier, Jesus had condemned the Pharisees for elevating their traditions to a level equal with Scripture (Mark 7:6–9; Matt. 15:7–9).

## THEIR MOTIVATION

The false teachers on Crete were driven, in part, by a desire for easy wealth (**dishonest gain**, v. 11). In addition, **their minds and consciences [were] corrupted** (v. 15). In both the area that determines rational thought (the mind) and the area that determines moral behavior (the conscience), these teachers had been corrupted. Because of this, evil

## LIFE CHANGE

### AUTHORITY OF SCRIPTURE

Whether the subject is choosing church leaders or rebuking false teachers, the key question for the church is this: Will you accept the authority of God's Word?

A leader must hold firmly to the trustworthy message as it has been taught (Titus 1:9), and false teachers must be rebuked because they are teaching things they ought not to teach (1:11) and are disobedient (1:16). In both cases, God's Word is the authority.

We may either submit to the instruction of God's Word or refuse to surrender to its authority. By doing the former, we line up with believers throughout the ages. By the latter, we reject God's best guidance for our lives and disqualify ourselves from leadership in His church.

thoughts and actions flowed from them.

To live in purity, one must think pure thoughts, for evil behavior flows from evil thoughts. Paul points out that **to the pure, all things are pure**, but **to those who are corrupted . . . nothing is pure** (v. 15). Jesus affirmed, "Nothing outside a man can make him 'unclean' by going into him. Rather, it is what comes out of a man that makes him 'unclean'" (Mark 7:15). A person with an impure mind tends to find evil in whatever he thinks about, whatever he says, whatever he touches.

A pure mind comes by the cleansing work of the Holy Spirit; purity cannot be attained by sheer discipline. The corruption of our minds is deeply rooted; only the power of the Holy Spirit can remove it. Thankfully, that power is available to us. As Paul writes to the Romans, "Those who live according to the sinful nature have their minds set on what that nature desires; but those who live in accordance with the Spirit have their minds set on what the Spirit desires. The mind of sinful man is death, but the mind controlled by the Spirit is life and peace" (Rom. 8:5–6).

## THEIR HYPOCRISY

Paul closes his indictment of the false teachers by exposing their hypocrisy. **They claim to know God, but by their actions they deny him** (Titus 1:16). The fact that these teachers sought to enrich themselves at the expense of the people should have been proof enough that they were unreliable.

The apostle reveals three negative traits of these people: **they are detestable, disobedient and unfit for doing anything good** (v. 16). Barclay points out that the Greek word translated *unfit* is elsewhere used to describe a counterfeit coin, a soldier who fails in battle because of cowardice, a candidate who is rejected by the voters, and a stone that is cast aside because it is unfit for building.[7] These false teachers are counterfeits, thoroughly worthless as religious leaders, worthy only of being rejected by those who seek the truth.

Paul's mention of **anything good** (v. 16) is the first of six references in Titus to good works (see also 2:7, 14; 3:1, 8, 14). In contrast to these worthless hypocrites, God's people should occupy themselves with doing good things.

## ENDNOTES

1. J. B. Phillips, *The New Testament in Modern English*, Student Edition (New York: Macmillan Publishing Company, 1972), p. 449

2. The instructions in this section appear to be directed to men only, which would lead to the conclusion that women were excluded from consideration as elders. That may not have been the case. It is true that Paul appears to have had specific reasons for excluding women from leadership in certain congregations. It is equally clear that many women did serve in leadership roles in the early church. See the notes on 1 Tim. 2:9–15 for a full discussion of this issue.

3. Cited by William Barclay, *The Letters to Timothy, Titus, and Philemon*, The Daily Bible Study Series (Philadelphia, Pa.: The Westminster Press, 1975), p. 237.

4. J. B. Phillips, *The New Testament in Modern English*, Student Edition (New York: Macmillan Publishing Company, 1972), p. 450

5. A. Berkeley Mickelsen, *Interpreting the Bible* (Grand Rapids, Mich.: Wm. B. Eerdmans Publishing Company, 1963), p. 342.

6. John R. W. Stott, *Guard the Truth: The Message of 1 Timothy and Titus* (Downers Grove, Ill.: InterVarsity Press, 1996), p. 181.

7. Barclay, *Letters*, p. 246.

# 3

# CHARACTER AND CONDUCT OF VARIOUS GROUPS

## Titus 2:1–10

I n the second chapter of Titus, Paul turns his attention to building Christian character into the believers on the island of Crete. Paul's remarks here are similar to certain passages in other epistles, which have come to be known as *house codes* because they deal with relationships within a household (see Eph. 5:21–6:9; Col. 3:18–4:1, and 1 Pet. 2:18–3:7). Paul's instructions to Titus are about Christian character and conduct in a more general sense.

### 1. TITUS'S TWO-FOLD ASSIGNMENT 2:1

A major part of Titus's responsibility was to **teach what is in accord with sound doctrine** (Titus 2:1). Paul's use of the word **you** at the beginning of this admonition is emphatic. He is saying, in effect, "I have told you what these false teachers are up to, but *you*, Titus, must teach something entirely different."

Paul once again stresses the importance of sound, or healthy, teaching (see comments on 1:9). In contrast to the false teaching that had infected the churches, Titus's responsibility was to communicate truth—good spiritual food that would build strength and health into the congregations.

Paul is really instructing Titus to teach two things: **sound doctrine** and **what is in accord with** it (2:1). He further explains that doctrine in

2:11–14, but first he gives Titus instructions on applying the practical teaching that flows from it. J. B. Phillips refers to this as "the sort of character which should spring from sound teaching."[1] All teachers and preachers must recognize the importance of this two-fold responsibility: teaching the truth and applying it. It is important that believers know what is true; it is also important that they know how to live based on that truth.

## 2. THE VARIOUS GROUPS 2:2–10

Paul organizes his instructions to Titus in six categories, covering various age groups and stations in life and including Titus himself.

### OLDER MEN

Paul begins with some words for the maturing people in the local congregations, starting with **older men** (2:2). While it is difficult to mature without growing older, it is quite common for people to age without maturing. Paul's advice to Titus was aimed to help him assist older people in acting like the mature persons they are supposed to be.

The word used for **older men** is not the same one translated *elder* in 1:6, so it does not refer to an office in the church but to the relative age of the men. Paul believed that older men should be an example to others, being **worthy of respect** (2:2), not simply because of their age but because of their conduct. They were to be **temperate** (v. 2), meaning sober as opposed to drunk. That temperance was also to be seen in their general conduct and judgment, as they were to be **self-controlled** (v. 2). One mark of maturity is that the gap narrows between what one knows he ought to do and what he actually does.

Paul continues his theme of spiritual health, urging that older men be **sound in faith, in love and in endurance** (v. 2). Their faith should be strong, they should not become resentful, and they must face adversity without breaking. As the body ages, health is difficult to maintain. Among these older men, however, there was to be no spiritual flagging. The spirit can grow stronger even as the body weakens.

## OLDER WOMEN

Using the adverb **likewise**, Paul indicates that he expects similar behavior of **older women** (v. 3). But there is more. In addition to displaying the character qualities he urges upon older men, older women must show they are **reverent** (v. 3). This Greek term appears only here in the New Testament and means "suited to a sacred character."[2] Elsewhere, the word is used to describe a priestess who devotes herself to temple service. It can refer to a person or object that is consecrated to God, or it can mean to behave as a holy person. Our self-image has a direct bearing on our behavior. If all Christians thought of themselves as holy and behaved accordingly, what an impact that change in attitude might have upon a watching world.

People of all ages ought to avoid slander; no one has license to spread gossip or vicious rumors about others. But Paul makes that point a matter of special instruction for older women: they must **not be slanderers** (v. 3).

Just as Titus was to instruct older men to be temperate, so he was to admonish older women to avoid **[addiction] to much wine** (v. 3). Given the proximity of this admonition to the advice on slander, one wonders if Paul implies a connection between slander and drunkenness. Certainly, overindulgence in alcohol has a detrimental effect on relationships.

On the positive side, older women were **to teach what is good** (v. 3). The phrase **teach what is good** is a single compound word in Greek and is found only here in all of Greek literature.[3] It refers not so much to formal teaching as to being a good role model in both teaching and behavior. In contrast to the false teaching already condemned by Paul, older women were to communicate—by their words and their deeds—the positive character of a Christian. Rather than using their words to slander, older women were to use them for teaching—especially for **teaching the younger women** (v. 4).

## YOUNGER WOMEN

The word translated **younger** (v. 4) carries a nuance of newness or freshness; it may refer to women who were newly married. In his first letter to Timothy, Paul seems to assume that Timothy will instruct the young women himself (1 Tim. 5:2, 11, 14). Here Paul indicates that the older women, not Titus, will instruct **younger women**. Paul's apparent shift in policy may have something to do with the moral climate in the Cretan churches. Edmond Hiebert writes, "Naturally prone to be lax and indifferent, the Christians were adversely influenced by the prevailing low moral standards in Crete."[4] In a culture where sexual sin was rampant, Titus would have been wise to avoid the appearance of evil by refraining from close contact with younger women.

In contrast to the brief instruction given for older women, Paul lists seven points on which younger women should be instructed. The first two have to do with their **husbands and children** (v. 4). In a culture where marriages usually were arranged by the parents of the bride and groom, young wives would need the wise counsel of their older counterparts to learn how to **love their husbands** (v. 4). The older women could advise the younger also on loving their **children** (v. 4).

The next point of advice for younger women is that they be **self-controlled and pure** (v. 5). Paul urges self-control for all the age groups mentioned except older women. Perhaps, as some have suggested, Paul held the opinion that older women had diminished sexual desire and saw no need to admonish them on self-control. That seems unlikely, for he implies a need for self-control in his strong caution against slander and overindulgence in alcohol. More likely is that Paul believed an admonition to self-discipline was implied when, after urging the older men to be self-controlled, he said, **Likewise, teach the older women** (v. 3).

The instruction for the younger women to be **pure**

---

 **MANNERS AND CUSTOMS**

THE ROLE OF WOMEN

In first-century Greek culture, a woman had few options for economic support and many were forced into prostitution. Lydia managed her own business (Acts 16:13–15), but she was probably an older woman with grown children. For younger women, a career outside the home was unlikely.

Paul does not suggest that women are inferior to men, for he says elsewhere that in Christ "there is neither Jew nor Greek, slave nor free, male nor female" (Gal. 3:28). His admonition for women "to be subject to their husbands and to be busy at home" (Titus 2:5) is in keeping with the cultural expectations of the day. Paul advises women (as he has elsewhere advised men and church leaders; see 1 Tim. 2:8; 3:1–10, 12; Titus 1:5–9) to avoid behaviors that would invite criticism of the church.

(v. 5) is probably a reference to sexual purity but might also imply wholesomeness in their thought life, speech, and general conduct.

When Paul stresses these women are **to be busy at home** (2:5), he is urging women who are wives and mothers to give the home the attention it needs. By making their homes their first priority, they would not only give proper attention to their families but also avoid the dangers of idleness and gossip, which Paul condemns in 1 Tim. 5:13–14.

All Christians are **to be kind** (2:5; Eph. 4:32), but Paul specifically urges kindness as a virtue for the younger women. Unless one maintains a kind attitude, it is easy to dwell on the intentional or unintentional slights so common in family life and consequently grow irritable and harsh. The ancient writer says of the "virtuous woman" that "in her tongue is the law of kindness" (Prov. 31:26 KJV).

Paul's instruction to be **subject to their husbands** (Titus 2:5) suggests voluntary submission. While that was the typical role of a wife in the first century, Christian women in any age are not to be bitter or resentful in their submission to their husbands. Here, as with the conduct of church leaders (see notes on 1:6–9), Paul's concern is with the reputation of the gospel. If Christian women were not loving and respectful of their husbands or did not adequately care for their families, others might have occasion to **malign the word of God** (2:5). The conduct of young women would be an advertisement of the power of the gospel.

## YOUNG MEN

Paul's instruction for **young men** is brief, consisting of a single sentence (v. 6). Beginning that sentence with the word **similarly** (v. 6), Paul implies a parallel to the responsibilities already outlined for other groups. Paul tells Titus to **teach** (vv. 2, 3) the older people but to **encourage** the young men (v. 6). Encouragement may be the most useful tool when making a point from one young man to another. However, the word translated **encourage** is not a weak one. It is a strong word, implying that Titus must urge this teaching upon them.

Paul's admonition to young men is as powerful as it is brief. He urges upon them a single virtue: **be self-controlled** (v. 6). What word so well embodies the very thing that all young men need—mastery of themselves? Paul's lone command encompasses every area of life: speech, temper, finances, ambition, sexuality. *Self-control* is only one word, but what a powerful word it is.

## TITUS HIMSELF

As Titus moved about the island of Crete, appointing leaders, challenging false teachers, instructing believers, and building disciples, he would need to keep himself spiritually fit. As Paul had urged Timothy to "watch [his] life and doctrine closely" (1 Tim. 4:16), he now advises Titus to guard his personal conduct and the content of his teaching.

In contrast to the false teachers, who were "unfit for doing anything good" (Titus 1:16), Titus was to **set them an example** (v. 7). Paul probably meant primarily that Titus was to be a role model for young men, but others would observe him as well. The Greek word translated **example** refers to a die or pattern and is the word from which we derive the English word *type*. The character of a Christian leader will be stamped upon those who follow him or her.

As a teacher with **integrity** (2:7)**,** Titus would not allow his message to be contaminated by false teaching. The Greek translated **integrity** is used only here in the New Testament; however, Paul elsewhere uses a form of the word to refer to persons who would "defile the temple of God" (1 Cor. 3:17 KJV). In Titus 2, Paul means that Titus should show integrity by being undefiled in his motives. His demeanor of **seriousness** (v. 7) would indicate the dignity of his teaching. As an ambassador of Jesus Christ, Titus must never descend

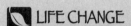

## LIFE CHANGE

### CHRISTIAN LIFESTYLE

Three times in Titus, Paul expresses a concern over the way our behavior impacts the world around us. He admonishes young women to live "so that no one will malign the word of God" (2:5), or, as J. B. Phillips puts it, so they will be "a good advertisement for the Christian faith." Paul challenges Titus himself to live and teach "so that those who oppose [him] may be ashamed because they have nothing bad to say" (2:8). Finally, Paul urges slaves to live so "they will make the teaching about God our Savior attractive" (2:10).

Whatever our station in life, we are observed by others. The manner in which we live will be our first witness to the power of the gospel.

to behavior or speech that would bring reproach upon his calling. In fact, his teaching must be characterized by **soundness of speech** (v. 8). The communication of every Christian teacher must be healthy and wholesome.

When Paul says that Titus's teaching must be such that it **cannot be condemned** (v. 8), he does not imply that Titus could control the reaction of others to him or to the gospel. It is not possible for a minister of the gospel to avoid opposition. However, he could ensure that their condemnation would have no basis in fact. Christian leaders can live and teach in such a way that when others oppose the gospel, they will **be ashamed because they have nothing bad to say about [them]** (v. 8).

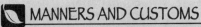

## MANNERS AND CUSTOMS

### THE ROLE OF SLAVES

Some scholars have estimated there were fifty million slaves living in the Roman Empire during the first century, comprising perhaps one third of the population. The institution of slavery was deeply enmeshed in Roman society. It would have been impossible to change this system suddenly without the collapse of the entire culture. In dealing with slavery, Paul does not suggest an open rebellion but a revolution from within. He calls on owners to provide their slaves with what is "right and fair" (Col. 4:1) and calls on slaves to treat their masters with respect (1 Tim. 6:1). Paul goes so far as to state that believing slaves and their Christian owners are brothers (1 Tim. 6:2). In the sight of God, Paul teaches, "there is neither Jew nor Greek, slave nor free, male nor female, for you are all one in Christ Jesus" (Gal. 3:28).

By **ashamed**, does Paul mean that opponents of the faith will be embarrassed when it turns out that Christians are innocent of any charges leveled against them? Or does Paul hope those opponents will be shamed into repentance when they see the virtue of believers? The precise meaning is uncertain, but it is certain that Christians must live with **integrity** (v. 7) and teach with **soundness of speech** (v. 8). Our words and deeds will be noticed by the world around us.

## SLAVES

Slavery was common in the Roman Empire. While not holding the same rank as family members, slaves were considered members of the household in which they served; therefore, Paul's instruction to Titus about what to **teach**

**slaves** (v. 9) is not out of place here. Having given instruction to several age groups and Titus himself, Paul now addresses slaves within the church.

There were stereotypes about slaves in the first century; they were often regarded as lazy, argumentative, and prone to thievery.[5] And some of them were. Yet Paul urges Christian slaves to rise above the stereotype and be a grand exception. Paul urges slaves to **be subject to their masters in everything** (v. 9). That was the role of a slave, naturally, but Paul advises them to submit willingly, **to try to please [their masters], not talk back to them, and not to steal from them** (v. 9).

Paul makes no distinction between slaves that had Christian masters and slaves who had pagan masters. He simply admonishes all slaves **to show that they can be fully trusted** (v. 10). They were to be so dependable that a master could entrust his slave both with his possessions and his business enterprise.

The Greek word translated **make . . . attractive** (v. 10) was used to describe the action of displaying jewelry in such a way as to show its beauty. By living exemplary lives, the slaves would "add lustre to the doctrine of God our Saviour" (v. 9 NEB).

## ENDNOTES

1. J. B. Phillips, *The New Testament in Modern English*, student ed. (New York: Macmillan Publishing Company, 1972), p. 450.

2. Ralph Earle, *Word Meanings in the New Testament*, vol. 5 (Kansas City, Mo.: Beacon Hill Press of Kansas City, 1977), p. 262.

3. Gordon D. Fee, *1 and 2 Timothy, Titus,* New International Biblical Commentary (Peabody, Mass.: Hendrickson Publishers, Inc., 1988), p.186.

4. D. Edmond Hiebert, *Titus,* The Expositor's Bible Commentary: Ephesians through Philemon (Grand Rapids, Mich.: Zondervan, 1981), p. 423.

5. Craig S. Keener, *The IVP Bible Background Commentary: New Testament* (Downers Grove, Ill.: InterVarsity Press, 1993), p. 638.

# 4

# DOCTRINAL BASIS FOR MORAL BEHAVIOR

## Titus 2:11–15

O n the heels of his teaching on proper behavior for various groups within the church, Paul presents the theological basis for his confident assertions. This ordering of material contrasts with that used in several of Paul's other letters (Romans, Ephesians, and Colossians), where he first gives the doctrinal basis for conduct then goes on to show how that correct belief leads to practical Christianity. Here the order is reversed. Paul is saying, in effect, "The reason I can speak so emphatically about the way you should behave is because I know what God has done. He has caused His **grace . . . that brings salvation [to appear] to all men**" (2:11).

### 1. THE GRACE OF GOD 2:11–12

The **grace of God** (v. 11) is His favor, attention, and goodwill, which are totally undeserved. Not only do we not deserve this grace but there is no way we can provide it ourselves. Grace operates in two ways in the life of the believer: it **brings salvation** (1:11), and it **teaches us . . . to live self-controlled, upright and godly lives** (2:12).

#### WHAT GRACE BRINGS

Only God can bring salvation, which He has dramatically done, causing it to appear **to all men** (2:11). In the original language, the phrase **has appeared** (v. 11) stands at the beginning of the sentence, giving it a position of prominence and strong emphasis. The word Paul uses is the one from which we derive our word *epiphany*. He uses this same word in Acts 27:20 referring to the appearance of the sun. God's good favor has burst into the darkness of the human condition like a brilliant sunrise. The incarnation of Christ has made God's love and goodwill toward us more vivid than mere words could ever have done. Jesus came as the embodiment of God's grace. Writing to Timothy, Paul makes it clear that the manifestation of grace involves more than Jesus' birth; it includes His death and resurrection as well (see 1 Tim. 2:9–10).

Obviously, God's intention is that **all men**, meaning everyone, should embrace this generous offer of **salvation** (Titus 2:11). Salvation is available for all; however, it requires a personal response by each individual. No one receives salvation accidentally or contrary to his own will. While it is **the grace of God that brings salvation** (v.11), it is appropriated to each person by a personal decision. "For it is by grace you have been saved," Paul wrote to the Ephesians, "*through faith*" (Eph. 2:8, emphasis added). By repenting (Luke 13:3) and putting our trust fully in Jesus Christ (Heb. 11:6), we can enjoy His **salvation**.

## WHAT GRACE TEACHES

The word Paul chose for **teaches** (Titus 2:12) may be literally translated "to train up a child." It means to educate or instruct, and implies the idea of discipline. Teaching has both positive and negative components.

Negatively, it **teaches us to say "No"** (v. 12) to the very things that kept us away from God in the first place. The importance of learning to "renounce" (RSV) "godless ways" (NEB) cannot be overstated. **Ungodliness** (v. 12) speaks of a mindset that leaves God out of the picture. **Worldly passions** (v. 12) are urges and cravings that are opposed to the way God wants us to think, act, and live.

On the positive side, God's grace **teaches us . . . to live self-controlled, upright and godly lives** (v. 12). Paul has already stressed the importance of living a **self-controlled** (1:8; 2:2, 5, 6) life. He emphasizes this point again not because living a life of high moral character is merely commendable but because it is essential that we link what we believe with the way in which we live.

To live an **upright** (2:11) life means to be in harmony with what the Scriptures teach about correct living. When the word *upright* is used of God (John 17:25; Rom. 3:26), it means that His conduct is in complete agreement with His nature. When it is used of others, it means their behavior is in keeping with the teachings of God.

God's grace also **teaches us . . . to live . . . godly lives** (Titus 2:12). The word **godly**, sometimes translated *devout*, is used to describe Cornelius the centurion (Acts 10:2), and Ananias, who ministered to Paul (then known as Saul) in Antioch (Acts 22:12).

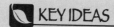

## KEY IDEAS

### SELF-CONTROL

One of the great paradoxes of the Christian life is that we are to surrender our will completely to Christ, yet He expects us to exercise self-control. This is not a minor issue, as Paul presses the need for self-control among all age groups mentioned in Titus 2:1–12. In Galatians, Paul concludes his list of the fruit of the Spirit with the twin qualities of gentleness and self-control (5:23). *Gentleness* may be translated *meekness* or *humility*. It implies surrender while *self-control* implies effort. God accepts the surrender of our selves by filling us with His Spirit, which enables us to exercise self-control (Rom. 8:1–2, 5). To control oneself by an act of the will is not possible. We can exercise self-control only under the direction of God's Holy Spirit.

Peter reminds his readers that God "knows how to rescue godly men from trials" (2 Pet. 2:9). As we resist evil, **ungodliness, and worldly passions** (Titus 2:12), God actually empowers us by the Holy Spirit to live **godly lives**.

This trio of virtues—self-control, uprightness, and godliness— reminds us that character influences behavior in three directions: toward ourselves, toward others, and toward God.

God's grace is able to sustain us, Paul says, even **in this present age** (v.12). People in every age have likely wondered if the temptations were too strong, the enemy too powerful, and the expectations too high; Christians have probably always wondered if God's grace is truly adequate. Paul's words remind Christians in every age that God's grace is sufficient, right here and right now.

## 2. THE BLESSED HOPE 2:13

The first appearance of Jesus Christ, when He descended into our world, submitted to human birth in a lowly manger, grew up to preach and teach, died on a cross, and rose again, was a manifestation of God's **grace** (2:11). His second coming will be a demonstration of God's glory. Meanwhile, **we wait for the blessed hope** (v. 13)—Christ's next appearing.

The word **wait** carries the idea of enthusiastic anticipation, not passive lingering or killing time.

The fact that the New International Version places a dash after the word **hope** indicates that **the glorious appearing** is, in fact, **the blessed hope** for which **we wait** (v. 13). At the present time, the world disregards and does not recognize Christ's glory. But a day is coming when there will be no way to deny His splendor.

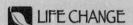

### LIFE CHANGE

#### LIVING "IN BETWEEN"

Paul writes about two great appearances of Jesus Christ. The first (Titus 2:11), an appearance in grace, occurred long ago. The second (2:13), an appearance in glory, will come in the future. We are living in between the two appearances—the Incarnation and the Second Coming.

The challenge of this in-between living is to neither be preoccupied with the past or the future but to live lives of self-control in anticipation of Christ's return. We are to pursue godliness and righteousness while we live in the present, reflect on the past, and hope for the future.

Across the centuries, a lively debate has occurred regarding the correct meaning of the phrase **great God and Savior** (v. 13). Some think it refers to both the Father (great God) and to Jesus (Savior). However, in the Greek manuscripts, there is only one article, which precedes both names. That seems to tie the two names together indicating a single person. Nowhere else in the New Testament does the Second Coming refer to the Father. It seems unlikely, then, that Paul is saying that both the Father and the Son will return in glory. Instead, the statement strongly affirms the deity of Jesus Christ. He is both our **Savior** and our **great God**.

# 3. THE REDEEMING CHRIST 2:14

In Titus 1:5, Paul reminds Titus of what he is supposed to be doing on Crete—appointing elders and straightening out what was left unfinished. In 2:14, we are told what Christ is doing—redeeming and purifying believers and instilling in them an eagerness to do what is good.

## REDEEMING

Paul describes **Jesus Christ** as One **who gave himself for us** (2:14). This is typical of Paul's phraseology in other letters. He wrote to the Galatians about "Jesus Christ, who gave himself for our sins to rescue us from the present evil age" (Gal. 1:3–4). Jesus Himself taught, "For even the Son of Man did not come to be served, but to serve, and to give his life as a ransom for many" (Mark 10:45).

In giving **himself for us**, Jesus paid the ultimate price **to redeem us from all wickedness** (Titus 2:14). The slaves about whom Paul wrote in 2:9–10 would have understood this reference to redemption. In the slave markets of the day, a buyer could approach the auction block, pay the agreed upon price for a particular slave, then remove the slave's chains and set him free. In the case of our deliverance, the chains from which Jesus freed us are the chains of **wickedness**. Anyone who has been enslaved to an addiction knows how difficult it is to break those chains. All of us are addicted to sin and incapable of breaking free from that wickedness without the power of Jesus Christ. The price for our redemption was Jesus' life, and He willingly **gave himself** in order to "rescue us" (v. 14 TEV) from an otherwise hopeless fate.

## PURIFYING

God not only provided for our redemption but also is concerned for our sanctification. Paul emphasizes this when he declares that Jesus **gave himself for us . . . to purify for himself a people that are his very own** (v. 14). God wants both to liberate us from the bondage of sin and to purify us from the nature of sin. He wants to take us out of sin (redemption) and then take sin out of us (sanctification).

## GREAT THEMES

### HOLINESS

In the Beatitudes Jesus commends those who are pure in heart, promising that "they will see God" (Matt. 5:8). But purity of heart seems to be an impossibly high standard. This has led some observers to conclude that because we are "only human," we can never really be pure. They reason that God simply treats us as if we were pure because He is merciful.

Yet why would Jesus command something that is impossible? Peter insists that God showed no distinction between Jews and Gentiles, but for both groups, He "purified their hearts by faith" (Acts 15:9). John taught, "If we confess our sins, he is faithful and just and will forgive us our sins and purify us from all unrighteousness" (1 John 1:9).

God does not simply treat us as if were pure in heart; He makes us pure.

Paul taught the Ephesians that Jesus gave Himself for the church, "to make her holy, cleansing her by the washing with water through the word, and to present her to himself as a radiant church, without stain or wrinkle or any other blemish, but holy and blameless" (Eph. 5:26–27). Just as we cannot redeem ourselves from the bondage of sin, we cannot purify ourselves from its contamination. That purification is a blessing made possible through the sacrificial death of Christ on the cross.

When Paul speaks of **people that are [God's] very own** (v. 14), he uses Old Testament terminology. God had promised the people of Israel that if they would obey Him fully and keep His covenant, then, out of all the nations, they would be His "treasured possession" (Exod. 19:5; see also Deut. 7:6, 14:2, 26:18; and 1 Pet. 2:9).

Paul seems to be making a special effort to tie the finished work of Christ to Old Testament images that would be of great significance to people of Jewish heritage. We assume that some of the Cretan Christians were Jews because Luke tells us that on the Day of Pentecost, "there were staying in Jerusalem God-fearing Jews from every nation under heaven" (Acts 2:5). Luke specifically includes Cretans in the list of nationalities represented (Acts 2:11). Paul reminds his audience also that Christ **gave himself for us** (Titus 2:14), which brings to mind the sacrifice of the lamb at Passover. The emphasis on the fact that Christ died **to redeem us** (2:14) would evoke images of the Exodus, when the Hebrew people came out of Egypt.

## INSTILLING EAGERNESS TO DO GOOD

Paul indicates that Jesus had a further motive in giving Himself as the sacrifice for our sins: he wanted to instill in us an eagerness **to do what is good** (v. 14). The only appropriate response to what Christ has done by redeeming us and purifying us is **to live self-controlled, upright and godly lives** (v. 12) as described in the practical instructions Paul gave the various groups in 2:2–10. After a person has made the decision to receive the **salvation** that comes from God's **grace** (v. 11), experience the joy of being redeemed and purified, and look forward to the **glorious appearing** (v. 13) of Christ, obeying God's word is not a drudgery. Instead, there is an eagerness **to do what is good**.

## 4. RESTATEMENT OF TITUS'S RESPONSIBILITY 2:15

Paul begins this chapter with the command to **teach** (2:1). He ends it with the same command but adds two imperatives for Titus: **encourage and rebuke** (v. 15). Paul uses the same two Greek words here that he earlier gave as mandates for church leaders (1:9). Titus was to be sure that church leaders understood that they should "encourage others by sound doctrine and refute those who oppose it." Encouragement is important as a teacher urges his disciples to put what they have been taught into practice. Rebuke is needed not only by those who oppose sound doctrine (1:9) but also by those who fail to live a godly life (2:12).

**These . . . things** that Titus was to **teach** (2:15) are probably the instructions given to various groups in 2:2–10 and given for leaders in 1:10–16. Titus was to exercise his duties **with all authority** (2:15) because Paul had given him this commission with the full authority of the apostle's influence and reputation behind it. Titus also had authority based on the truth of what he would offer. He would not spout his own opinions but would communicate sound doctrine that would produce healthy Christians on Crete.

Paul further instructs Titus, **Do not let anyone despise you** (v. 15). This statement may indicate that Titus was older than Timothy, because when Paul wrote to Timothy he gave a similar admonition but added, "because you are young" (1 Tim. 4:12). Paul makes no reference to Titus's age. Paul does, however, urge Titus not to tolerate disrespect, either for Titus himself or for his message. If this letter was read in the churches on Crete, as many observers think, then Paul's words may have been intended as much for the Cretans as for Titus himself. Christians on Crete would have heard that message loud and clear: the leader of God's church deserves respect.

# 5

# CHARACTER AND CONDUCT IN THE MARKETPLACE

## Titus 3:1–11

So far in the letter to Titus, most of Paul's instruction has been directed at Christian character and conduct either in the church or at home. Now Paul now turns his attention to beliefs and behaviors in the marketplace. The Christian life is not lived in isolation. The world around us observes our conduct and forms an opinion about our character accordingly. The opinion that nonbelievers have about us will dramatically affect their view of the hope we offer.

## 1. HOW WE OUGHT TO LIVE 3:1–2

Ancient historians report that people on Crete were notorious for their unruly attitudes toward government. They had a reputation for being constantly involved in rebellions, murders, and even deadly conflicts among themselves. Against that backdrop, Paul gives Titus instructions on how the Christian **people** (3:1) on Crete should behave.

Paul's use of the word **remind** (v. 1) shows that this was not the first time the Cretan Christians had heard this information. The Greek tense used carries the idea of continuing to remind, repeatedly urging the people to fulfill their responsibilities. Christian teachers often need to repeat what their hearers already know because it is human nature to forget our obligations or fail to live up to them.

Paul asks Titus to remind the people of six qualities that every Christian should embrace. First is the call **to be subject to rulers and authorities** (v. 1). Paul is talking about voluntary submission, not a grudging surrender. We must submit first of all to God, yet we must remember that He delegated authority to civil governments (Rom. 13:1). In other places in the New Testament, both Paul (Rom. 13:4) and Peter (1 Pet. 2:13, 14) define the responsibility of civil government to promote good and punish evil. That responsibility extends to anyone who has a legitimate place of authority in our lives.

Concerning this passage in Titus, John Wesley writes that Christians are to obey government authorities actively, so far as conscience permits.[1] Soon Christians would face a severe test of their consciences and their loyalties. Rome would require its citizens throughout the empire to express their allegiance by offering a pinch of incense and declaring, "Caesar is Lord." No person who believes that Christ alone is Lord could do that. Many believers became martyrs rather than deny the lordship of Christ. Christians must cooperate with government authorities and submit to them when to do so glorifies God, but when the position of the government conflicts with the teachings of Christ, Christians must remain true to our Lord.

The second quality Paul calls for in Christians is cooperation with civil authorities. Paul urges believers **to be ready to do whatever is good** (Titus 3:1). The comment indicates that Christians are not to be passive bystanders but should be actively involved in promoting things that uphold the general welfare of their community. Paul calls on Christians to be a constructive force, to be givers and not just takers in their society.

The third quality is that we must not **slander** (v. 2) anyone. A Christian should not throw curses or angry, demeaning words at others or about them. Good words must accompany our good deeds.

The fourth quality of Christian social conduct is that we must be **peaceable** (v. 2), which literally means nonfighting. This is not a prohibition against standing up for what one believes. Yet while doing so, a Christian must recognize the rights of others persons to have differing viewpoints. Even when facing opposition from others, a sincere believer will resist developing an argumentative attitude or a tendency to fight (see v. 9) but will instead promote peace.

The fifth quality is that Christians should be **considerate** (v. 2). They will be thoughtful, courteous, and gracious, not insisting on having their own way. This teaching urges believers to be people who do not insist on enforcing the letter of the law but are willing to give and take, finding a middle ground if that can be done without compromising a moral principle.

The sixth quality of Christian conduct is **to show true humility toward all men** (v. 2). Paul calls believers to reject any tendency to be selfishly assertive and never to assume a harsh demeanor. The Greek word translated **humility** is rendered *meek* in other places. It is a word that describes Jesus Himself (Matt. 11:29; 21:5), and it is one of the Beatitudes (Matt. 5:5). This behavior is to be shown **toward all men,** not just fellow Christians. Paul's admonition has evangelistic overtones. Our conduct toward others in the marketplaces of life can provide a winsome witness for the Savior.

## 2. HOW WE USED TO LIVE 3:3

There is a vast difference between how Christians ought to live and how they used to live. Paul often urges his readers to live a holy life, but he is never holier-than-thou. He admits that **at one time we too were foolish** (Titus 3:3). He seems to be saying, "What is true of the unsaved Cretans was once true of us as well." Given Paul's agreement with the ancient prophet's negative assessment of the Cretans (1:12), it is a little surprising that he so readily identifies with them. We might wonder how this admission by Paul fits with his statement to the Philippians that he had been "a Hebrew of Hebrews," implying that he was deeply religious and faultless in his righteousness (Phil. 3:5–6). Yet Paul understood the difference between what he had appeared to be and what he actually was. In his earlier life, Paul had been a seemingly righteous person, commendable in the eyes of the community. But when enlightened by the Holy Spirit, Paul better understood his earlier motivations and comprehended what lay beneath the surface of his behavior. He knew that he, too, had been selfish, stubborn, and opposed to God—in a word, **foolish.**

By foolish, we often mean silly, unwise, thoughtless, or even irrational. But in using that term, Paul means having no spiritual understanding or sensitivity toward God. Elsewhere Paul refers to unbelievers as those who "are darkened in their understanding and separated from the life of God because of the ignorance that is in them due to the hardening of their hearts" (Eph. 4:18–19).

Paul says we also were once **disobedient** (Titus 3:3). That describes a person who willfully refuses to obey God's law and chafes under authority. It is the same word Paul used earlier to depict the false teachers (1:16).

A **deceived** (3:3) person is one who is duped, misled, and following the wrong spiritual guides. In his second letter to Timothy, Paul warned that young man about "evil men and imposters" who "go from bad to worse, deceiving and being deceived" (2 Tim 3:13). The Apostle John describes Satan as one "who deceives the whole world" (Rev. 12:9 NKJV).

A person who is deceived may easily become **enslaved** (Titus 3:3). Enslavement is the natural result of being caught up in **all kinds of passions and pleasures** (v. 3). Paul writes to Timothy about people he hopes will "escape from the trap of the devil, who has taken them captive to do his will" (2 Tim. 2:26). This is the only place Paul uses the word *pleasures,* although Jesus used it to describe people who "are choked by life's worries, riches and pleasures" (Luke 8:14).

The twin characteristics of **malice and envy** (Titus 3:3) describe people who have ill will toward others and are jealous of their success. We are not surprised when people who live this way find themselves **being hated and hating one another** (v. 3). Paul describes persons who are repulsive and disgusting even to those who are likeminded. They are antisocial and invite mutual antagonism. It is impossible to form wholesome relationships with others when we resent them and wish them ill.

The antisocial characteristics mentioned in v. 3 describe the former character of Christians. That character is seen in three relationships. The first is our relationship toward God, in which we were **foolish** and **disobedient**. The second is our attitude toward ourselves; we were **deceived and enslaved**. The third is our relationship toward others; we were filled with **malice and envy, being hated** as well as **hating one another**. Paul's description of human character is extremely negative, but he does accurately assess it.

# 3. WHY WE CHANGED 3:4–6

The conjunction **but** (3:4) gives us hope that the way we used to live will not be the way we always live. In his writings, Paul often indicates a contrast between what we are now and what we once were (see Rom. 6:17–23; 1 Cor. 6:9–11; Eph. 2:1–13; 5:7–12; Col. 1:21–23; 3:7–10). What accounts for the change?

## HE SAVED US

Humanly, there was no chance of escape from the dismal condition in which we found ourselves. **But,** Paul begins, **when the kindness and love of God our Savior appeared, he saved us** (Titus 3:4–5a). Paul uses the same term for **appeared** that he employs in 2:11, where he speaks of the appearance of God's grace. At the same time God's grace appeared, His **kindness and love . . . appeared** as well.

Jesus accomplished our salvation on the cross. That simple fact can be stated in three words—**He saved us** (v. 5)—yet its ramifications have occupied theologians for centuries. Paul quickly reminds us that our salvation came **not because of righteous things we had done** (v. 5). This reminder is similar to Eph. 2:8–9, where Paul says that salvation comes by grace through faith, "and this is not from yourselves, it is the gift of God" (see also Rom. 4:4, 5; Gal. 2:16–17). Having said so much in this letter to Titus about the value of doing good things, Paul seemed to feel it was necessary to re-emphasize God's grace and mercy. This reminder provides balance and establishes once again that works do not save us (see also Luke 18:9ff; Phil. 3:7ff; 2 Tim. 1:9). Our own righteousness is "like filthy rags" (Isa. 64:6).

Salvation comes **because of [God's] mercy** (Titus 3:5). Instead of giving us what we deserve—punishment—He extends **mercy** (v. 5), **kindness and love** (v. 4).

## HE GAVE US A REBIRTH

The **washing of rebirth** (v. 5) probably means water baptism. The Greek word translated **washing** appears only one other place in the New Testament. Paul uses the word to explain that Christ makes the church

255

holy, "cleansing her by the washing with water through the word" (Eph. 5:26). In both instances the act of baptism is used as a symbol for the true **washing of rebirth** that takes place when Christ forgives our sin and washes away its defilement. Baptism itself does not save us. In the New Testament, believers were baptized after they were saved, not in order to be saved. After Cornelius and his household showed evidence of faith, Peter said, "'Can anyone keep these people from being baptized with water? They have received the Holy Spirit just as we have.' So he ordered that they be baptized in the name of Jesus Christ" (Acts 10:47–48). Baptism is an outward symbol of what Christ has already done in our hearts. The term *rebirth* signifies new life, that marvelous change that Christ brings within us. It is not too much to say we are new creations (see 2 Cor. 5:17). Christ doesn't simply repair us; He makes us new.

## HE RENEWED US

Paul goes on to declare that God accomplishes this **renewal** in us **by the Holy Spirit** (Titus 3:5). Jesus "gave himself for us to redeem us" (2:14), but it is the Holy Spirit who convicts us of our sins (John 16:7–11), enlightens us about the truth in Christ (John 16:13), and actually washes and renews us within. This renewal occurs when we take the advice Paul gave the Romans: "Offer your bodies as living sacrifices, holy and pleasing to God—this is your spiritual act of worship. Do not conform any longer to the pattern of this world, but be transformed by the renewing of your mind" (Rom. 12:1–2).

God made this kind of renewal possible by the **Holy**

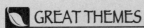

### GREAT THEMES
#### THE HOLY SPIRIT'S WORK

Some commentators see the renewal by the Holy Spirit mentioned in Titus 3:5 as a reference to the cleansing work of the Holy Spirit that brings about entire sanctification (see 1 Thess. 5:23). In other words, Paul may be talking both about how Jesus saved us (Titus 3:5) and about how He sanctifies us through the renewal by the Holy Spirit. Jesus promised inner "streams of living water" for those who will follow Him without reservation (John 7:38, 39). The person who makes a full surrender of his or her life to Christ and continues to walk in obedience will find deep reservoirs of grace, blessing, empowerment, and renewal for every life situation.

**Spirit, whom he generously poured out on us** (vv. 5–6). Paul uses the same word for **poured out** that Luke uses to describe the coming of the Holy Spirit on the day of Pentecost (Acts 2:17, 18, 33). It is the same word Paul uses when he declares that "God has poured out his love into our hearts by the Holy Spirit, whom he has given us" (Rom. 5:5). It is a dramatic word, indicating that God freely dispenses forgiveness and cleansing to all who open their hearts. The outpouring of the Holy Spirit at Pentecost was a significant event in history, but it did not exhaust God's ability to bless those who are ready to receive. God bestows none of these blessings apart from the finished work of **Jesus Christ our Savior** (Titus 3:6).

## 4. WHAT WE BECOME 3:7–8

Because Christ **saved us** (3:5), we receive great benefits from Him. The little phrase **so that** (v. 7) indicates that God has a purpose for what He has done. Jesus did not die in vain. His death on the cross shows the great wickedness of humankind, but it ultimately accomplishes a greater purpose.

We have **been justified by [God's] grace** (v. 7). **Justified** is a legal term. It indicates that God, the Judge, has declared us righteous. He has done so because of **his grace**, the favor He chooses to show apart from any merit of our own. God was able to justify us without compromising His righteous standard because Jesus satisfied the demands of justice on the cross.

God's purpose was that **we might become heirs** (v. 7). God is so magnanimous that He not only forgives us but also adopts us into His family, making us "heirs of God, and joint-heirs with Christ" (Rom. 8:17 KJV). Furthermore, he has given us **the hope of eternal life** (Titus 3:7). That we are **heirs** (v. 7) is an established fact (see Rom. 8:16–17). Typically, an heir receives an inheritance upon the death of the benefactor. In our case, our Benefactor will never die. Instead, we receive our inheritance upon our own death. We partake of **eternal life** here and now, but we will inherit its full benefits in the future, which is why we have **hope**.

One can almost imagine Paul reflecting on what he had just written in vv. 4–7, being satisfied with the statement, and pronouncing it a **trustworthy saying** (v. 8). Some scholars think he may have been quoting a hymn or creed. Whether recited or created by Paul under divine inspiration, it is a beautiful statement of faith.

 **WHAT OTHERS SAY**

*Be careful to excel in good works—* Though the apostle does not lay these for the foundation, yet he brings them in at their proper place, and then mentions them, not slightly, but as affairs of great importance. He desires that all believers should be *careful—* Have their thoughts upon them: use their best contrivance, their utmost endeavours, not barely to practise, but to *excel*, to be eminent and distinguished in them: because, though they are not the ground of our reconciliation with God, yet they are amiable and honourable to the Christian profession.

—John Wesley, *Explanatory Notes upon the New Testament*

Passionate communicators of God's truth learn **to stress [important] things** (v. 8), placing "line upon line" and "precept upon precept" (Isa. 28:13) for the purpose of building solid Christian character in their disciples. Paul wants those **who have trusted in God** to translate their belief into behavior, to **devote themselves to doing what is good** (v. 8). If we do not put belief into practice, our heavenly religion will be no earthly good. As Jo Anne Lyon points out, "God doesn't set people apart for no reason. He sanctifies people (makes them holy) for a purpose. When we are blessed by God, we are singled out for a reason, a purpose, a mission."[2] As Paul might have put it, it's not enough for Christians to *be* good—they must also *do* good.

Paul describes **these things**, the concepts that he has just emphasized to Titus, as **excellent** (v. 8). These teachings encompass the three dimensions of our salvation: past, present, and future. We have been **saved**, reborn, renewed, and **justified**, which is past (vv. 5–7), we live a life of **good** works in the present (v. 8), and we look forward to the full inheritance of **eternal life** He has promised us, which is in the future (v. 7).

**These things** are also **profitable for everyone** (v. 8). Wherever Christianity has been practiced conscientiously and consistently, it has brought great spiritual and humanitarian benefits. Hospitals, hunger relief programs, improved treatment of women and minorities, and human rights advocacy have been created wherever Christ has worked through His people to touch the world.

# 5. WHAT WE MUST AVOID 3:9–11

While we don't know the exact nature of the problems on Crete, it appears that some people were doing research into the Old Testament **genealogies** and then instigating **controversies** (3:9) by drawing false conclusions about them. Concerning these contentious teachers, John Stott observes, "They were certainly speculators. They treated the law (that is, the Old Testament) as a happy hunting ground for their conjectures. To Paul their whole approach was frivolous."[3] Paul deals with a similar problem in his first letter to Timothy (see Introduction to 1 Timothy and 1 Tim. 1:3–7).

There always seem to be some people in the church who have "an unhealthy interest in controversies and quarrels" (1 Tim. 6:4). These people love to engage in debates, but their arguments never produce a positive result. They lead only to **quarrels** and **controversies** (Titus 3:9) that alienate one believer from another. In Greek, the words *quarrel* and *sword* are derived from the same root. Quarreling over meaningless things too often divides God's people.

Quarreling or discord was a widespread enough problem in the early church that Paul warns against it in several of his letters (Rom. 1:29; 13:13; 1 Cor. 3:3; 2 Cor. 12:20; Gal. 5:20). In contrast to the **things** Paul declared **profitable** (Titus 3:8), these controversial squabbles were decidedly unprofitable.

Paul's recommendation to Titus for dealing with controversy was first of all to **warn a divisive person** (v. 10). The Greek word translated **divisive** is the one from which we derive the word *heretic*. Paul uses the term to indicate a person who takes a minor point and makes a major problem of it. A divisive person can generate tremendous difficulty in the church because he or she lacks a sense of proportion. Instead of building bridges, such a person divides believers into opposing camps.

Paul's sound advice is to **warn a divisive person once** and even **a second time. [But] after that, have nothing to do with him** (v. 10). Paul knew that further time spent on such an individual would be wasted. Indeed, such people often thrive on attention. Paul believed that such people were **warped** (v. 11), meaning twisted in their thinking. Ultimately, they are

## LIFE CHANGE

### CONFLICT RESOLUTION

Conflict resolution is a messy business. It is so difficult that many Christians do not have the inner fortitude to do it.

Nevertheless, Jesus teaches that we must confront those who have sinned against us (Matt. 18:15–17). First, there is to be a conversation only between the two parties involved. If that is not productive, witnesses are to be included. If the divisive person still won't listen, the entire church should be involved, presumably the church's ruling body. If even that action is not successful, the person is to be treated as "a pagan or a tax collector" (v. 17).

Paul instructs Titus to do much the same with a divisive person: warn him twice, and, if the warnings are not heeded, avoid him (Titus 3:10). If this procedure were followed conscientiously, fewer disagreements would develop into full-blown divisiveness.

**self-condemned** because their behavior is **sinful** (v. 11).

This advice may seem harsh, but it is much less severe than his instructions to Timothy concerning certain others who were causing problems in the early church. Paul refers to some who have rejected "faith and a good conscience" and consequently "shipwrecked their faith" (1 Tim. 1:19). He goes on to name Hymenaeus and Alexander, whom he had "handed over to Satan to be taught not to blaspheme" (1 Tim. 1:20). Each instance of church discipline warrants its own, appropriate response (see Rom. 16:17–18; 2 Thess. 3:14–15; 2 Tim. 2:25–26).

## ENDNOTES

1. John Wesley, *Explanatory Notes upon the New Testament* (London, Charles H. Kelly, N.D.), p. 802.

2. Jo Anne Lyon, *The Ultimate Blessing* (Indianapolis: Wesleyan Publishing House, 2003), p. 70.

3. John R. W. Stott, *Guard the Truth: The Message of 1 Timothy and Titus* (Downers Grove, Ill.: InterVarsity Press, 1996), p. 44.

# 6

# CLOSING REMARKS

## Titus 3:12–15

Paul closes most of his letters with personal remarks, and this letter is no exception. The closing remarks are about the same length as the introduction to this letter, occupying just four verses. That contrasts with 2 Timothy, in which his closing remarks, instructions, and final greetings comprise fourteen verses.

## 1. APPEAL TO TITUS 3:12

Apparently, Paul considered Titus's work on Crete to be temporary. While his mission there was extremely important, Paul had other assignments in mind. As soon as the apostle could make arrangements to send a replacement, Titus was to join Paul. The replacement would be either **Artemas or Tychicus** (3:12), but at the time Paul wrote the letter, he had not yet decided which of the two to send.

We know nothing further about Artemas, as he is not mentioned anywhere else in Scripture; however, we know a great deal about Tychicus, who was one of Paul's trusted coworkers. When Paul returned from Greece to Asia Minor on his third missionary journey, Tychicus was among the group of brothers who accompanied him (Acts 20:4). When Paul needed someone to carry his letter to the Ephesians, Tychicus, whom Paul called a "dear brother and faithful servant in the Lord" (Eph. 6:21), took the letter, provided encouragement to the church, and gave the people an update about Paul (Eph. 6:22). Tychicus provided the same service by carrying Paul's letter to the Colossians, accompanied by Onesimus (Col.

4:7–9). According to 2 Tim. 4:12, Paul eventually sent Tychicus to Ephesus, so it seems likely that it was Artemas who went to Crete to relieve Titus.

Paul conveys urgency to Titus about joining him, telling the younger man, **do your best to come to me . . . as soon as** a replacement arrives (Titus 3:12). Paul directs Titus to come to **Nicopolis** (v. 12). Although several cities in the ancient world bore that name, nearly all scholars agree that Paul meant the city known as Epirus on the west coast of Greece. Situated about two hundred miles northwest of Athens, Nicopolis was a place whose name literally meant Victory City. It was so named when Augustus founded the city after his victory over Mark Antony at Actium in 31 B.C. It is obvious that Paul is not writing from **Nicopolis** because he says that he has **decided to winter there** (3:12). The implication is that he was elsewhere when he wrote to Titus.

## 2. REMINDER TO HELP OTHERS 3:13

Paul's letter was probably brought to Titus by **Zenas the lawyer and Apollos** (3:13). Some believe that Zenas, who bore a Greek name, may have been a convert from Judaism. If so, the term *lawyer* would indicate that he was an expert in Mosaic law. On the other hand, Zenas may have been a Gentile convert, in which case he would likely have been a Roman jurist.

**Apollos** was a well-known, educated Jew from Alexandria. He worked with Aquila and Priscilla at Ephesus, where "they invited him to their home and explained to him the way of God more adequately" (Acts 18:26). Apollos later went to Corinth, where he had an effective ministry (Acts 18:27–19:1).

Paul urged Titus, **Do everything you can to help [these men] on their way and see that they have everything they need** (Titus 3:13). Rendering hospitality was characteristic of early Christians (Acts 15:3; Rom. 15:24; 1 Cor. 16:6; 2 Cor. 1:16; 3 John 6). The good works that Paul writes so much about in this short letter are practical things that meet real needs for real people.

## 3. RATIONALE FOR DOING GOOD 3:14

Paul was always on the lookout for opportunities to teach believers the importance of living deeper, stronger, more Christlike lives. Zenas and Apollos presented just such an opportunity—one in which **good** works could be put into action. By emphasizing that **people must learn** (3:14), Paul reminds Titus to take advantage of this teachable moment.

Good works should never be an afterthought. They must be part of the lifestyle to which believers **devote themselves** (v.14). By assisting Christian workers, God's people would advance the gospel and, at the same time, develop their own character.

An alternative rendering of the phrase **devote themselves to doing what is good** is "enter honorable occupations" (3:14 RSV margin). That reading is in harmony with the idea of working to **provide for daily necessities** (v. 14) and fits with Paul's admonition that Christians must **not live unproductive lives** (3:14; see also 2 Thess. 3:10–12). However, given Paul's strong emphasis throughout the letter on **doing what is good**, it is most likely that the phrase is yet another reference to the importance of demonstrating Christian character through wholesome behavior.

## LIFE CHANGE

### Doing Good

*Doing good* is a recurring theme in Paul's letter to Titus. This strong emphasis cannot be an accident. Like our Master, who "went around doing good" (Acts 10:38), the Christian leader must be one who loves what is good (Titus 1:8). While good works can never be the basis for our salvation (3:5), Paul calls Christian leaders to set an example by doing good (2:7), in contrast to the false teachers who are "unfit for doing anything good" (1:16). In the dark night of the Cretan culture, those who did good works in the name of Jesus would shine like stars—as they will today.

## 4. FINAL GREETINGS 3:15

In some of Paul's letters, he identifies those who are with him and those who send greetings to the letter's recipients. In this case, he simply says, **Everyone with me sends you greetings** (3:15). **Zenas** and **Apollos** (v. 13) would probably have given a more detailed report upon their arrival, including personal greetings from others who were with Paul.

Without mentioning names, Paul asks that Titus **greet those who love us in the faith** (v. 15). Paul was confident of the Christian affection the believers of Crete felt for him. Those of "like precious faith" (2 Pet. 1:1) have a genuine, divinely inspired affection for their spiritual leaders and their brothers and sisters in Christ.

Finally, Paul concludes with a brief and typically Pauline statement: **Grace be with you all** (Titus 3:15). The blessing of grace that Paul bestows upon Titus in the beginning of his letter, (1:4), the grace "that brings salvation" (2:11), and the grace by which we are justified (3:7), he now confers upon Titus and upon **all** the believers of Crete (3:15).

In Greek, the word **you** (v. 15) is plural, which suggests that Titus is to communicate Paul's greetings to the rest of the church family, perhaps by reading the letter to the various churches in Crete.

So Paul concludes his brief letter with its strong emphasis on Christian character and conduct. Whether in the church, the family, or the marketplace, character and conduct go hand in hand. Consistency between the two is crucial to a Christian's witness in any age.

# PHILEMON

# INTRODUCTION TO PHILEMON

The letter to Philemon is one of only two personal, private letters preserved in the New Testament. The Apostle John's letter to Gaius, which we know as 3 John, is the other. Undoubtedly, Paul wrote many personal letters, but this one to his friend Philemon is the only one to survive.

## AUTHORSHIP

Hardly anyone questioned that Paul was the author of this letter until F. C. Bauer did so in 1835. Bauer, who also rejected Paul's authorship of the Pastoral Epistles, suggested that the letter to Philemon was written pseudonymously in the second century to help the church handle the issue of slavery. That view never gained popular acceptance.

W. C. van Manen, who did not accept Paul's authorship of any New Testament epistle, proposed that the letter to Philemon was a Christian rewrite of an earlier, secular letter written by the Roman author Pliny the Younger to his friend Sabinianus on behalf of a slave whom Sabinianus had set free. Apparently, the slave had offended Sabinianus and sought Pliny's help in bringing reconciliation. However, the idea that Philemon is based on Pliny's letter is pure conjecture. Most scholars accept Paul's authorship of the letter to Philemon.

## RECIPIENT

Philemon was a wealthy resident of Colosse, a city in Phrygia, a province of Asia Minor. Colosse was located on the Lycus River, about twelve miles from Laodicea. We may conclude from Paul's comment to Philemon, "You owe me your very self" (Philem. 19), that Philemon had come to faith in Christ under the ministry of the Apostle Paul. Since we have no record of a visit to Colosse by Paul, we may further conclude that the two met during the apostle's lengthy ministry in Ephesus (Acts 19:1–10), which was approximately one hundred miles west of Colosse.

Some scholars believe Philemon may have been married to Apphia and that Archippus may have been their son (Philem. 2).

## DATE OF WRITING

The traditional view is that Paul wrote the letter to Philemon at the same time he wrote the letter to the Colossians, which would place it sometime during Paul's first imprisonment in Rome, approximately A.D. 59 or 60, perhaps as late as A.D. 62. Several facts support this view. First, the recipients of both letters lived in the same locale. Colossians is addressed to the entire church at Colosse, Philemon to a member of that church. Second, both letters refer to Paul's imprisonment (Philem. 1, 13; Col. 4:3, 18). Third, the author mentions that Timothy joins him in sending both letters (Philem. 1; Col. 1:1). Finally, the closing greetings of each epistle are similar, and the same five fellow workers are named in both letters (Philem. 23–24; Col. 4:10–14).

Some scholars, however, think the letter to Philemon may have been written prior to the letter to the Colossians, perhaps sent from Ephesus as early as A.D. 55 or 56. (See the map on page 36.) Because Ephesus was a major city that would have contained a large population of slaves, it would have been relatively easy for Onesimus to flee to Ephesus and find anonymity. Rome was twelve hundred miles away. To reach Rome required a hazardous journey, and the longer travel time would have increased the likelihood that Onesimus would be caught.

Those who favor a separate date for the writing of each letter point out that Paul asks Philemon to "prepare a guest room" for him (Philem. 22). Obviously Paul hoped to visit Colosse soon; however, in the letter to the Colossians, he makes no mention of a planned visit but simply asks them to pray "that God may open a door for our message" (Col. 4:3). Surely, scholars contend, if Paul had been planning a trip to Colosse, he would have mentioned it to the church there.

A third possibility is that Paul wrote both letters from Caesarea during his two-year imprisonment there (see Acts 23:33–24:27). But this proposal is speculative and must be rejected due to lack of hard evidence.

The traditional view is the most likely, placing Paul's authorship of Philemon in Rome around A.D. 59 or 60.

## PURPOSE

Onesimus was a fugitive slave, having run away from his master, Philemon, a prominent member of the church in Colosse. As a slave from the province of Phrygia, Onesimus would have been considered a slave of the lowest order. Apparently he had stolen from his master (Philem. 18–19) and fled to Rome. Because it was a vast metropolis of some two million people, perhaps a third of them being slaves, Rome might have seemed like the perfect place for Onesimus to melt into the crowd and become anonymous.

It is not certain how Paul and Onesimus came into contact in Rome, but we do know that Paul led the runaway slave to a saving knowledge of Christ. Onesimus became the apostle's willing servant, nearly a son to Paul.

While Paul enjoyed Onesimus's attention to his needs, he was aware that the slave belonged to Philemon. The right thing to do was to send him back. Paul did so, along with a letter encouraging the master to treat his errant slave with kindness.

We don't know if Philemon honored Paul's request to receive Onesimus as a Christian brother, but it seems likely that he complied. If he had not done so, the letter probably would not have survived. It would have been suppressed by Philemon, if not destroyed.

## MAJOR THEMES

The letter to Philemon was written on the subject of the treatment of a runaway slave, but it is about much more than slavery. This brief epistle shows how Christians must treat one another, regardless of their rank or station in life.

Slavery is abhorrent to us today, yet it was a reality in the first century Roman world. If any new religion, such as Christianity, had called for the abolition of slavery, that religion would have been strongly opposed if not destroyed.[1] Paul deals with the subject of slavery within that context, appealing for Philemon to act on the basis of his heart as a brother in Christ.

In this letter, we see three Christian men, each from a different background, all grappling with the same issue. Paul, formerly a legalistic Jew, was dramatically saved by the grace of God and became an apostle to the Gentiles. Philemon, a converted Gentile from Asia Minor, was a wealthy man and host of a house church in Colosse. Onesimus, a runaway slave, occupied the lowest rung of the social ladder. But the three had one thing in common: they had received Christ as Savior. Their status in Christ brought a unity otherwise unthinkable in the world in which they lived.

Why was this letter preserved? One intriguing possibility is hinted at by the fact that Ignatius, a Christian martyr, wrote to the Ephesians early in the second century and refers to Onesimus as the bishop of Ephesus. It is not certain that this was the same Onesimus, yet it is not impossible that the slave obtained his freedom and rose in the ranks of the church's leadership. We know that the first collection of Paul's letters was assembled at Ephesus. If Onesimus was a bishop there, he may have had a hand in including this short letter in the collection, "in order that all men might know what the grace of God had done for him."[2]

## ENDNOTES

1. Arthur A. Rupprecht, *Philemon,* The Expositor's Bible Commentary: Ephesians through Philemon (Grand Rapids, Mich.: Zondervan, 1981), p. 457.

2. William Barclay, *The Letters to Timothy, Titus, and Philemon*, The Daily Bible Study Series (Philadelphia, Pa.: The Westminster Press, 1975), p. 275.

# OUTLINE OF PHILEMON

### I. Greetings and Gratitude (1–7)

A. Greetings (1–3)

B. Gratitude (4–7)

### II. Paul's Appeal on Behalf of Onesimus (8–21)

A. A Multifaceted Appeal (8–16)

B. Benefit in the Lord (17–21)

### III. Personal Remarks and Benediction (22–25)

A. A Promised Visit (22)

B. Personal Greetings (23–24)

C. Benediction (25)

# 1

# GREETINGS AND GRATITUDE

## Philemon 1~7

The Apostle Paul wrote this brief letter to his friend Philemon, a wealthy slave-owner in Colosse, to request that Philemon treat his runaway slave, Onesimus, with Christian kindness. Apparently, the slave had fled to Rome, where he encountered Paul. The apostle befriended him and sent him back to his master bearing this letter.

### GREETINGS

In many of Paul's epistles, he refers to himself as an apostle—but not in this one. Instead, Paul refers to himself as a **prisoner** (v. 1), a self-identification he uses in the salutation of no other letter. Paul mentions his chains, meaning his status as a prisoner, five times in this short letter (vv. 1, 9, 10, 13, 23). By doing so, he eloquently makes the point that he is one slave making an appeal on the behalf of another slave. While technically a prisoner of the Roman Empire, Paul always chose to think of himself as a **prisoner of Christ Jesus** (v. 1); the apostle knew that he was in prison as part of God's sovereign plan. Indeed, wherever believers find themselves, they are bound by love to Christ Jesus.

As an apostle, Paul had authority to make demands on **Philemon** (v. 1), yet Paul did not approach Philemon on the basis of authority. He approached him as a friend, and Paul strengthened his appeal by mentioning **Timothy** (v. 1) at the outset of the letter. It is likely that by this time, Timothy was commonly recognized as a protégé of **Paul** and as a leader in his own right.

Successful Christian leaders know that ministry is about relationships. Paul seems to have enjoyed a warm relationship with Philemon, whom he calls a **dear friend and fellow worker** (v. 1). There is no record of a visit by Paul to Colosse. That has led to conjecture that **Philemon** may have traveled the to Ephesus, some one hundred miles away, and there found Jesus Christ through Paul's ministry (see v. 19).

**Apphia** (v. 2) was probably Philemon's wife, and, according to the custom of that day, she would have had responsibility for day-to-day oversight of the household's slaves. Therefore, whatever Philemon decided about the fate of Onesimus would affect **Apphia** and her management of the household.

**Archippus** (v. 2), also mentioned in Colossians (Col. 4:17), was a leader in the community and may have been a pastor. He must have worked with Paul at one time because he is recognized as a **fellow soldier** (Philem. 1). The apostle describes only one other person in that way, Epaphroditus of Philippi (Phil. 2:25). Some scholars believe that Archippus was the son of Philemon and Apphia.

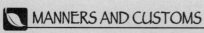

## MANNERS AND CUSTOMS

### HOUSE CHURCHES

Paul mentions house churches in several of his letters. A church met in the home of Priscilla and Aquila in Rome (Rom. 16:5) and another in the home of Nympha in Colosse (Col. 4:15). There seem to have been two types of house churches in the early years of the Christian Church. Some congregations consisted of a single, large household. Others comprised worshipers from several households. Christians worshiped in homes until about the third century, when they began meeting in church buildings.

In his opening greeting, Paul mentions **the church** (v. 2) that meets in Philemon's home. This does not imply that the letter was to be read to the entire church. The letter is personal in nature, dealing with a sensitive issue. Paul is simply saying, "Please convey my blessing **to the church that meets in your home**" (v. 2). **Grace . . . and peace** (v. 3) is Paul's typical greeting.

# GRATITUDE

Paul's expression of gratitude for Philemon is similar to that in some of his other letters (Rom. 1:8–10; Phil. 1:3–11; Col. 1:3–8; 1 Thess. 1:2–5). He tells Philemon that he gives thanks **always** (v. 4), and he tells the reason: **because I hear about your faith . . . and your love** (v. 5). The Greek word **you** (v. 4) is singular both here and in verse 6, reinforcing the idea that this is a personal letter to Philemon, not intended for public reading. Barclay observes, "Doubtless Paul must have written many private letters but of them all only *Philemon* has survived."[1]

Paul must have had a very long prayer list, for he often told people, **I remember you in my prayers** (v. 4; see also Rom. 1:9–10; Eph. 1:16; Phil. 1:4; Col. 1:9; 2 Thess. 1: 11; 2 Tim. 1:3).

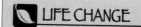

## LIFE CHANGE

### SHARING THE FAITH

In praying for Philemon to be active in sharing his faith (Philem. 6), Paul touches on a growth point for every believer. When sincere unbelievers ask us hard questions, it drives us back to the Word and to prayer. As we study in order to find the answers, two things happen. First, we are enabled to provide responses to the seeker. Second, our own understanding of the truth expands. When we share our faith with others, it grows!

We do not know what Philemon did to express his **faith** or to show his **love for all the saints** (v. 5), but from these few details, we picture a warm, openhearted individual who was a great asset to the church at Colosse.

Verse 6 is difficult to translate because the Greek word rendered **sharing** in the New International Version may have a variety of meanings. One meaning refers to a business partnership, so Paul may be saying that Philemon's partnership in the gospel will strengthen his faith. Another meaning indicates fellowship. In that case, Paul may be saying that Philemon's fellowship with other believers will cause him to go deeper with Christ. Also, the word can be interpreted as an act of sharing. In that case, Paul may be wishing that Philemon would show hospitality, which is certainly implied in verse 7. The phrase **sharing your faith** (v.

6) could also be a reference to witnessing to others about Christ. If it is, we must realize that a person need not have perfect **understanding of every good thing we have in Christ** (v. 6) in order to share the gospel. In fact, the very act of witnessing will increase the desire to know more about the benefits we have in Christ.

Paul's wisdom is evident as he precedes a heavy request with equally profound compliments. The apostle does not say how Philemon's **love** provided such **great joy and encouragement**, nor does he mention how Philemon **refreshed the hearts of the saints** (v. 7), other than by opening his home as a meeting place for the church (v. 2). Even so, the statement is a significant tribute to the man whom Paul calls a **brother** (v. 7).

The Greek word translated here as **refreshed** (v. 7) is rendered as *rest* in Jesus' invitation, "Come to me, all you who are weary and burdened, and I will give you rest" (Matt 11:28). Paul received this blessing of refreshment from other Christian workers also (1 Cor. 16:17–18; 2 Tim. 1:16).

Paul hopes that Philemon, a man of **faith** and **love** (v. 5), a man who opens his home to others (v. 2), a man who refreshes the **hearts** of fellow believers (v. 7), will rely on those honorable qualities when dealing with Onesimus.

## ENDNOTES

1. William Barclay, *The Letters to Timothy, Titus, and Philemon*, The Daily Bible Study Series (Philadelphia, Pa.: The Westminster Press, 1975), p. 269.

# 2

# PAUL'S APPEAL ON BEHALF OF ONESIMUS

## Philemon 8–21

In the body of this letter, Paul makes an irresistible appeal on behalf of Onesimus. That Onesimus must go back to his master, Philemon, was never in question. The conditions under which he would be received, however, were very much in doubt. Yet when Paul is finished with his appeal, it seems that Philemon had little choice but to do what the apostle suggests. Though Paul's appeal is never forceful, it is often subtle, and he frequently implies rather than openly reveals his motivations. He does not make the request itself until verse 17, choosing to set the stage by marshaling the rationale for his request. Paul's letter to Philemon is a masterpiece of tactful entreaty.

## A MULTIFACETED APPEAL

Paul could have appealed to Philemon on the basis of spiritual authority. Paul knew that **in Christ**, he had the authority to order Philemon to do **what [he] ought to do** (v. 8). As an apostle, Paul had tremendous authority in all matters relating to the church and spiritual issues. Although he does not assert that authority, the mere suggestion that he could do so reminded Philemon of the balance of power in their relationship.

Paul makes his appeal first **on the basis of love** (v. 9). Rather than banging the fist of spiritual authority, Paul chose to appeal to Philemon's heart.

2. The apostle appeals also on the basis of age, calling himself **an old man** (v. 9). The Greek word meaning *ambassador* is nearly the same as the word translated here as **old man**, causing some scholars to think Paul was referring to himself as an ambassador. But the personal nature of this letter fits better with an appeal based on age rather than position. Paul was probably between fifty-five and sixty years of age when this letter was written, and was certainly considered a wise and mature man. His appeal would be given serious consideration.

3. Third, Paul appeals to Philemon on the basis of need. Paul reminds Philemon that the apostle was **a prisoner of Christ Jesus** (v. 9). This reminder was sure to evoke feelings of sympathy for Paul, living under house arrest in Rome.

4. A fourth basis of Paul's appeal is his relationship to Philemon. The entire letter is focused on relationships. There is Paul's relationship to Philemon; Paul calls him a "dear friend and fellow worker" (v. 1), a **brother** (vv. 7, 20) and a **partner** (v. 17). There is also Paul's relationship to **Onesimus** (v. 10), whom he refers to as his **son** (v. 10). In that era, people often applied the terms *father* and *son* to a teacher and his student or to an evangelist and a convert (1 Cor. 4:17; 1 Tim. 1:2; 2 Tim. 1:2; Titus 1:4). Paul refers to Onesimus as **my very heart** (v. 12), showing the depth of the relationship between them. Paul also mentions Philemon's relationship to the runaway slave. Paul Rees suggests that Onesimus's plight might be summarized in three phrases: he was socially without status, criminally without excuse, and personally without hope.[1] Despite his shortcomings, Paul recommends Philemon receive Onesimus as a **dear brother** (v. 16).

5. Fifth, Paul prepares the way for his appeal with humor. The name **Onesimus** (v. 10) means profitable or useful and was a fairly common name for slaves. Paul makes a clever play on words when he tells Philemon, "Useful" used to be **useless to you**, but he has now become truly **useful both to you and to me** (v. 11). As a runaway slave, Onesimus was in a grave situation, so it was wise of Paul to lighten the mood with a bit of humor.

Sixth, Paul appeals to Philemon on the basis of altruism. Paul has already described Philemon as having a benevolent spirit (see vv. 2, 5, 7). Paul implies that Philemon will want to be of help to the apostle in much the same way Onesimus was, helping him while he was in **chains for the gospel** (v. 13).

Seventh, Paul appeals to Philemon on the basis of friendship. One of Paul's motives for writing to Philemon was to convince him to trust Onesimus as something more than a slave. When Paul declares, **I am sending him . . . back to you** (v. 12), he knew

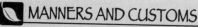

## MANNERS AND CUSTOMS
### RUNAWAY SLAVES

In the Roman Empire of the first century, a slave had few rights. He was a living tool, and his master had absolute power over him. It was considered unforgivable for a slave to run away. When caught, he would certainly be flogged, and his owner might brand him with an F, meaning *fugitivus*, runaway. The slave might even be crucified. A runaway slave's only recourse was to find someone to intercede for him. The intercessor was obligated to return the slave to his owner. If this was impossible, the slave might be sold and the proceeds sent to the owner. Although he would have preferred to keep Onesimus with him, Paul followed Roman law by sending him to his master along with a letter entreating Philemon to treat the runaway with mercy.

that he was doing only what was required by law. In doing so, however, Paul was losing his **very heart** (v. 12). Onesimus had become **very dear** (v. 16) to him.

Eighth, Paul appeals to his friend on the basis of respect. Onesimus belonged to Philemon, and Paul did **not want to do anything** in regard to the slave **without [Philemon's] consent** (v. 14). The apostle preferred a response that was **spontaneous and not forced** (v. 14).

Ninth, Paul makes his appeal on the basis of providence. While he never suggests that Onesimus's theft and desertion were appropriate, he does seem to imply that God was at work throughout the scenario. He contrasts the temporary separation—**a little while** (v. 15)—with the permanence of Onesimus's return. What we may see as a human failure, God may see as a divine opportunity.

Finally, Paul appeals to Philemon's magnanimity. It would require a great generosity of spirit, a certain nobility, to treat a **slave . . . better**

**than a slave—as a dear brother . . . in the Lord** (v. 16). (For more specific teaching on the Christian behavior of slaves and masters, see Col. 3:22–4:1).

## BENEFIT IN THE LORD

Paul finally comes to the point of making his request. In doing so, he appeals to Philemon's partnership with him and the prospect of mutual benefit because of Philemon's generosity. The word translated **partner** (v. 17) refers to a business relationship, a business partner. It implies that Paul and Philemon have common interests.

Paul, Philemon's partner, pleads with him to **welcome** Onesimus as he would welcome Paul. The Greek word translated **welcome** implies reception into a circle of friends. Paul asks Philemon to welcome Onesimus into their partnership.

Paul closes his appeal by hinting at the obligation that Philemon has to the apostle. First, Paul indicates that he will stand behind any obligation Onesimus has to Philemon—**if he . . . owes you anything, charge it to me** (v. 18). Then Paul then reminds Philemon of his debt to the apostle—**you owe me your very self** (v. 18). This is likely a reference to Philemon's conversion under the ministry of Paul.

By stating that he is **writing this with [his] own hand** (v. 19), Paul emphasizes his statement of obligation. The letter serves as his promissory note.

Interestingly, Paul never directly accuses Onesimus of theft and never calls him a runaway. Rather, he speaks in a conditional way—**If he has done you any wrong** (v. 18). Yet from these verses it may be assumed that Onesimus stole something—money or some object of value—from Philemon. Or it may be that by running away, the slave had deprived his master of the value of his work. It is significant that Paul never suggests that Philemon should simply ignore Onesimus's transgressions, whatever they might have been. While the past may be forgiven, its consequences linger.

Again, Paul makes a subtle play on words by suggesting that Philemon give him **some benefit** (v. 20); the name *Onesimus* and the word *benefit* are derived from the same root. In verse 7, Paul compliments Philemon as one who "refreshed the hearts of the saints." Now he asks for that same refreshment, which will come if Philemon receives Onesimus. I've given "Useful" back to you, Paul is saying, now perhaps you can give some benefit to me.

Although Paul did not give Philemon any specific command, he was **confident of** his friend's **obedience** (v. 21). Indeed, Paul seems sure that Philemon **will do even more than** he asks (v. 21). What more could Philemon do than receive Onesimus as a Christian brother? Paul may be implying that Philemon could return Onesimus to the apostle so that the servant could continue to meet Paul's needs. Perhaps Philemon might even set Onesimus free.

### ENDNOTES

1. Paul S. Rees, *The Epistles to the Philippians, Colossians, and Philemon,* Proclaiming the New Testament, vol. 4 (Grand Rapids, Mich.: Baker Book House, 1964), p. 132.

# PERSONAL REMARKS AND BENEDICTION

## Philemon 22–25

In concluding this letter, Paul makes a final request, sends greetings on behalf of his friends, and offers a benediction.

### A PROMISED VISIT

Paul's last request of Philemon is that he **prepare a guest room** because Paul's **hope** (v. 22) was to return to Colosse in the future. There is no record of such a visit, so it cannot be said with certainty that it ever took place. Given that the Greek words **you** and **your** (v. 22) are plural, Paul's hope was, no doubt, based on the **prayers** (v. 22) of the entire congregation. Although this is a private letter, Paul would have depended on his friend to communicate his greeting to the church that met in his house and solicit their prayers on the apostle's behalf. If Philemon had a home large enough to accommodate the church gathering (see v. 2), preparing a guest room for Paul should have posed no problem.

### PERSONAL GREETINGS

Paul gives the names of five comrades in the faith who also sent **greetings** (v. 23). We do not know why **Epaphras** (v. 23) was in prison with Paul. Some have conjectured that he was a voluntary **prisoner** (v. 23) so that he could work with and for Paul. **Epaphras** was responsible for taking the gospel to Colosse (Col. 1:7), and he was both a hard worker and a prayer warrior who wrestled in prayer on behalf of the Colossian church (Col. 4:12, 13).

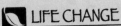

## LIFE CHANGE
### THE VALUE OF TEAMWORK

Paul surrounded himself with people. Many were protégés, people who were learning how to do ministry by watching the apostle at work. Others are coworkers, like Barnabas and Silas, who accompanied Paul on missionary journeys. Paul was fond of calling these companions his "fellow workers." As an apostle, Paul had spiritual authority over those with whom he worked, but he was always a team player. Others learned from him, and he benefited from their assistance. Paul's life is a model of the truth that ministry is best done with a team.

**Mark** (v. 24), a relative of Barnabas, had deserted Paul at Pamphylia during his first missionary journey (see Acts 15:37–40). Consequently, Paul refused to allow the young man to accompany him on a second missionary journey; however, about five years after Paul wrote the letter to Philemon, Paul wrote to Timothy saying that Mark was helpful to him in his ministry (2 Tim. 4:11). That same Mark became the author of the second gospel.

**Aristarchus** (v. 24) was with Paul during the riot at Ephesus (Acts 19:29). He was with Paul later in Greece (Acts 20:4), and he accompanied Paul on his journey to Rome (Acts 27:2). At one point, Paul refers to him as a "fellow prisoner" (Col. 4:10).

**Luke** (v. 24) is the physician who accompanied Paul on his various travels. He wrote both the Gospel that bears his name and the book of Acts. At one point he was the only companion Paul had during his second imprisonment in Rome (2 Tim. 4:11).

**Demas** provides the one sad story among Paul's **fellow workers** (v. 24). He ultimately deserted Paul "because he loved this world" (2 Tim. 4:10).

## BENEDICTION

Paul frequently closes his letters with a benediction in which he confers **the grace of the Lord Jesus Christ** (v. 25). As Thomas Hale observes, "The Lord's grace includes the Lord's mercy, His love, the fruits of the Spirit, and the power of the Spirit. When we pray for the Lord's grace for ourselves and for others, all these things are given to us."[1]

So ends a warm, personal letter issued by Paul to his friend Philemon on behalf of the slave Onesimus, the "very heart" of the apostle.

## Endnotes

1. Thomas Hale, *The Applied New Testament Commentary* (Colorado Springs, Colo.: Chariot Victor Publishing, 1997), p. 689.

# SELECT BIBLIOGRAPHY FOR TITUS & PHILEMON

Barclay, William. *The Letters to Timothy, Titus, and Philemon*, The Daily Bible Study Series. Philadelphia: The Westminster Press, 1975.

Bruce, F. F. *The Epistles to the Colossians to Philemon and to the Ephesians*, The New International Commentary on the New Testament. Grand Rapids, Mich.: William B. Eerdmans Publishing Company, 1984.

Clarke, Adam. *The New Testament of our Lord and Saviour Jesus Christ*. New York: G. Lane & P. P. Sandford, 1842.

Dunnam, Maxie D. *Galatians, Ephesians, Philippians, Colossians, Philemon*, The Communicator's Commentary, vol. 8. Waco, Tex.: Word Books, Publisher, 1982.

Earle, Ralph. *Word Meanings in the New Testament*, volume 5. Kansas City, Mo.: Beacon Hill Press of Kansas City, 1977.

Failing, George E. *Philemon,* The Wesleyan Bible Commentary, volume 5. Grand Rapids, Mich.: William B. Eerdmans Publishing Company, 1965.

Hale, Thomas. *The Applied New Testament Commentary.* Colorado Springs, Colo.: Chariot Victor Publishing, 1997.

Keener, Craig S. *The IVP Bible Background Commentary: New Testament*. Downers Grove, Ill.: InterVarsity Press, 1993.

Lockyer, Herbert, ed. *Nelson's Illustrated Bible Dictionary*. Nashville, Tenn.: Thomas Nelson Publishers, 1986, CD-ROM.

Matthews, Victor H. *Manners and Customs in the Bible*. Peabody, Mass.: Hendrickson Publishers, Inc., 1988.

Patzia, Arthur G. *Ephesians, Colossians, Philemon*, New International Biblical Commentary, vol. 10. Peabody, Mass.: Hendrickson Publishers, Inc., 1984.

Rees, Paul S. *The Epistles to the Philippians, Colossians, and Philemon,* Proclaiming the New Testament, vol. 4. Grand Rapids, Mich.: Baker Book House, 1964.

Rupprecht, Arthur A. *Philemon,* The Expositor's Bible Commentary: Ephesians through Philemon. Grand Rapids, Mich.: Zondervan, 1981.

Smith, David. *The Life and Letters of St. Paul.* New York: Harper & Brothers.